Lecture Notes
in Business Information Processing   336

More information about this series at http://www.springer.com/series/7911

Krzysztof Wnuk · Sjaak Brinkkemper (Eds.)

Software Business

9th International Conference, ICSOB 2018
Tallinn, Estonia, June 11–12, 2018
Proceedings

 Springer

Editors
Krzysztof Wnuk
Blekinge Institute of Technology
Karlskrona, Sweden

Sjaak Brinkkemper
Utrecht University
Utrecht, The Netherlands

ISSN 1865-1348   ISSN 1865-1356   (electronic)
Lecture Notes in Business Information Processing
ISBN 978-3-030-04839-6   ISBN 978-3-030-04840-2   (eBook)
https://doi.org/10.1007/978-3-030-04840-2

Library of Congress Control Number: 2018962543

This Springer imprint is published by the registered company Springer Nature Switzerland AG
The registered company address is: Gewerbestrasse 11, 6330 Cham, Switzerland

Preface

Conference theme: How Digitalization Impacts Software Business

Although the business of software shares common features with other international knowledge-intensive businesses, it carries many inherently unique features. It is making it a challenging domain for research. The examples of many successful companies show that software provides a unique benefit to its users. Moreover, software has spread all over the world and has permeated in many industries that are not usual for software. Software companies have to depend on one another to deliver a unique value proposition to their customers or a unique experience to their users. Companies that were engineering-driven have become software-intensive and struggle to keep up with the required speed of development and planning.

The 9th International Conference on Software Business was held in Tallinn, Estonia, and co-located with the 30th CAiSE conference of June 11–12, 2018. ICSOB 2018 focused on digitalization and its impact on the speed of business models and business modeling and realization of these business models.

The conference was opened by a keynote by Dr. Slinger Jansen on "What Is Next After Software Ecosystems?" and concluded by a summary presentation from the Dagstuhl Seminar 18182 "Software Business, Platforms, and Ecosystems: Fundamentals of Software Production Research" by Professor Sjaak Brinkkemper.

During the two days of the conference, 12 papers (selected from 34 submissions) were presented in the areas of software product management, start-ups, business models, and software ecosystems. Each presentation was followed by a discussion session where a discussant assigned for each paper asked questions, followed by the questions for the audience.

October 2018

Krzysztof Wnuk
Sjaak Brinkkemper

Organization

Conference Chairs

Sjaak Brinkkemper   Utrecht University, The Netherlands
Krzysztof Wnuk   Blekinge Institute of Technology, Sweden

Program Committee

Jan Bosch	Chalmers University of Technology, Sweden
João M. Fernandes	University of Minho, Portugal
Georg Herzwurm	University of Stuttgart, Germany
Slinger Jansen	Utrecht University, The Netherlands
Casper Lassenius	Aalto University, Finland
Eetu Luoma	University of Jyväskylä, Finland
Ricardo J. Machado	University of Minho, Portugal
Tiziana Margaria	University of Limerick and LERO Institute, Ireland
Björn Regnell	Lund University, Sweden
Pasi Tyrväinen	University of Jyväskylä, Finland
Anna Lena Lamprecht	LERO Institute, Ireland
Andrey Maglyas	Lappeenranta University of Technology, Finland
Arto Ojala	University of Jyväskylä, Finland
Sergey Avdoshin	National Research University Higher School of Economics, Russia
David Callele	University of Saskatchewan, Canada
Samuel A. Fricker	University of Applied Sciences and Arts Northwestern Switzerland
Thomas Hess	Munich School of Management, Germany
Thomas Kude	University of Mannheim, Germany
Stig Larsson	Effective Change AB, Sweden
Ulrike Lechner	Universität der Bundeswehr München, Germany
Konstantinos Manikas	University of Copenhagen, Denmark
John McFregor	Clemson University, USA
Rory O'Connor	Dublin City University, Ireland
Efi Papatheocharous	SICS, Sweden
Samuli Pekkola	Tampere University of Technology, Finland
Wolfram Pietsch	Aachen University of Applied Sciences, Germany
Karl Michael Popp	SAP AG, Germany
Dirk Riehle	Friedrich-Alexander University of Erlangen-Nürnberg, Germany
Matti Rossi	Aalto University, Finland
Kari Smolander	Lappeenranta University of Technology, Finland

Richard Berntsson Svensson   Blekinge Institute of Technology, Sweden
Tobias Tauterat   University of Stuttgart, Germany
Pasi Tyrväinen   University of Jyväskylä, Finland

Contents

Software Ecosystems

Individual People as Champions in Building an Emerging Software Ecosystem

Katariina Yrjönkoski[1], Marko Seppänen[1], and Sami Hyrynsalmi[2]($\boxtimes$)

[1] Laboratory of Industrial and Information Management,
Tampere University of Technology, Pori, Finland
{katariina.yrjonkoski,marko.seppanen}@tut.fi
[2] Laboratory of Pervasive Computing, Tampere University of Technology,
Pori, Finland
sami.hyrynsalmi@tut.fi

Abstract. An increasing amount of software service providers tend to evolve their platforms into business ecosystems. In the mainstream of extant literature, the ecosystems have been seen as an interconnected system of organizations, mainly ignoring the individual level. However, some previous studies have suggested that collaboration—such as building a new ecosystem—may be depending on individual key persons who are development-oriented and capable of seeing the ecosystem's value potential already in its early phases. Based on the results of a single-case study, this short paper proposes a new conversation on an unexplored area of key persons as enablers—'champions'—for a new ecosystem creation. The empirical analysis was based on a single case study on a recently launched new software business ecosystem. As a result, four different capability areas and six, partly overlapping, roles for a champion, were identified. In future work, the findings on individual's roles and required capabilities may provide fruitful research avenues to understand better the process of emergence of new ecosystems.

Keywords: Business ecosystem · Software ecosystem
Emerging ecosystem · Champion · Strategic management
Role · Capability

1 Introduction

Software ecosystems are complex socio-technical constructs involving often hundreds of companies and persons from different fields. For example, in the case of mobile application ecosystems—i.e., Google Play for Android devices and Apple App Store for iOs devices—the number of involved organization is counted in hundreds of thousands (e.g. [1]). Yet, individual people, their skills and competences might be crucial for an ecosystem during its life-cycle.

© Springer Nature Switzerland AG 2018
K. Wnuk and S. Brinkkemper (Eds.): ICSOB 2018, LNBIP 336, pp. 3–9, 2018.
https://doi.org/10.1007/978-3-030-04840-2_1

In his seminal work, Moore [2] identified four distinct stages in the life-cycle. In Moore's life-cycle model, the phases are: *(i)* Birth, *(ii)* Expansion, *(iii)* Struggle for Leadership, and *(iv)* Renewal or Death. During an emergence of an ecosystem, i.e., in its birth and expansion phases, individual persons might important role in the development of the ecosystem. That is, commitment to the ecosystem in its early phases by promoting it and by innovating new content by individuals might be a vital condition for the ecosystem as a whole.

The extant ecosystem literature has highlighted some unexplored observations of different individual behavior and its potentially crucial impact on building a new ecosystem. Some researchers have recognized that relational attributes such as trust and commitment are different at company and individual level (e.g. [3–5]). Such key persons ant their amount have seen as an important factor in different collaborative contexts [6] Nevertheless, the importance of individuals and their skills in the emergence of an ecosystem are still mainly unexplored area.

This short paper aims to uncover what kind of role an individual might have in an emergence of an ecosystem and, furthermore, what kind of mindset is needed. Thus, we focus on the following research question:

RQ What are the roles and characteristics of individuals that boost the development of an emerging ecosystem?

This study introduces our findings at individual level mindset differences when building an ecosystem forward from the birth phase. The paper is based on a single case: an ecosystem connecting public and private sector actors. The primary data consists of 15 interviews of users working in private sector and using the services of the core platform. We analyzed the data and outlined four themes the key persons typically emphasize.

On one hand, most individuals related to the emergence of a new ecosystem may not even recognize or see its benefits – or even drawbacks. On the other hand, key persons (hereafter labeled as *'champions'*) are development-oriented participants who might have a significant role in the emergence or death of an ecosystem. Champions rise from different parts of an emerging ecosystem. These kinds of champions are aware of the existing new ecosystem, might have better understanding of its benefits, and are more willing to develop the emerging ecosystems further.

The rest of this paper is structured as follows. Section 2 presents the empirical setting of this study and Sect. 3 goes through the results. Section 4 discusses on implications of the results and Sect. 5.

2   Research Process

This empirical inquiry is based on a case study research. In the following, we will first presents the case environment and then continue with research process.

2.1   The Case Ecosystem

COMPANY LTD (name anonymized due to confidentiality reasons) is a Finnish startup firm, that was established in 2017 as a spin-off of another software company. Its core business is to develop and orchestrate an ecosystem for digitalizing certain public administration processes, which are typically participated by companies and local authorities. The ecosystem is based on open source; the source code is available in GitHub platform (https://github.com/open-source). The product is delivered as a cloud service. Currently, there are also a few external data services integrated. By following the definition of a software ecosystem by Jansen et al. [7], the COMPANY LTD's ecosystem can be described as a software ecosystem. There are external actors, cooperation done between different parties and a software platform which is central for the ecosystem.

The ecosystem is aimed to generate new business to COMPANY LTD by implementing the digital processes on its business area. At the moment, they have approximately 200 public organization customerships and several business organization customers related to each public organizations. COMPANY LTD has a vision of creating and orchestrating an ecosystem around their core business area. Based on the ecosystem life-cycle model by Moore [2], the ecosystem seems to be in the expansion phase—it has bypassed the birth phase as it has stable business running and some customers. This study is based on COMPANY LTD's customer satisfaction questionnaire, conducted in May 2017, that was addressed to company's cloud service users.

2.2   Research Process

The study was conducted by interviewing 15 persons from companies using the cloud service. The data were collected by non-structured theme interviews. All the interviewees either use the service as part of their daily routines or they are system administrators of the service in their organization. The sample (n = 15) was selected by COMPANY LTD, as they wanted to get feedback from the most significant and active customers. Each interview lasted approximately for an hour. Afterwards, the interviews were transcribed and analyzed by the researchers.

The interview questionnaire was divided into two main parts. The first part gathered customer feedback for product development and marketing. In the second part, the interviewees were asked about the collaboration and ecosystem; for instance, do they see it beneficial, what kind of expectations they have for it, do they have some ideas about the future actors and services in the ecosystems, etc. Furthermore, their willingness and commitment to collaboration with other users and ecosystem orchestrator was mapped, also by offering a forum for that in the near future. Since the interviewees were not ecosystem specialists, the need emerged to replace the concept of 'ecosystem' partially with more familiar concepts such as 'networking' or 'collaboration'. This change was done in order to keep discussion going smoothly forward—and it was carefully considered when analyses were conducted.

3   Results

As the ecosystem is still in expansion phase, the most of the users did not recognize the ecosystem and they did not say that they have a relation to an emerging ecosystem. They were rather describing it in a terms of traditional customer-supplier-relationship. In their answers, the emphasis was on getting their daily work done and reaching some benefits of streamlining it. When asked, they considered collaborative innovation and user feedback as a critical factor for developing the ecosystem, but they still were not ready to invest their own time. They still were not able to see much advantages of the ecosystem. Also, they were not able to recall many services or actors they would see beneficial. They had only a minor communication with the orchestrator; the communication related typically to some specific problem of use.

However, a smaller group among the interviewees differed from the mainstream. They emphasized different issues in their answers when compared to other respondents. They showed more interest in the ecosystem and being active in developing it. They were seemingly more committed and agreeable to contribute the ecosystem although fast returns are not to be expected. In general, their mindset on the ecosystem is more development-oriented and more persistent. Due to this remarkable different approach these people could be considered as *'champions'*; persons who are important enablers and promotors for an emerging ecosystem.

Certain topics that sum up the champions' approach were convergent through the answers of all champions. They can be classified in four main themes, to the capabilities to understand:

1. *the long-term value creation*;
2. *the inherent nature and challenges of developing software for different users of the software development*;
3. *the insight of other user companies and a tendency to improve the practices of the whole industry*; and
4. *importance of communication* and information and best practices sharing.

While these abilities are not uncommon, they were found to be important for promoting the emerging ecosystem as well as supporting its development.

4   Discussion

This study contributes to the business and software ecosystem literatures by showing that there are more roles than currently characterized in the extant literature. Previous research has suggested the following four roles during ecosystem birth: the *'communicator'*, *'entrepreneur'*, *'regulator'*, and *'lobbyist'* [8]. In addition, several other roles were proposed, such as *'expert'*, *'regulator'*, *'ecosystem leader'*, and *'champion'* that may come to prominence more often than others in driving the genesis process [9]. It seems rather likely that champions may have a different focus in their ecosystem support activities, depending on their position, job and personal characteristics. Based on our findings, we identified three different champion profiles:

Promotor provides the 'faces' for the ecosystem, markets and promotes the ecosystem and attracts actors to join.
Powerhouse keeps up the spirit, vision, motivates and supports towards ecosystem's targets.
Gatekeeper selects and guides ecosystem members as well as maintains (usually informal) 'rules of the game' in and for the ecosystem.

In the early phase of ecosystem birth a champion, in some of the above roles, may mainly work inside her own organization. The champion thus modifies the processes to fit the ecosystem wherever it is possible, communicates the ecosystem related issues as a positive manner and, at all, takes an active role in ecosystem-related actions and co-operation. As the ecosystem evolves further, these roles may expand and start to promote the ecosystem on the whole ecosystem level. Furthermore, we assume that three more champion roles may emerge:

Insulator protects the ecosystem from external disturbances, align external presumes.
Fertilizer fosters the growth of the ecosystem, and acquires more energy, money and resource for the ecosystem.
Evangelist promotes and fosters the ecosystem through blogging, vlogging, presenting and speaking of as well as creating demonstrations for the ecosystem.

These roles have been identified and described based on an expanding phase of an ecosystem. Even though some of those are same as previous works by [8, 9], previous works had firms as their level of analysis. Thus, this individual perspective suggested in this study is different and changes the definitions of above roles. The competences that were needed in the birth phase need to be changed and increased, since the requirements on next phase are different – as discussed by Moore [2] related to his ecosystem life-cycle model. The diffusion adoption process [10] has a similar idea where the needs of adopters change when adoption goes further in diffusion process. One possible way when an ecosystem grows is that instead of a single person as a champion, more individuals will be needed. In other words, the champion will not wear so many hats anymore but there will be separate persons for couple of those roles, for instance, Fertilizer's role will be time-consuming thus that may require rather soon more person-months and -years.

Another topic that emerges from our findings is that an ecosystem is different than a network. A network is characterized by its structural holes that affect on its formation and how linkages between actors are built. An ecosystem is biased to its outcome - an ecosystem is *"the alignment structure of the multilateral set of partners that need to interact in order for a focal value proposition to materialize"* [11]. This distinction is crucial for people working in business ecosystems. The way how the champion considers ecosystem fits well on this perspective, and

in accordance all other individuals should see the entire ecosystem and understand the possibilities and obstacles that current and future ecosystem will need.

There are certain limitations worth of notion. This study was based on the
empirical investigation of one emerging ecosystem. The case ecosystem, as almost
all of the ecosystems, is unique and thus the results should not be generalized but
instead they offer insight on individuals' roles. Further, the investigation may be
biased based on the research setting (i.e., interview query, also conceptual mix-
ing, for instance some interviewees seemingly mixed ecosystems and networks in
their perceptions). This bias has been attempted to avoid with exposing the data
and analyses for careful analyses of three researchers. Finally, typical case-based
research limitations apply to (e.g. small sample, single country) that further
research may tackle.

5   Conclusion

By studying an emerging software ecosystem, we were able to identify a new
kind of group among the ecosystem. We labeled these individuals as 'champions' as they are individual persons in the organizations who are able boost the
development of the ecosystems. Based on the interviews, we also identified some
capabilities that may be needed for being a successful champion. This study
contributes to the ecosystem literature by adding more details in the previous
studies of roles in ecosystems especially at individual level. Most of previous
ecosystem studies focus on at organizational or industry level. Thus, this study
is among the first ones to emphasize individuals and relevance of their actions
for the ecosystem's development. Nevertheless, this study is requesting further
work to analyze the impact of individual persons as well as the role their skills
and competences in the business and software ecosystems.

References

1. Hyrynsalmi, S.: Letters from the war of ecosystems – an analysis of independent
   software vendors in mobile application marketplaces. Doctoral dissertation, University of Turku, Turku, Finland, December 2014. TUCS Dissertations No 188
2. Moore, J.F.: Predators and prey: a new ecology of competition. Harvard Bus. Rev.
   71(3), 75–86 (1993)
3. Ojasalo, J.: Key account management at company and individual levels in business-
   to-business relationships. J. Bus. Ind. Mark. **16**, 199–220 (2001)
4. Hurni, T., Huber, T.L., Dibbern, J.: Coordinating platform-based multi-sourcing:
   introducing the theory of conventions. In: Carte, T., Heinzl, A., Urquhart, C., (eds.)
   Proceedings of the International Conference on Information Systems - Exploring
   the Information Frontier, ICIS 2015, Fort Worth, Texas, USA, 13–16 December
   2015. Association for Information Systems (2015)
5. Valença, G., Alves, C.: Understanding how power influences business and requirements decisions in software ecosystems. In: SAC 2016, pp. 1258–1263. ACM, New
   York (2016)

6. Rese, A., Gemünden, H., Baier, D.: 'Too many cooks spoil the broth': key persons and their roles in inter-organizational innovation. Creat. Innov. Manag. **22**, 390–407 (2013)
7. Jansen, S., Finkelstein, A., Brinkkemper, S.: A sense of community: a research agenda for software ecosystems. In: 31st International Conference on Software Engineering – Companion Volume, ICSE-Companion 2009, pp. 187–190. IEEE, May 2009
8. Dedehayir, O., Ortt, R.J., Mäkinen, S.J., Chakrabarti, A.: The process of ecosystem genesis: a tale of two drugs, pp. 1–11. The International Society for Professional Innovation Management (ISPIM), Manchester, July 2016
9. Dedehayir, O., Mäkinen, S.J., Ortt, J.R.: Roles during innovation ecosystem genesis: a literature review. Technol. Forecast. Soc. Change **136**, 18–29 (2016)
10. Rogers, E.M.: Diffusion of Innovations. Simon and Schuster, New York (2010)
11. Adner, R.: Ecosystem as structure: an actionable construct for strategy. J. Manag. **43**(1), 39–58 (2017)

Modeling Support for Strategic API Planning and Analysis

Jennifer Horkoff[1,2]([envelope]), Juho Lindman[1], Imed Hammouda[2,3], Eric Knauss[1,2],
Jamel Debbiche[1], Martina Freiholtz[1], Patrik Liao[1], Stephen Mensah[1],
and Aksel Strömberg[1]

[1] University of Gothenburg, Gothenburg, Sweden
{jennifer.horkoff,eric.knauss}@gu.se, juho.lindman@ait.gu.se
[2] Chalmers Institute of Technology, Gothenburg, Sweden
[3] Mediterranean Institute of Technology, South Mediterranean University,
Tunis, Tunisia

Abstract. APIs provide value beyond technical functionality. They enable and manage access to strategic business assets and play a key role in enabling software ecosystems. Existing work has begun to consider the strategic business value of software APIs, but such work has limited analysis capabilities and has not made use of established, structured modeling techniques from software and requirements engineering. Such modeling languages have been used for strategic analysis of ecosystems and value exchange. We believe these techniques expand analysis possibilities for APIs, and we apply them as part of a cross-company case study focused on strategic API planning and analysis. Results show that goal, value, and workflow modeling provide new, API-specific benefits that include mapping the API ecosystem, facilitating incremental API planning, understanding dynamic API-specific roles, identifying bottlenecks in API change workflows, and identifying API value.

Keywords: APIs · Strategic analysis · Conceptual modeling

1 Introduction

Traditionally, software APIs (application programming interfaces) have been viewed from a technical perspective, as a means to separate implementation from functional calls – a way to define a contract of software functionality. More recently, it has become apparent that APIs are able to play a key role as part of a strategic business plan for software-intensive companies, noted by both academia [1,2], and industry [3–5].

In this work, we introduce and evaluate the use of established conceptual modeling approaches from requirements and software engineering in order to understand and analyze APIs from a strategic business perspective. Existing work, has facilitated various forms of API analysis, e.g., when to open an API [3], how to use APIs as part of a business model [4–6], and assessing API readiness

© Springer Nature Switzerland AG 2018
K. Wnuk and S. Brinkkemper (Eds.): ICSOB 2018, LNBIP 336, pp. 10–26, 2018.
https://doi.org/10.1007/978-3-030-04840-2_2

as part of software ecosystems [1]). However, such work has not made use of structured conceptual models to capture, understand and analyze APIs. Such models open new possibilities for API analysis. There is a rich body of literature in the use of conceptual models for strategic software analysis, particularly capturing the interplay between technologies and the organizational or business domain, e.g., [7–9] Such work allows one to map goals and dependencies in a software ecosystem [10], evaluate reciprocal value flows between actors in a value network [8], and capture organizational processes [9]. These approaches show promise for strategic analysis of APIs, but must be evaluated for this context.

Our main driving research question is: *what are the benefits and drawbacks of applying established modeling notations to strategic API analysis?* In describing our methods and experiences, we make it possible for others to replicate our modeling process, to whatever degree it is possible in a different context, performing strategic API analysis using structured models, allowing for novel types of API analysis.

More specifically, we have conducted a cross-company case study with four software-intensive companies working in the embedded systems domain. For each company, we have focused on a specific API, either established or a in planning. Via several cross-company and in-company workshops, we have worked through understanding and analyzing the strategic plans and challenges of each API using goal modeling [11], e^3 value modeling [8], and workflow modeling using UML activity diagrams [9]. We have selected these particular notations due, in part, to their appropriateness for strategic software analysis in a business context and, in part, due to the interests and requests of our particular companies, who were especially interested in ecosystem mapping, value and workflow analysis.

In this paper we present the results of our API analysis using (anonymized) examples, highlighting several benefits of conceptual modeling for strategic API analysis. Namely, modeling the ecosystem of an API in conjunction with our layered API architecture from [12] allowed the companies to find gaps in their plans, and to see the changing roles of various strategic actors depending on the API of focus. Modeling allowed us to conduct incremental planning for API deployment, and to evaluate bottlenecks in API workflows. Finally, we conducted an analysis of API value, understanding why an existing API was or was not used in a particular company. We also consider the drawbacks of the modeling approaches applied in this context, and discuss which aspects of our findings are particular to APIs, or more general for any software modeling. The primary contribution is to illustrate how widely known modeling approaches can be used in a not-yet-explored way: strategic API analysis.

Our overall goal in this continuous project is to build a framework to provide structured guidance for strategic API analysis, including the use of conceptual models. In [12] we give an early and broad overview of our framework, focusing on a 4-layer strategic API architecture. In [13], we work with some of the same results as described in this paper, but purely from the perspective of comparing the effectiveness of various modeling approaches in practice, ignoring the issues and findings related to APIs. The current submission describes further aspects of the planned framework, including ecosystem mapping, incremental API planning, workflow and value analysis. Other components, to be elaborated in future work, include API governance, metrics, and life cycle.

This paper is organized as follows: Sect. 2 describes background and related work. In Sect. 3 we describe how our industrial modeling sessions were conducted and how our results were validated. Section 4 describes the results of our modeling efforts, organized into key findings. Section 5 discusses our results, while Sect. 6 concludes the paper and discusses future work.

2   Background and Related Work

API Analysis. APIs have been studied from an academic perspective, although the body of work in this area is not extensive, and does not make use of conceptual modeling. De Souza and Redmiles looked at how APIs help to facilitate software coordination by providing contracts and boundary objects, facilitating communication [2]. Particular attention has been paid to the use of Open APIs, particularly as a way to stimulate R&D and generate new revenue streams [6]. In this light, our study is unique in that we focus APIs in very large organizations (our partner companies range from thousands to tens of thousands of employees). As such, there is focus on internal APIs, which, due to the size of the organizations, reside in complex ecosystems.

Level	Layer
4	Product, system, services embedded in **Domain**
3	API Usage
2	API
1	Business Asset

Fig. 1. Strategic API layered architecture [12]

Initial work has considered APIs from the point of view of software ecosystems, pointing out that the fast-pace changes within an ecosystem require guidance to continually assess and modify APIs [1]. In our past work we have begun to develop a framework for strategic API analysis, including a layered architecture, to understand API business value and usage, shown in Fig. 1. Here, an API protects and strategically exposes business assets. The API is used by software application(s), either internal or external, and the API usage is embedded in a domain, occupied by strategic actors and motivated by businesses cases. In previous work we have applied this general framework to several company cases, identifying elements in each layer. This analysis was helpful to map API ecosystems at a high level, but in this work we find greater insight in combination with structured modeling notations.

Several reports from industry offer useful practical design considerations for APIs, including advice on collecting usage data, monetization strategies, and at what point to open an API to external parties [3–5]. The existing body of API work provides useful input to our overall framework for strategic API analysis (e.g., when to change, improving usability, when/if to open). However, these approaches do not make use of established, structured, modeling frameworks to facilitate API analysis. Given strategic API concerns, existing modeling languages with a focus on strategic analysis, such as goal or e^3 value modeling, may be able to provide additional analysis power. In this work we evaluate the utility of such tools via application to industrial cases.

Ecosystem Mapping. Over the last decade, inspired by open source and cooperative business communities, software analysis has taken an ecosystem perspective (e.g., [14–16]). Further work has focused on capturing and evaluating ecosystems with structured models. For example, Boucharas et al. provide a formal modeling language for software supply network modeling, including products, platforms, mediums, customers, and suppliers [14]. Handoyo et al. focus on capturing software ecosystems via value chains, using software supply network diagrams from [14] as a foundation [17]. Other work has used goal models to capture and understand software ecosystems [10] and tradeoffs in the degree of openness in software platform data [18].

Although work has focused on modeling software ecosystems, we are not aware of work focusing on API ecosystems in particular. As the supply network diagrams from [14,17] focus on trade relationships, not easily applicable to API analysis, we opt to use a goal modeling ecosystem approach in this work [11]. In this way, we capture a more general concept of dependencies between actors, as well as internal actor motivations for participating in the ecosystem, including problems and challenges.

Incremental Modeling. The practice of capturing as-is vs. to-be is wide-spread in conceptual modeling. Although API analysis has considered various stages of API design or release (e.g., private to public [3]), we have not seen examples of incremental planning using conceptual models specifically for APIs.

Workflow Analysis. Modeling and analysis of workflows (business processes, activities) is widespread in both software and business (e.g. [9]). To our knowledge, we have not seen specific consideration of API-related workflows, e.g., the process of updating or changing an API. In this work we apply UML activity diagrams for this purpose.

Value Analysis. The emphasis on value as part of agile methods, as well as the focus on value in, for example, value-based software engineering [19], has provoked a recent academic focus on value analysis and modeling. Several value-oriented modeling approaches have been introduced, including [17]. In this work we use e^3 value modeling as per Gordijn et al. [8]. We select this language due to its simple visual syntax, continued application, development in research (e.g., [20]), and availability of tool support.

3 Methodology

In this section we describe the research context, including a brief description of our anonymized companies and their APIs of focus, and a description of our modeling methodology.

3.1   Research Context and Case Companies

This research is carried out as part of the Chalmers Software Center (SWC)[1]. Work in the center is organized into half-year sprints, renewable as part of continuous projects. Projects involved interested software center companies, including many of the leading software companies in Northern Europe.

The high-level goal of the research sprint (January to May 2017) was continue to develop aspects of the strategic API framework while providing analytic value in API management and strategies to our four partner companies. All project companies (C1–C4) are SWC partner companies working in the embedded systems domain. Each company selected a particular API for more in-depth work as part of the project. We describe the APIs of focus for each company in Table 1.

Table 1. Case company API description

Company	Description
Company 1 (C1)	C1 offers many APIs to its physical devices as well as a through cloud services. The API of focus, a cloud API, was in the planning stages during this study
Company 2 (C2)	C2 supplies databases to its customers that are used in the generation of reports that support tasks such as quality control. The API of focus, a reporting API, was in the planning stages
Company 3 (C3)	The investigated API is mainly internal and related to the reuse of common function signatures across products. The API of focus, a profile API was in partial operation
Company 4 (C4)	The studied API was internal and encompassed global software design rules handling faults and alarms. The API of focus was in use

3.2   Model Creation and Validation

Modeling and analysis was conducted as part of three SWC thesis projects [21–23]. The thesis groups (G1–G3) each worked with 1–2 companies, continually sharing results with the research team in weekly meetings. Based on the interests of each company, different modeling methods were applied. As all companies were interested in mapping their API ecosystem, inspired by work using goal modeling for ecosystem mapping [10], goal modeling was used in all cases. C3 was particularly interested in API workflow analysis, thus activity diagrams were applied to this case. C4 was interested in understanding the value of their API to potential users, thus we applied e^3 value modeling in this case.

The project started with a cross-company coordination workshop. Each of the three groups conducted a series of group and individual workshops and interviews in order to collect qualitative data to facilitate modeling. G1 and G2 conducted

---

[1] https://www.software-center.se/.

workshops on location with the company, as well as follow-up online interviews. G3 was situated within C4 for a period of roughly three months.

Information gathered from workshops and interviews, including a selection of technical documentation, was used to create models. It was agreed with the companies that the first round of modeling should focus on a particular scenario or user story, to keep the scope of the models in check. Each group attempted to classify their resulting models in terms of the layered API architecture reported in [12]. The modeling process was iterative, with the students receiving iterative feedback from someone knowledgeable in the modeling approaches (the first author), researchers knowledgeable about the cases, and the company contacts. The general elicitation process can be summarized as follows:

1. **Introductory Group Interview:** Necessary to understand the API ecosystem of the companies.
2. **Off-site Modeling:** Using available context knowledge and the API usage scenario of focus (user story) to create initial model versions.
3. **Interactive Workshop:** Starting with initial models, expand and correct the models interactively using group input.
4. **Follow-up Online Interview(s):** Finalize data collection and fill gaps discovered while modeling. Discuss experiences with modeling approaches.
5. **Dissemination Workshop:** Summarize modeling and analysis results in a workshop with all company representatives present.

Company workshops had 3–6 company participants including roles such as developer engineers, development managers, software engineers, product managers, and expert engineers, i.e., those involved with and familiar with the development or operation of the API. Participants had a technical background, and were generally familiar with software modeling, although not specifically with goal or value modeling. Online interviews were conducted with individual representatives from each company, who had been present in the workshops. Workshops lasted three hours, while individual interviews were typically one hour.

G3 also conducted an introductory group interview with C4, but gathered further data with individual semi-structured interviews and a survey, selecting participants involved in the API Framework (FW). Ten interviews and two surveys were conducted with the same questions, with interviews lasting 45 min. G3 also had access to archival data concerning their API of focus.

For G1 and G2 model creation was iterative and continuous, with workshops and interviews presenting and receiving feedback on the models. G3 explicitly used member checking to improve the accuracy, credibility and validity of the collected data [24]. Four new interviews were scheduled with previous participants, each lasting around an hour, during which G3 described and went through the models step by step, receiving feedback. Further member checking was conducted when the authors elicited feedback and general impressions on modeling results from each company in the final shared workshop. More information on the modeling method and company participants can be found in the full theses [21–23].

4 Results

We describe our results, grouping them into categories.

API Ecosystem Mapping. For each case, the teams used goal modeling to map the ecosystem of the API, including the API itself, the company, and the various internal and external actors in the ecosystem. For each actor, the actor's motivations and dependencies on other actors were considered. A high-level view of the resulting ecosystem map for C1 can be seen at the top of Fig. 3 and for C2 (with layers) in Fig. 5. A more detailed view of part of a resulting model for C3, analyzing the situation before API workflow redesign, can be seen in Fig. 2 (see [11] and red annotations for language constructs). This figure focuses on the process of approving changes to the profile, the API equivalent construct in this case, enabling a common interface for specifying device functionality. The model uses qualitative goal model analysis (as described in [25], legend on top right of figure) to determine the satisfaction level of quality goals based on the contributions of tasks/goals.

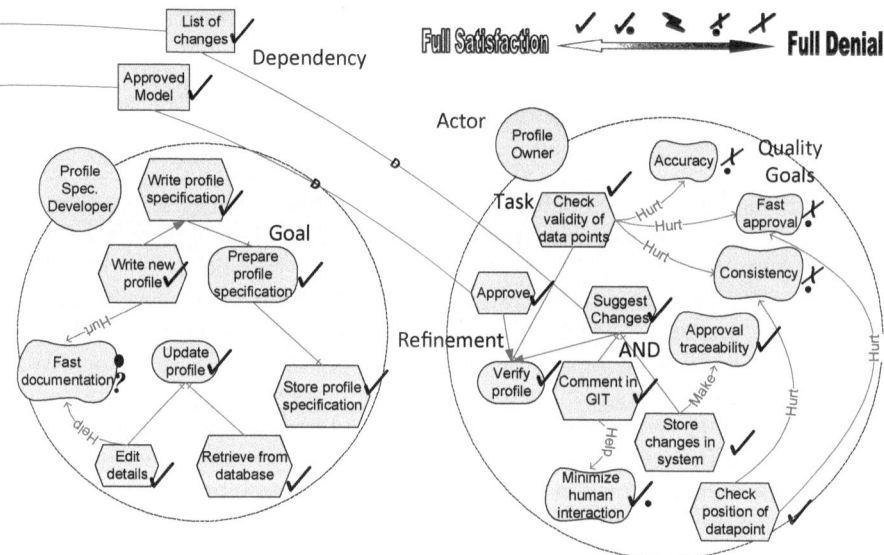

Fig. 2. Selected details of the goal model for C3, capturing the as-is situation before workflow redesign (Color figure online)

Although the models were complex, much of the modeling was done as part of company workshops, in a participatory manner with direct input from participants. Thus, company partners were generally engaged, and found this type of modeling useful to have a high-level view of the ecosystem. For example, C1 stated that it helped them understand the needs and wants of the various types of customers in their API ecosystem (top of Fig. 3).

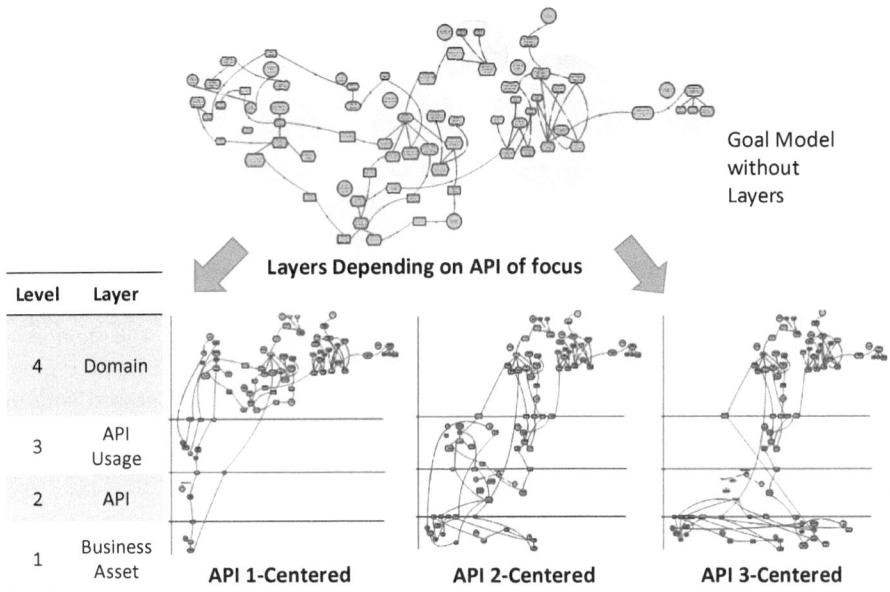

Fig. 3. Layering of goal model using API layers from [12] showing different API-centric views for C1 (high-level view, details obscured)

The process of iterative ecosystem modeling helped to show gaps in the modeler's knowledge. For example, for C2, several questions arose: what is the role particular module in API design? The relevance of the cloud? Who accesses the API? When? etc. Most of these questions could be answered easily by the customer partners, but as this case was an API in development, forcing the C2 participants to hammer out details was often seen as helpful.

Summary: Ecosystem modeling with goal models was helpful in mapping out and understanding the domain, including participating actors, and in solidifying details. Drawbacks included model complexity.

Ecosystem Mapping with API Layers. The teams made an effort to take each of the models created as part of the API analysis and sort the model elements as per the layers of the strategic API architecture described in Sect. 2. We found that making this division for workflow or e^3 value models was difficult (more detail described in [13]). However, this was possible for goal models by assigning API-related actors to layers. See Fig. 3 for a high-level view of how this was performed for C1. Note that the details of this figure are deliberately obscured to hide details of the company analysis. Figure 4 (described in next section) gives a simplified view showing only the actors.

The participant companies found that mapping API ecosystem actors to API layers was a helpful exercise in understanding the roles of the ecosystem actors, as they related to the API. In some cases, this mapping revealed significant gaps in our ecosystem goal models. For example, in the initial C1 model, we had neglected to include the assets protected and managed by the device API.

Summary: Mapping ecosystem models to API layers helped to identify the API-centered roles of the actors, and in some cases to reveal missing actors. The drawbacks were that this was not easily possible with e^3 or workflow models.

Changing API Ecosystem Perspectives. When mapping our API ecosystem models to the API layers, it was challenging to map actors to layers, as their role was contextual. This was particularly true when an ecosystem contained more than one API. For example, in C1 the C1 ecosystem contains three APIs: the low-level device API which allows one to access content on the device(s), the raw content cloud API which provides device content to third party cloud developers, and the processed content cloud API which takes processed content from third party developers and provides it to the end customers.

In this case, ecosystem actors such as third party developers (gray circle in Fig. 4) could be placed on many layers depending on the API of focus. From the perspective of the Device API, this actor is part of the domain (left figure), a user of the raw content cloud API which uses the Device API. From the raw content API perspective, it is part of the App SW layer (middle), as the software which uses the raw content cloud API. While from the perspective of the processed content API, it is part of the Business Asset layer (right), as an asset used by the processed content cloud API. We show the different allocation of domain actors to layers depending on the API of focus at a high-level in Fig. 3 and with more abstraction in Fig. 4. In Fig. 4, each actor is a different color, so that the position of the actors can be traced across figures.

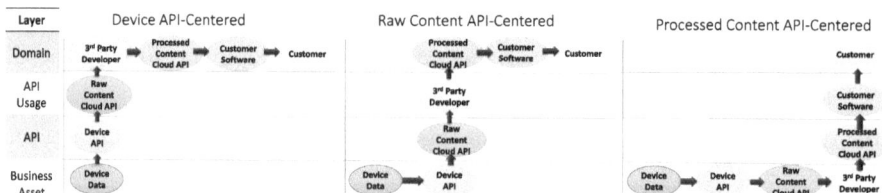

Fig. 4. API layers from [12] showing different API-centric views from the goal model for C1 (simplified view of Fig. 3 where each circle is represents a different actor) (Color figure online)

This type of analysis allows companies to understand the dynamic roles of the actors in their API ecosystem, particularly if the ecosystem is complex and contains different APIs. Similar situations can be found in some of the other companies, such as C3, with a communication API at a low level and a profile API (referenced in Fig. 2) at a higher level.

Summary: Mapping ecosystem models to strategic API layers allowed us to understand the changing roles of ecosystem actors, depending on the API of focus. Drawbacks were that this would only apply in cases with multiple APIs.

Incremental API Planning. In the case of C2, the analysis focused on planning a new API. C2, a large, international company, found planning global API deployment to be a particular challenge. Should the API be deployed globally in all locations? In some locations? With partial functionality? Should the old way of accessing data be preserved in parallel?

In this case an incremental planning approach using the layered ecosystem mapping models proved useful for the company. We took our initial ecosystem model, and with company input, modified it to show the incremental development and deployment of the API. A high-level view of the output is shown in Fig. 5. In the current (as-is) situation, there is no API (the API layer is empty), and several problems exist (e.g., customers often request custom reports, labor intensive for C2 employees). In the near future, the API is available as an option, some employees may use it, alleviating some problems, but others may choose to access data in the old way. In the near future, only the API is available to access data, thus there is a transition period to ease employees into API use. In the future, customers may use the reporting API directly. We show the details and changes for one actor in Fig. 6.

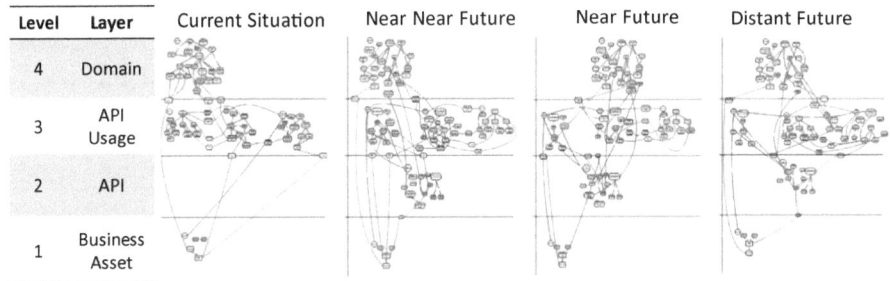

Fig. 5. Incremental planning of case API for C2 via goal models (high-level view)

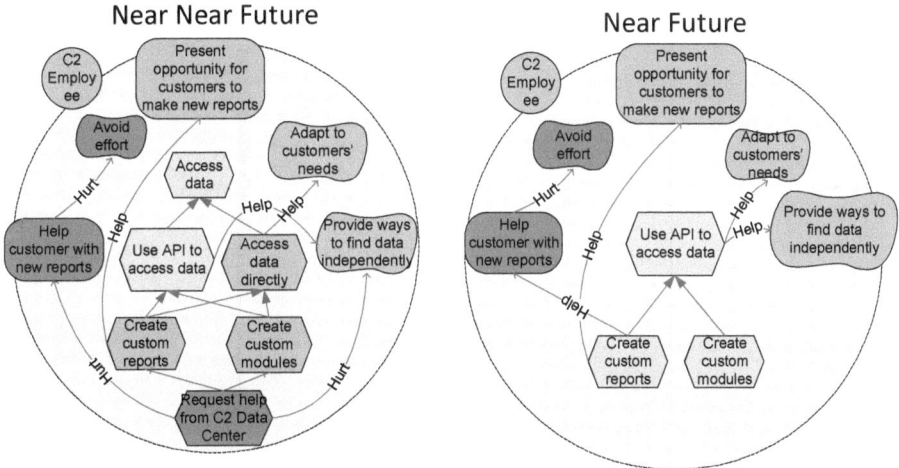

Fig. 6. View of one actor from Fig. 5, C2 case, near near vs. near future

In this case, colors (teal, orange) were used to show problematic goals, and how these problems were mitigated with subsequent API deployment steps. Although C2 found the process of creating these figures helpful in understanding the benefits of this form of incremental deployment from an ecosystem actor-centric view, such models were not easily able to cover technical details. For example, which data to expose via the API first? It is possible the model could help to evaluate this question, but detail would need to be added, which is difficult given the complexity of the model as is.

Summary: Goal ecosystem models allowed us to show incremental changes in plans over time, including goals that were satisfied/problems that were solved. Drawbacks include difficulty in representing technical detail.

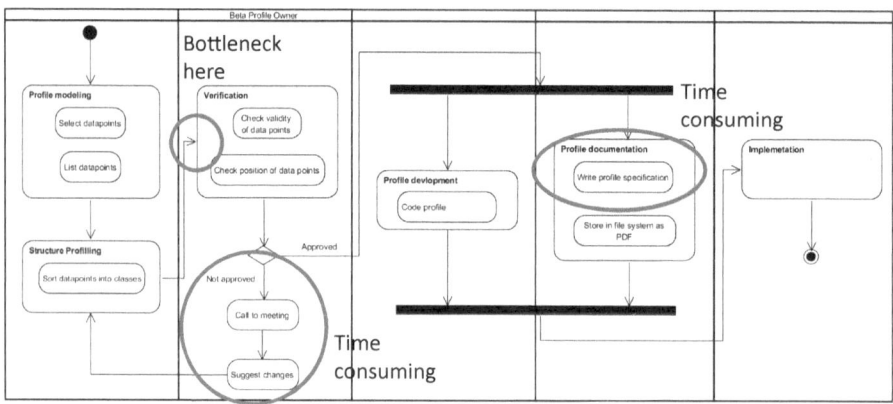

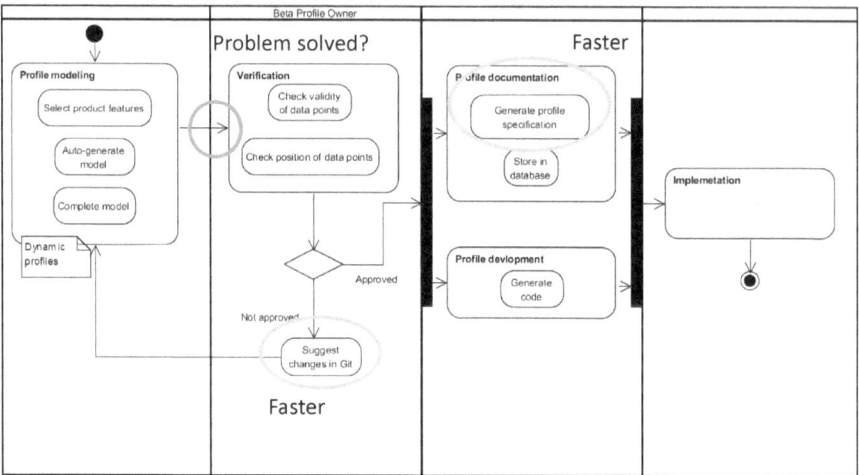

Fig. 7. As-is and to-be API modification process for C3 (some details removed)

API Workflow Analysis. C3 was particularly interested in understanding the workflow of processing requested changes to their API. In this case, they had an existing workflow and a new, planned workflow for their profile-based API. In addition to ecosystem modeling via goal models (Fig. 2), we performed workflow modeling for the as-is and to-be (planned) cases. Although we were not able to perform formal or quantitative workflow analysis (e.g., simulation, see [13] for more details), we were able to use the models to indicate bottlenecks and problematic flows for the as-is scenario, and to show how these problems would be at least partially alleviated in the new plan. See Fig. 7 for details. For example, in the as-is flow, the steps when the profile (API) owner rejected new additions or changes was time consuming. In the planned workflow, this part of the process was sped up by use of git. In other cases it was not clear if or how bottlenecks were solved by the new process design, and these cases were discussed with C3. Mapping back to qualities in the goal model, we found that the new design achieves maintainability, extensibility, and (partial) flexibility, but did not directly improve accuracy, consistency or fast approval.

Summary: Applying workflow modeling to APIs helped to understand the process of changing an API, including bottlenecks and planned process improvements. Drawbacks include an inability to perform workflow simulation.

API Value Analysis. In the case of C4, the company wanted to know why internal partners were motivated to use or not use an internal API enforcing software design rules. Use of the API was considered a good practice, but was not mandatory. In this case, it was agreed with the company that it would

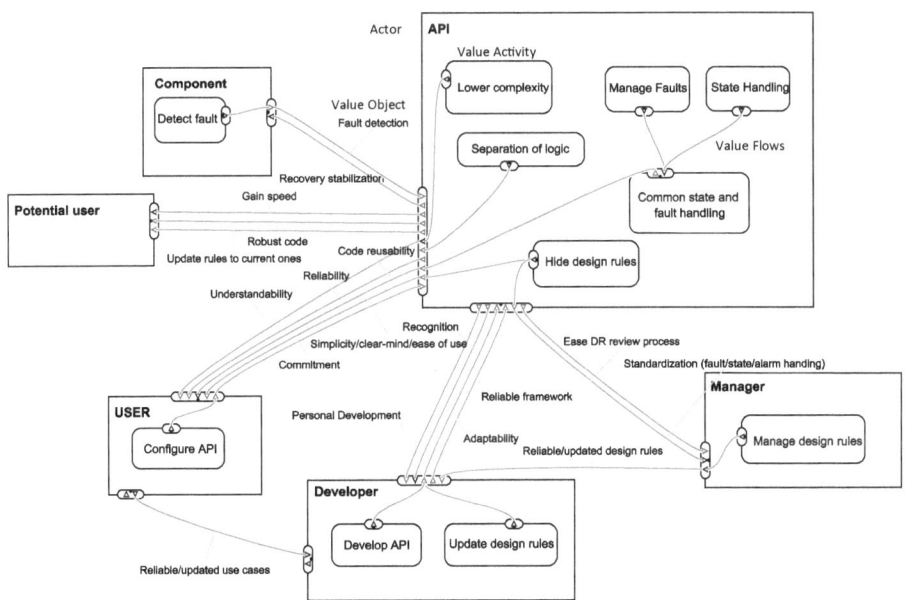

Fig. 8. e^3 value model for case API for C4 (some details changed) (Color figure online)

be useful to evaluate the value of the API, and as such, e^3 value modeling was applied. The result (some details changed), is shown in Fig. 8 (language annotations in red, more detail in [8]). The process of value modeling helped to highlight advantages/values of the API, showing why various actors would be motivated to use the API (e.g., robust code, standardization).

We note that the model did not necessarily capture the disadvantages of the API, including the learning curve, and difficulties in testing. We are currently continuing the project from both a goal and value-oriented perspective, at the request of the companies.

Summary: Value analysis was useful for understanding why people were motivated to use an API, in a relatively simple view. Drawbacks included an inability to show problems or missing values.

5   Discussion

Modeling Summary. We answer our initial research question, *what are the benefits and drawbacks of applying established modeling notations to strategic API analysis?* by summarizing the benefits (B) and drawbacks (D) of applying selected established modeling techniques to analysis of APIs from a strategic, business perspective (Table 2).

Table 2. Summary of benefits and drawbacks for API modeling

Benefits	Drawbacks
B1: Iterative modeling helped to reveal gaps in knowledge, both for the researchers and company partners	D1: Modeling, particularly goal modeling, can be complex and take some time to understand
B2: Mapping of ecosystems of goal modeling facilitates an understanding of API actors and motivations	D2: Goal models could not easily capture some of the specific technical detail needed for strategic analysis
B3: Division of ecosystem maps into strategic API layers helped to find gaps in knowledge and better understand the roles of various API actors	D3: Workflow models needed additional annotation to indicate the presence of problems or bottlenecks
B4: Dividing ecosystem models into layers helped to show the dynamic API-specific roles of various actors when multiple actors are involved	D4: e^3 value models could not easily capture drawbacks or reasons not to use a particular API
B5: Ecosystem models can be used to show incremental API planning, including gradual access to and use of the API	
B6: Issues in API workflows, such as bottlenecks, can be understood and addressed via workflow modeling	
B7: e^3 value modeling can help to understand the value (or lack of value) of APIs for actors in the ecosystem	

We have shown that by using structured models, we gain analysis benefits beyond existing API-related work (Sect. 2), including a visual mapping of API ecosystems, visualized incremental API planning, an analysis of the dynamic roles of API actors, API workflow and value analysis.

API Maturity. Our cases covered APIs of differing maturity. We can observe that ecosystem mapping was particularly useful for APIs in the planning stage (C1, C2), although it still provided some value to the other companies. Workflow modeling was applicable when workflows were established or planned (C3); such modeling would have been less applicable to those cases in the early planning stages (C1, C2). Value modeling was useful to capture value exchanges for an established case (C4), but could also be useful in planning stages.

Open/Closed APIs. Most of the APIs in our cases were internal (closed). However, because the companies were large, internal users could in some ways be treated as external: they were often geographically distributed and not personally known to our business contacts. As such, they were similar to open APIs.

API-Specific Results. One could question how many of our benefits and drawbacks are API-specific, or could occur in any strategic modeling exercise for a software-intensive company. B1 and B2 could be considered quite general, findings which are likely to appear in a software-related modeling exercise, while B3-B5 are more specific to APIs. B6 and B7 could be found for the analysis software in general; however the issues of bottlenecks in B6 is exaggerated by the presence of an API guardian, which is less common for general software. Value analysis in B7 is particularly useful in the case of APIs, as API value is often less obvious than with regular software. In this case, the value is not in a direct provision of functionality, but more subtly, in the enforcement of good coding principles. All of our found drawbacks are general, not specifically related to APIs. We consider this positive: use of the modeling techniques for APIs does not introduce additional significant challenges compared to general use of the modeling notations.

Threats to Validity. In terms of *Construct Validity*, the student modelers and the company representatives may have misunderstood the syntax or semantics of goal, workflow, or value models. We mitigated this threat by giving an overview of the modeling language at multiple points in the study. In this study, we worked with companies who were particularly interested in API analysis, including ecosystem, value and workflow analysis. In other cases, with less company buy-in, the modeling activities may be less fruitful.

Considering *Internal Validity*, all groups used some form of triangulation, collecting data from workshops, documents, archival data, and interviews. For C1, C2 and C3, validation rounds after the interactive workshop only involved one person per company. However, we mitigate this effect by collecting impressions from more people and multiple companies in the final cross-company workshops.

Examining *External Validity*, all case companies are located in Scandinavia; however, the companies are international. Applying the same modeling process to different companies with different APIs may produce differing observations.

However, we mitigate this possibility by involving a number of people from four different companies. Furthermore, all companies are in an embedded system domain, involving hardware in their products. We believe our results would be transferable to pure software companies. Our companies are also large; API modeling may be less beneficial for smaller companies. It is also likely that our results would not hold if different modeling notations were used.

Finally, considering *Reliability*, our study had the participation of a goal model expert, a co-author of [11]. However, most models in the studies were created by the student modelers.

6   Conclusions

We have used existing established modeling techniques in a novel way, demonstrating novel types of API analysis from a strategic business perspective. We have found several benefits of this application, including API-specific benefits, often related to the combination of structured modeling with our API layered architecture introduced in previous work. Drawbacks are common to most modeling efforts, including model complexity and expressive limitations.

Our findings are being incorporated into our framework for strategic API analysis. We are currently working with our industry partners to develop modeling methods, API metrics, and guidance in terms of API governance.

Acknowledgments. Thanks to company contacts and the Chalmers Software Center for support.

References

1. Hammouda, I., Knauss, E., Costantini, L.: Continuous API-design for software ecosystems. In: Proceedings of 2nd International WS on Rapid and Continuous Software Engineering (RCoSE 2015 @ ICSE), Florence, Italy (2015)
2. de Souza, C.R.B., Redmiles, D.F.: On the roles of APIs in the coordination of collaborative software development. CSCW **18**(5), 445 (2009)
3. Nordic API: Developing the API mindset: a guide to using private, partner, & public APIs (2015). https://nordicapis.com
4. IBM Institute for Business Value: Evolution of the API economy. Adopting new business models to drive future innovation (2016)
5. Oracle Communications: Making money through API exposure. Enabling new business models (2014). http://www.oracle.com/us/industries/communications/comm-making-money-wp-1696335.pdf
6. Aitamurto, T., Lewis, S.C.: Open innovation in digital journalism: examining the impact of open APIs at four news organizations. New Media Soc. **15**(2), 314–331 (2013)
7. Eric, S.: Social Modeling for Requirements Engineering. MIT Press, Cambridge (2011)

8. Gordijn, J., Akkermans, H., Van Vliet, J.: Designing and evaluating e-business models. IEEE Intell. Syst. **16**(4), 11–17 (2001)
9. Dumas, M., ter Hofstede, A.H.M.: UML activity diagrams as a workflow specification language. In: Gogolla, M., Kobryn, C. (eds.) UML 2001. LNCS, vol. 2185, pp. 76–90. Springer, Heidelberg (2001). https://doi.org/10.1007/3-540-45441-1_7
10. Yu, E., Deng, S.: Understanding software ecosystems: a strategic modeling approach. In: Proceedings of the Third International Workshop on Software Ecosystems, IWSECO-2011 Software Ecosystems 2011, Brussels, Belgium, pp. 65–76 (2011)
11. Dalpiaz, F., Franch, X., Horkoff, J.: iStar 2.0 language guide. arXiv preprint arXiv:1605.07767 (2016)
12. Lindman, J., Hammouda, I., Horkoff, J., Knauss, E.: Emerging perspectives to API strategy. IEEE Software (Under revision). https://tinyurl.com/yaofetrx, https://www.computer.org/csdl/mags/so/preprint/08501965-abs.html
13. Horkoff, J., et al.: Goals, workflow, and value: case study experiences with three modeling frameworks. In: Poels, G., Gailly, F., Serral Asensio, E., Snoeck, M. (eds.) PoEM 2017. LNBIP, vol. 305, pp. 96–111. Springer, Cham (2017). https://doi.org/10.1007/978-3-319-70241-4_7
14. Boucharas, V., Jansen, S., Brinkkemper, S.: Formalizing software ecosystem modeling. In: Proceedings of the 1st International Workshop on Open Component Ecosystems, pp. 41–50. ACM (2009)
15. Bosch, J.: From software product lines to software ecosystems. In: Proceedings of the 13th International Software Product Line Conference, pp. 111–119. Carnegie Mellon University (2009)
16. Jansen, S., Finkelstein, A., Brinkkemper, S.: A sense of community: a research agenda for software ecosystems. In: 2009 31st International Conference on Software Engineering-Companion Volume, ICSE-Companion 2009, pp. 187–190. IEEE (2009)
17. Handoyo, E., Jansen, S., Brinkkemper, S.: Software ecosystem modeling: the value chains. In: Proceedings of the Fifth International Conference on Management of Emergent Digital Ecosystems, pp. 17–24. ACM (2013)
18. Sadi, M.H., Yu, E.: Modeling and analyzing openness trade-offs in software platforms: a goal-oriented approach. In: Grünbacher, P., Perini, A. (eds.) REFSQ 2017. LNCS, vol. 10153, pp. 33–49. Springer, Cham (2017). https://doi.org/10.1007/978-3-319-54045-0_3
19. Biffl, S., Aurum, A., Boehm, B., Erdogmus, H., Grünbacher, P.: Value-Based Software Engineering. Springer, Heidelberg (2006). https://doi.org/10.1007/3-540-29263-2
20. Gordijn, J., Petit, M., Wieringa, R.: Understanding business strategies of networked value constellations using goal-and value modeling. In: 14th IEEE International Conference on Requirements Engineering, pp. 129–138. IEEE (2006)
21. Debbiche, J., Strömberg, A., Liao, P.: Applying goal modeling to API ecosystems: a cross-company case study. Bachelor thesis (2017). http://hdl.handle.net/2077/52649
22. Bedru, F., Freiholtz, M., Mensah, S.: An empirical investigation of the use of goal and process modelling to analyze API ecosystem design and usage workflow. Bachelor thesis (2017). http://hdl.handle.net/2077/52648

23. Hussein, M., Lundén, A.: An industrial assessment of software framework design: a case study of a rule-based framework. Master's thesis (2017). https://tinyurl.com/y9td34v6
24. Harper, M., Cole, P.: Member checking: can benefits be gained similar to group therapy? Qual. Rep. **17**(2), 510–517 (2012)
25. Horkoff, J., Yu, E.: Interactive goal model analysis for early requirements engineering. Requir. Eng. **21**(1), 29–61 (2016)

Software Ecosystem Health
of Cryptocurrencies

Matthijs Berkhout, Fons van den Brink, Mart van Zwienen,
Paul van Vulpen, and Slinger Jansen[✉]

Utrecht University, Princetonplein 5, 3584 CC Utrecht, The Netherlands
{m.j.a.berkhout, f.vandenbrink2,
m.a.vanzwienen}@students.uu.nl,
{p.n.vanvulpen, slinger.jansen}@uu.nl

Abstract. Background: Cryptocurrencies are highly valued without understanding the health of the underlying ecosystems. Previous work shows factors
which determinate the exchange rate. However, the technological determinants
show decreasing significance. **Objective:** This paper explores whether the
Open-source Software Ecosystem Health Operationalization (OSEHO) framework can be used to extend the given technology factors. **Method:** By conducting the OSEHO in a case-study on three distinct cryptocurrency ecosystems,
this paper gives a better insight in the ecosystem's value, longevity and
propensity for growth and the relation of these factors to the cryptocurrency
value. **Results:** The 'healthiest' cryptocurrency ecosystem also shows the
highest economic health. Two metrics from the OSEHO show strong positive
significant correlation with the exchange rate. **Conclusion:** Metrics from the
OSEHO show promising indications to be technological determinants for the
exchange rate. This research can be used as a foundation for further econometric
tests or research on other aspects of cryptocurrencies.

Keywords: Cryptocurrency · Software ecosystems · Ecosystem health
Bitcoin · Ethereum · Ripple

1 Introduction

Cryptocurrencies have attracted significant attention in recent years [1]. These cryptocurrencies are based on blockchain technology, wherein a blockchain is essentially "*a
public ledger with potential as a worldwide, decentralized record for the registration,
inventory and transfer of all assets*" [2]. The reason these blockchain technologies are
so popular is because its central attributes provide security, anonymity, and data
integrity [3], while building on computer cryptology and a decentralized or peer-to-peer
network. Therefore, no centralized institutes are necessary to ensure trust among the
users. Using blockchain technology for financial transactions, as cryptocurrencies do, is
merely one of the possible applications, as the blockchain technology may be used for
the transfer of all possible assets, as is stated by Swan [2].

There is research on the exchange rate and value of cryptocurrencies, such as the
work of Li and Wang [1], but there is little research on the health of the technology

K. Wnuk and S. Brinkkemper (Eds.): ICSOB 2018, LNBIP 336, pp. 27–42, 2018.
https://doi.org/10.1007/978-3-030-04840-2_3

behind the cryptocurrencies. Li and Wang propose technical factors that determinate the exchange rate. However, these factors show decreasing significance as the technology becomes more mature. This paper proposes the health of the cryptocurrency ecosystems as a new technological factor for determining the exchange rate.

In order to assess the health of cryptocurrency technologies, this paper approaches the cryptocurrencies from a software ecosystem point of view, wherein a software ecosystem is defined by Jansen [4] as "*a set of actors functioning as a unit and interacting with a shared market for software and services, together with the relationships among them. These relationships are frequently underpinned by a common technological platform or market and operate through the exchange of information, resources and artifacts*".

Looking at cryptocurrencies as software ecosystems, it is possible to use a measurement framework to assess the health of cryptocurrency ecosystems. The Open Source Ecosystem Health Operationalization framework (OSEHO) by Jansen [5] can be used to establish the health of software ecosystems. This makes it possible to compare the cryptocurrency ecosystems health, based on a framework, with the currency exchange rate. There are signs of field maturity identified by the increase in published journal articles and the number of existing ecosystems studies.

The increase in published journal articles and the number of existing ecosystem studies are signs of growing field maturity. However, the tools specific for software ecosystems may still need further research to be generalised, as Manikas identified [6].

Therefore, the contribution of this paper is twofold. Firstly, the application of the OSEHO on the cryptocurrency software ecosystems helps generalising the framework. Secondly, this paper explores another use of the OSEHO by examining the metrics in the framework for possible indicators for extending the model by Li and Wang [1]. This leads to the following research question:

Research question: *What are the possibilities of using the health of cryptocurrency software ecosystems as an influencing factor on the exchange rate of cryptocurrencies?*

This research question will be answered based on a case-study of the three highest-valued distinct cryptocurrencies, where value is expressed in market capitalisation [7]. These are Bitcoin, Ethereum and Ripple at the time of writing. The basis for this choice is two-fold: on the one hand, the choice has been made to focus on distinct coins, rather than hard forks or multiple coins built on the same blockchain, and on the other hand the choice has been made to focus on coins for which most information is available.

Bitcoin (BTC) is the oldest of the three cryptocurrencies, being launched in 2007, and in fact the first actual application of blockchain technology as a means of a decentralised, electronic cash system [2]. Ethereum is the newest of these blockchains, which launched in 2015. Aside from the currency, the Ether (ETH), this ecosystem offers a vast range of possibilities in the form of smart contracts and as a decentralised application platform [8]. The last cryptocurrency considered in this study, Ripple (XRP), was launched in 2012 by Ripple Labs, a for-profit enterprise and offers a faster and more robust transaction protocol than other cryptocurrencies [7, 9].

The work in this paper is continued in the next section with a literature review. Section 3 describes the research methodology, such as the data collection methods. In Sects. 4 and 5 the results are presented and analysed. Subsequently, the limitations of the study are discussed in Sect. 6. Finally, the conclusion on the application of the ecosystem health of cryptocurrency ecosystems as a technological factor in the framework by Li and Wang is made in Sect. 7.

2   Related Works

This section describes the context of this research from three perspectives, starting with an introduction of the blockchain technology, after which the cryptocurrencies, as part of the blockchain, and software ecosystems are elaborated upon.

2.1   Blockchain

Swan [2] puts the blockchain in the computing paradigm as the fifth disruptive paradigm since the mainframe in the 1970s. Yli-Huumo [3] states that the blockchain is a decentralized or peer-to-peer environment for transactions, where all the transactions are recorded to a public ledger, visible to everyone. The goal of the blockchain is to provide anonymity, security, privacy, and transparency to all its users.

This is possible because the public ledger cannot be modified or deleted after the data is approved by all nodes [3]. This strong point, data integrity, is the reason why it is the fifth disruptive computer paradigm [2]. Next to this strong point, Swan [2] also defines technical challenges for the adaption of blockchain, these are: (1) Throughput, (2) Latency, (3) Size and bandwidth, (4) Security, (5) Wasted resources, (6) Usability, and (7) Versioning, hard forks, and multiple chains.

2.2   Cryptocurrencies

Cryptocurrencies are digital assets, secured on a blockchain by cryptography. Most of the cryptocurrencies to date are created by private individuals, organisations, or firms [7]. Bitcoin for example relies on two fundamental technologies from cryptography, as explained by Böhme et al. [10]. These two are public-private key cryptography to store and spend money, and cryptography validation of transactions.

Cryptocurrencies are no traditional fiat currencies, whose value is determined by law, but they operate resembling a free market system [11]. White [7] shows that the value of cryptocurrencies can be expressed in a market cap (price per unit multiplied by number of units outstanding). Since the cryptocurrencies are no traditional fiat currencies, a curiosity derived on which determinants define the value of the cryptocurrencies. Related works show determinants for the Bitcoin exchange rates (which is the price per unit), most of them are summarised in the work by Li and Wang [1] as shown in Table 1. The economic factors are researched and determined in previous works that are elaborated by Li and Wang [1]. They also show that these economic factors have a significant impact in determining the exchange rate.

Table 1. Determinants for the USD Exchange Rate of Bitcoin by Li and Wang [1]

Technology factors	Economic factors
Public recognition	Economic indicators of the foreign country
Mining difficulty	Bitcoin economy
Mining technology	Market activity

The technology factors as determinants are based on the work of Kristoufek [12, 13], and Garcia et al. [14]. The public recognition is proved to be a significant factor for determining the exchange rate by Kristoufek [12]. The other technological factors however show that their impact diminishes over time [1]. This leaves a gap in the research field on which technological factors influence the exchange rate of cryptocurrencies and may therefore be used to replace the mining technology and-difficulty in a more mature ecosystem. Li and Wang also state that there is room for extension in this model, in terms of other determinants.

2.3   Software Ecosystem Health

Software ecosystems, or at least its concept first appeared in the book by Messerschmitt and Szyperski [15] in 2003. Since then, and especially since 2007, the area has been gaining popularity in the research field by rapidly evolving both in volume and empirical focus [6, 16].

A specific theory on software ecosystems is its health, one of the first definitions of software ecosystem health is given by Lucassen et al. [17] being: "*longevity and a propensity for growth*". This definition is derived from the work of den Hartigh [18], covering the health of business ecosystems. In the work of den Hartigh, three determinants of ecosystem health from Iansiti and Levien [19] are defined as:

- *Robustness*, the capability of an ecosystem to face and survive disruptions.
- *Productivity*, the efficiency with which an ecosystem converts inputs into outputs.
- *Niche creation*, the capacity to create meaningful diversity and thereby novel capabilities.

The OSEHO by Jansen [5] operationalises the three determinants for software ecosystems. Apart from the three pillars being the determinants Jansen added two layers in the OSEHO, the network level and project level. The network level operationalises the determinants for the ecosystem domain whereas the project level covers the analysis of projects within the software ecosystem. When using the OSEHO, it is important to first set goals about what you want to accomplish with the health measurement. After a goal is set, one can start with selecting the scope and metrics. When these are selected, there follows an assessment on whether there is sufficient data available. If this is the case, the data collection can start. The last, but certainly not the least part is analysing the data and satisfy the goals set in the first place [5].

Previous studies on e-commerce ecosystems [20], content management systems [21] and an open source framework [22] assessed these ecosystems with the OSEHO framework. More applications of OSEHO are needed to generalise the framework, which would fill a gap in the field of software ecosystems as identified by Manikas [6].

3   Research Method

The goal of this research is to find out if the health of a cryptocurrency ecosystem influences the exchange rate of the cryptocurrency. Therefore, this study hypothesises that there are metrics in the OSEHO framework that show significant relations with the exchange rate. To be able to check this hypothesis, two sub questions are drawn up:

RQ1.1: *How can the OSEHO framework be used to assess the health of the cryptocurrency ecosystem?*

RQ1.2: *Which metrics in the OSEHO framework show signs that they are related with the exchange rate?*

Cryptocurrencies are relatively young and exist since 2007. The research field is still nascent and therefore the focus of this study is explorative [2]. To accomplish the research goal, a case study approach has been chosen, where a number of cryptocurrencies have been chosen for which data will be collected. The collected data will be used to fill in the OSEHO framework.

The case study consists of five steps to be able to answer the research questions. Step one to four are needed to answer sub question one and step five is needed to answer sub question two.

Step one is to select the scope of the study, in this case three ecosystems in the shape of cryptocurrencies: Bitcoin, Ethereum, and Ripple. Step two is to select metrics from the OSEHO framework to measure the health of the cryptocurrency ecosystems. Step three is the gathering of data where whenever possible the data consists of a number of data points over time. This is necessary to see if that metric influences the exchange rate. Step four is filling in the data in the OSEHO framework and analysing it. The last step, step five, is to see if the metrics over time are influencing the exchange rate. In this step the metrics over time are set against the exchange rate to see if there is any relation between them. To test this relation a statistical analysis is performed.

3.1   Ecosystem Health Metrics

The metrics are split in three categories: Productivity, Robustness and Niche creation, as shown in Table 2. Not all metrics in the OSEHO framework were used for this study. Instead a selection has been made based on the relevance of the metrics of this topic the availability of data, and previous research.

The first metric that will be collected is the *number of new projects (1)* for each cryptocurrency. This will tell how many related GitHub projects, such as plug-ins or wallets are released from January 1st, 2017 till December 15th, 2017. This number contribute to the productivity of the ecosystem. The second metric collected is the *added knowledge (2)*. When developers can ask questions on knowledge bases (e.g. Stack Overflow), the ecosystem will benefit from it by the fact that there is a community within an ecosystem where people help each other with questions regarding the development [23]. This metric is measured by collecting the number of questions with the tag of the cryptocurrency attached. Apart from StackOverflow, both Bitcoin and Ethereum have a distinct stack exchange where questions can be asked. The number of questions from these exchanges are also measured. Another metric to measure the productivity from developers within an ecosystem is the *lines of code over time* (3) [17]. The number of lines of code added over time tells something about how productive the development of an ecosystem is. The *spinoffs and forks* (4), *number of tickets (5)* and *number of patents (6)* are also measured to compare the productivity of developers within an ecosystem.

To measure the robustness of an ecosystem other metrics are used. First the cohesion (7) of the ecosystem is measured by collecting the number of distinct APIs for the ecosystem [24]. APIs make it possible to connect software within or even outside an ecosystem, which enables better communication between clients and the ecosystem. Another metric that can be used to measure the robustness of an ecosystem is the number of active developers (8). The number of active developers shows how dependent an ecosystem is on individual developers. A higher number of active developers shows that the ecosystem is relatively more robust. An active developer is defined as a developer who has committed one or more lines of code to the respective cryptocurrency repositories within the last year. The second metric for robustness is the number of users of an ecosystem (9). This metric shows how many users were actively trading the cryptocurrencies in the last year. The number of transactions (10) is measured over time to see if the ecosystem still grows. The last metric for robustness is the search statistics (11). This metric shows which ecosystem was the most popular search term on Google and which ecosystem has the most interest over time. Van Lingen et al. [21] defines the findability on Google an indicator of ecosystem health, but only if the ecosystems are compared with each other. This data cannot be used to compare with the exchange rate, because this data is relative, but it can be used to compare the cryptocurrencies among themselves.

For the niche creation, the variety in the ecosystem is important to capture. This study uses two metrics which are derived from Lucassen et al. [17]. The first metric is the *variety in development technologies (12)*, which shows how many different programming languages are used to develop the software in the repository. The second metric is the *variety in projects (13)*. This is measured to compare how many projects are building upon the technology and thus extending the ecosystems. To measure variety, wallets are excluded as niche-projects, because wallets are focused on the main purpose of the ecosystem, which is the cryptocurrency, whereas for example the blockchain- and smart-contract applications provide a better insight in the niche-creation within an ecosystem.

3.2 Data Collection

The data was collected through different sources on December 15th, 2017. Data collected from GitHub was retrieved with GHTorrent [25] and gitstats[1]. The GHTorrent project is created by a research group of the TU Delft. It provides a MySQL database which can retrieve information by entering queries using the DBLite web-based client. For every new project using one of the cryptocurrencies the name and creation date is retrieved. Because GHTorrent is an archive, not all data is up to date on the repository

---

[1] https://github.com/matthijsberk/gitstats-ng

level. Therefore, another tool is used to inspect the repositories itself. Gitstats[1] is used to gather specific information within a repository, for example the number of contributors and lines of codes added over time. This application is written in Python and produces a JSON file. For Bitcoin and Ripple the core application was used. For Ethereum there are five different implementations of the blockchain, out of which Go-Ethereum was the most-popular and only actively-supported repository at the time of writing. Therefore, the information about Ethereum is collected solely from this repository, to prevent duplicity in the data set.

The data from the website Stack Overflow was gathered by using the data dump which is released every month. This dataset can be searched using SQL queries.

The number of patents is retrieved for each cryptocurrency from the Google patent database. For the data directly related to the cryptocurrency itself (e.g. value, number of transactions) a dataset from Kaggle is used which retrieved the data from several sources, for example different coin exchanges. Kaggle is a website where datasets are published. The last method used for retrieving data is collecting search statistics. To measure this, a Google trend analysis is executed to retrieve the number of times there has been searched for a certain cryptocurrency. This data is relative instead of absolute and therefore no hard conclusions can be drawn from this metric. A summary of the metrics per category and the corresponding sources can be found in Table 2.

Table 2. Overview of the selected SECO health metrics

	Metric	Source
Productivity	Number of new projects* (1)	GitHub
	Added knowledge (2)	StackOverflow
	Lines of code added over time* (3)	GitHub
	Spin offs and forks (4)	GitHub
	Number of tickets (5)	GitHub
	Number of patents (6)	Google
Robustness	Cohesion (number of APIs) (7)	ProgrammableWeb
	Number of active developers* (8)	GitHub
	Number of users (9)	Kaggle
	Number of transactions* (10)	Kaggle
	Search statistics (11)	Google trend analysis
Niche creation	Variety in development technologies (12)	GitHub
	Variety in projects (13)	GitHub

*The data from the metrics with an asterisk are available as data over time

4   Results

The results from the data collection are presented in this chapter. Each subsection elaborates on the different parts of the OSEHO framework being productivity, robustness and niche creation.

4.1 Productivity

The first six metrics used from the OSEHO as listed in Table 2 account for the productivity. The data about the productivity metrics is presented in Table 3. The first thing that draws attention are the missing metrics on Ripple. It became clear when mining the data, that there are numerous other applications with a naming that contains 'Ripple', other than the cryptocurrency. The search results for XRP were not complete and would give distorted results, for the search terms for the other metrics were complete. Therefore, to prevent incorrect data and/or data pollution, this study does not include the data for Ripple for these metrics.

Table 3. Results of the metrics per cryptocurrency

	Metric	Bitcoin	Ethereum	Ripple
Productivity	Number of new projects (1)	5499	345	-
	Added knowledge (2)	1117 17,470	721 12,496	-
	Lines of code added over time (3)	420,121	779,818	1,142,042
	Number of forks (4)	12,646	3100	518
	Number of tickets (5)	3535	2771	299
	Number of patents (6)	569	741	-
Robustness	Cohesion, number of APIs (7)	353	7	3
	Number of active developers (8)	147	133	20
	Number of users (9)	714,349 (unique)	10,557,839 (total)	-
	Number of transactions (10)	269,460,981	78,973,725	-
	Search statistics (11)	100	9	6
Niche creation	Variety in development technologies (12)	58	52	98
	Variety in projects (13)	466	1170	2

Since 01/01/2017, cumulatively 5499 new projects were added on GitHub where 'Bitcoin' was mentioned, respectively 345 for Ethereum. The added projects are shown in Fig. 1, which clearly shows a strong increase in the new projects added for Bitcoin near the end of 2017.

The added knowledge came from mining Stack Overflow, where there were 1117 questions asked about Bitcoin and 721 for Ethereum on Stack Overflow. Bitcoin and Ethereum are having an own stack exchange where questions can be asked. On these exchanges Bitcoin has 17,470 questions and Ethereum has 12,496 questions on their stack exchange. The lines of code added over time derived from mining the repositories of the cryptocurrencies in GitHub. The data on the lines of code is available since GitHub started to document the data about lines of code or since the opening of the repository in GitHub. For Bitcoin, this was on the 28th of April 2013, Ethereum on the 7th of August 2015 and Ripple on the 5th of August 2013. The number in the table

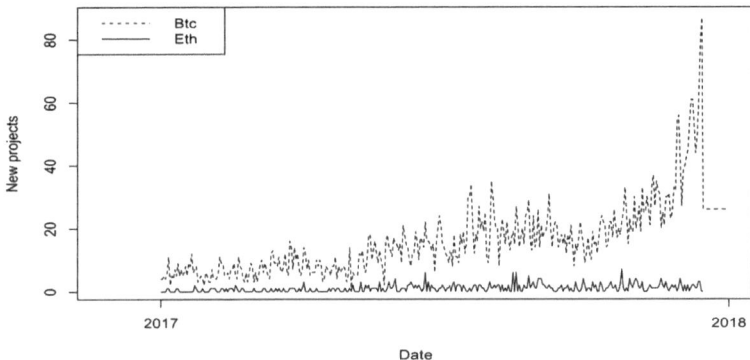

Fig. 1. Number of new projects

represents the total lines of code on the date of data collection, where Ripple has the highest number of 1,142,042 lines, followed by Ethereum with 779,818 lines and finally Bitcoin with 420,121 lines. From the same repositories, the number of forks and tickets were collected. With the number of forks being 12,646 for Bitcoin, 3100 for Ethereum, and 518 for Ripple. Bitcoin also shows the highest number of tickets with 3535, followed by Ethereum with 2771, and Ripple with 299. The patents that were published on Google for the cryptocurrencies were collected, where Ethereum has more published patents than Bitcoin, having 741 against 569 patents.

4.2   Robustness

The level of robustness on the cryptocurrencies are measured with the five metrics as described in Sect. 3. The results of the data collection for these metrics are presented in Table 3. This time, the lack of data for Ripple was caused by data scarcity. Where Kaggle had data sets on Bitcoin and Ethereum, there were no data sets available with information on these metrics for Ripple. ProgrammableWeb provided the data for the cohesion metric, where the number of APIs defined the cohesion. Bitcoin had 353 APIs, where Ethereum had 7 and Ripple 3.

Active developers were collected from GitHub repositories, where anyone who contributed in the year 2017 was considered an active developer. Again, Bitcoin takes the lead with 147 active developers, Ethereum follows with 133, and finally Ripple has 20 active developers. The active developers over time provides a slightly different view, as Fig. 4 shows that the number of active developers per month for Bitcoin is significantly higher, although Ethereum does show an upward trend in 2017.

Because of data scarcity, it was not possible to collect either the unique daily or the number of total unique users for the three cryptocurrencies. For Ethereum the total number of unique users came down to 10,557,839 where Bitcoin showed 714,349 unique daily users. Thus, the number of *new* unique users may be derived from the Ethereum data, but this does not compare to the daily unique users of Bitcoin. For Ripple, this information was not readily available.

The number of transactions is the total number of transactions on the blockchain at the time of data collection, being 269,460,981 for Bitcoin and 78,973,725 for Ethereum.

Bitcoin was searched the most, followed by Ethereum and Ripple. These relative statistics can be quantified as shown in the works of Kristoufek [12]. Although possible, this is not necessary for the comparative nature of this study and therefore left out of scope.

4.3   Niche Creation

This subsection elaborates on the results from the data collection on the niche creation of the cryptocurrencies, the last two metrics, variety in development technologies and projects are presented in Table 3. For niche creation, both metrics were available for Ripple as well. The development technologies were defined as the different programming languages in the GitHub repositories. Ripple shows the highest number with 98 languages, where Bitcoin is second with 58, and Ethereum last with 52.

The variety in projects derived from search results in GitHub. When searching for the wallets of the cryptocurrencies, Bitcoin showed the highest number of results, however, this is not the point of interest for niche creation. Therefore, this metric shows the sum of search results containing either 'blockchain' or 'smart contract' and excluding the term 'wallet'. Ethereum came up on top with 1170 results, out of which a big part, 518 projects, mentioned smart contracts. Bitcoin came second, with 466 results, out of which 12 contained a smart contract tag, and Ripple came last, with 2 blockchain projects.

5   Analysis

In this chapter, the results from the data collection are analysed. This is divided in two subsections; the first subsection is dedicated to analysing the metrics from the OSEHO framework. From this analysis, a comparison between the cryptocurrencies and their ecosystem health is made. The second subsection explores the metrics with values over time and the correlation of these with the USD exchange rate in order to see if these may be used as an extension on the model of Li and Wang [1].

5.1   Health Comparison

Looking at valuation of the cryptocurrencies at December 14th, 2017 as shown in Table 4, one would say that Bitcoin, next to being the oldest ecosystem, is financially the most successful cryptocurrency at that time. This is in line with the OSEHO framework, where Bitcoin appears to be the healthiest ecosystem, as it shows the best results for 8 out of the 13 metrics. When looking at this in the 3 different levels of the OSEHO framework, Bitcoin has the highest productivity and robustness, but not the highest niche creation. Therefore, this subsection elaborates on the metrics where Bitcoin does not show the highest value and on the metrics with noteworthy findings which arose during the data collection.

Table 4. Valuation of cryptocurrencies on 14 December 2017 (Retrieved from https://coinmarketcap.com [accessed December 15, 2017])

	Bitcoin	Ethereum	Ripple
USD EXCHANGE rate	$16,564.00	$695.82	$0.86
Market cap	$274,269M	$67,483M	$18,233M

The metrics where Bitcoin did not show the highest value are: (1) Lines of code added over time, (2) Number of patents, (3) Variety in development technologies, and (4) Variety in projects.

Ripple had the most **lines of code over time**. An explanation for this can be that Ripple is a protocol, which is slightly different from blockchains such as Bitcoin and Ethereum. Ethereum has more lines of code than Bitcoin, probably since the blockchain of Ethereum is more comprehensive: Ethereum example allows the use of smart contracts whereas Bitcoin does not. For both Ripple and Bitcoin, the lines of code increase gradually over time, whereas Ethereum sees a major drop in the lines of code of over 2.5 million lines of code, caused by a major clean-up on July 12th, 2017.

The highest **number of patents** is claimed by Ethereum with 741 patents, Bitcoin shows 569 patents. This indicates that the technology of the Ethereum blockchain shows more promising applications than that of the Bitcoin. On this point, the Ethereum software ecosystem scores better than the Bitcoin software ecosystem, in terms of new technologies and blockchain applications.

For the **variety in development technologies**, Ripple shows the highest number of development languages. However, the data collection for Ethereum only took place on Go-Ethereum, where other repositories for Ethereum are written in other languages. Therefore, it is hard to conclude that Ripple supports the most languages, as Ethereum might exceed them. One thing is clear though, which is that Bitcoin is built upon the least variety in development technologies. This shows that the interest in the Bitcoin core from the developers' perspective is narrow compared to the other ecosystems.

For the **variety in projects**, Ethereum has the most variety in projects (1170) followed by Bitcoin (466). When looking at the number of new projects Bitcoin has the most, 5499, followed by Ethereum with 345. This can be explained by the fact that Bitcoin is popular and a lot of people copy the repository of Bitcoin to their own repository. However, to develop applications Ethereum is the most popular blockchain technology, showing a higher variety in the projects produced. This is in line with the number of patents, both show that Ethereum is a promising software ecosystem.

Another noteworthy metric is the **added knowledge**. Bitcoin and Ethereum both have their own Stack exchange for sharing knowledge, for which the results are given in the table as well. Here should be mentioned that this does not mean that the Stackexchange only contains questions regarding the respective cryptocurrency. In fact, both contain questions regarding the 'other' cryptocurrency and in the case of Bitcoin an even higher number of other cryptocurrencies, and on StackOverflow numerous questions also contain both tags.

5.2   Exploring Indicators

The ecosystem health metrics which were captured over time are the number of new projects (1), the lines of code added over time (3), the number of active developers (8) and the number of transactions (10). The number of active users has been found, but given the different numbers obtained for this metric, the metric has been left out of the research.

To find correlations between the metrics available over time and the exchange rate, a Pearson's product-moment correlation test was conducted. The results from the correlation tests is shown in Table 5.

Table 5. Pearson's product-moment correlation tests

Cryptocurrency	Metric	t-value	df	Pearson coefficient	p-value
Bitcoin	Number of new projects	31.529	348	0.86	<2.2e−16*
Bitcoin	Lines of code	24.321	1692	0.51	<2.2e−16*
Bitcoin	Number of active developers	−0.722	54	−0.10	0.4732
Bitcoin	Number of transactions	44.235	1652	0.74	<2.2e−16*
Ethereum	Number of new projects	7.581	347	0.38	3.162e−13
Ethereum	Lines of code	−29.133	861	−0.70	<2.2e−16*
Ethereum	Number of active developers	5.839	26	0.75	3.737e−6*
Ethereum	Number of transactions	82.404	803	0.95	<2.2e−16*
Ripple	Lines of code	10.533	1065	0.31	<2.2e−16*
Ripple	Number of active developers	−5.090	51	−0.58	5.22e−6*

*. Correlation is significant at the 0.01 level (2-tailed)

The correlation tests show interesting results. The only metric that shows no significant correlation with the exchange rate is the number of active developers on Bitcoin. The number of transactions is also a determinant from the model by Li and Wang [1], the strong, positive, and significant correlations shown in Table 5 confirm their findings.

The lines of code also show significant correlations with the exchange rate on all cryptocurrencies. Unfortunately, Ethereum shows a negative correlation, this can be explained by the enormous drop in the lines of code due to a major clean-up on July 12th, 2017. Possibly the difference in lines of code, rather than the actual lines of code, is correlated to the exchange rate. A metric that is significantly positive for Bitcoin as well as for Ethereum is the number of new projects, showing potential as an indicator for the exchange rate. The number of active developers however shows mixed results for the different cryptocurrencies, possibly because the number of active developers does not show a lot of variation over time.

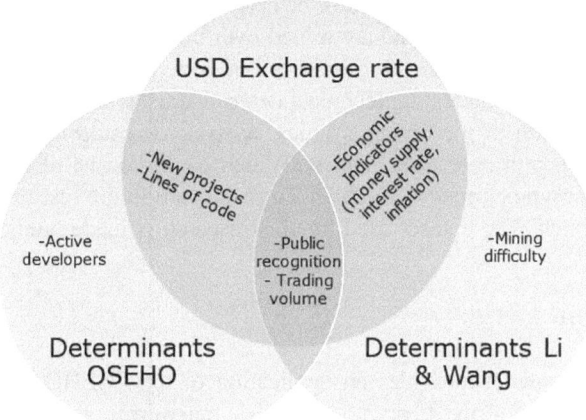

Fig. 2. Venn diagram determinants

Figure 2 visualises the possible future determinants for the exchange rate of cryptocurrencies. Mining difficulty is becoming less significant and is therefore left out as determining factor. There was no positive correlation found in the metric active developers, therefore that one is also left out as a determinant.

6 Discussion

Every research has limitations, this one is not an exception. The first limitation is the fact that this study only focuses on one Ethereum implementation, and therefore only mined the data from the most popular and most used repository of Ethereum, while there are other Ethereum repositories on hand. Bitcoin and Ripple only have one implementation, and therefore do not have this problem. When comparing Ripple with the other two cryptocurrencies it stands out that it is different. Ripple is more of a platform with value instead of a cryptocurrency. The ecosystems are not around that long, especially Ethereum, and not only are the software ecosystems not yet mature, the markets of the corresponding cryptocurrencies are also highly volatile.

This research shows some interesting results. However, to draw conclusions on whether the metrics from the OSEHO can actually extend the model by Li and Wang [1], more econometrical tests are needed. The statistical tests used in Subsect. 5.2 showed significance but are not strong enough to conclude that the changes in the price are caused by the metric, for example since it doesn't keep time series in mind. This leaves possibilities in future research, where this research can be used as a foundation so that future research doesn't have to start from scratch.

This is the first suggestion for future research, which would be using our data set and the results from this study and perform a more fitting statistical analysis to draw conclusion on extending the model by Li and Wang [1]. The second suggestion is to extend the research on the health of the cryptocurrency ecosystems. This extension could be twofold, one where more sorts of cryptocurrencies are considered, and one where more metrics of the OSEHO are mined over time. For example, the patents and the variety in projects are interesting metrics but currently not mined over time, and these might prove to be interesting technical determinants as well. The extension of the research on the health of the cryptocurrency ecosystems could result in a cryptocurrency ecosystem health operationalization. Which could consist of metrics from both the OSEHO and cryptocurrency literature. To make sure future research does not have to start from scratch. The dataset used for this research is made public[2].

7 Conclusion

This exploratory research provides an application of the OSEHO framework on the software ecosystems of three cryptocurrencies, answering the following research question: *What are the possibilities of using the health of cryptocurrency software ecosystems as an influencing factor on the exchange rate of cryptocurrencies?*

Three case studies, where data was mined from different sources showed that Bitcoin has the healthiest software ecosystem at the time of data collection. Some other interesting findings were that Ethereum shows a potential for growth in its productivity and niche creation, even outweighing Bitcoin on some metrics in the OSEHO framework.

With the metrics from the OSEHO correlation tests were performed to see if there are signs that these metrics have significant relations with the exchange rate of the cryptocurrencies. This would indicate that they are possible extensions on the model by Li and Wang [1]. The results show at least two potential metrics, being number of new projects and lines of code. However, stronger econometric statistical tests are needed to confirm this and to be able to predict exchange rates. Nevertheless, this research extended the model by Li and Wang with two possible determinants and verified parts of the model on other cryptocurrencies. The OSEHO framework showed to be a useful tool to not only measure the health of software ecosystems, but also to provide a foundation of quantitative data for statistical tests.

This research contributes to science by further adopting the OSEHO framework, by not only using it for health measurement, but also for further investigation on characteristics of software ecosystems. The second contribution is a verification and extension on the model by Li and Wang [1]. Indication show that metrics from the OSEHO framework can be used to extend the model. The third contribution is filling a gap in a nascent field of cryptocurrencies, by performing case studies on the three cryptocurrencies. The findings in this research can be used as a foundation for further scientific research on cryptocurrencies as a whole or by diving deeper in the determinants for the exchange rate of cryptocurrencies.

---

[2] https://www.github.com/matthijsberk/crypto_oseho.

References

1. Li, X., Wang, C.A.: The technology and economic determinants of cryptocurrency exchange rates: the case of Bitcoin. Decis. Support Syst. **95**, 49–60 (2017)
2. Swan, M.: Blockchain: Blueprint for a New Economy. O'Reilly Media, Sebastopol (2015)
3. Yli-Huumo, J., Ko, D., Choi, S., Park, S., Smolander, K.: Where is current research on blockchain technology? - a systematic review. PLoS ONE **11**, 1–27 (2016)
4. Jansen, S., Finkelstein, A., Brinkkemper, S.: A sense of community: a research agenda for software ecosystems. In: 2009 31st International Conference on Software Engineering-Companion, pp. 187–190 (2009)
5. Jansen, S.: Measuring the health of open source software ecosystems: beyond the scope of project health. Inf. Softw. Technol. **56**, 1508–1519 (2014)
6. Manikas, K.: Revisiting software ecosystems research: a longitudinal literature study. J. Syst. Softw. **117**, 84–103 (2016)
7. White, L.H.: The market for cryptocurrencies. Cato J. **35**, 383–402 (2015)
8. Buterin, V.: Ethereum white paper (2013)
9. Schwartz, D., Youngs, N., Britto, A.: The Ripple Protocol Consensus Algorithm. Ripple Labs Inc White Paper, pp. 1–8 (2014)
10. Böhme, R., Christin, N., Edelman, B., Moore, T.: Bitcoin: economics, technology, and governance. J. Econ. Perspect. **29**, 213–238 (2015)
11. Bouoiyour, J., Selmi, R.: What does Bitcoin look like? Ann. Econ. Financ. **16**, 449–492 (2015)
12. Kristoufek, L.: BitCoin meets Google Trends and Wikipedia: quantifying the relationship between phenomena of the Internet era. Sci. Rep. **3**, 1–7 (2013)
13. Kristoufek, L.: What are the main drivers of the Bitcoin price? Evidence from wavelet coherence analysis. PLoS ONE **10**, 1–15 (2015)
14. Garcia, D., Tessone, C.J., Mavrodiev, P., Perony, N.: The digital traces of bubbles: feedback cycles between socio-economic signals in the Bitcoin economy. J. R. Soc. Interface. **11** (2014)
15. Messerschmitt, D.G., Szyperski, C.: Software Ecosystem: Understanding an Indispensable Technology and Industry. MIT Press, Cambridge (2003)
16. Manikas, K., Hansen, K.M.: Software ecosystems-a systematic literature review. J. Syst. Softw. **86**, 1294–1306 (2013)
17. Lucassen, G., van Rooij, K., Jansen, S.: Ecosystem health of cloud PaaS providers. In: Herzwurm, G., Margaria, T. (eds.) ICSOB 2013. LNBIP, vol. 150, pp. 183–194. Springer, Heidelberg (2013). https://doi.org/10.1007/978-3-642-39336-5_18
18. Den Hartigh, E., Tol, M., Visscher, W.: The health measurement of a business ecosystem. In: ECCON 2006 Annual Meetingm, vol. 2783565, pp. 1–39 (2006)
19. Iansiti, M., Levien, R.: Strategy as ecology. Harv. Bus. Rev. **82**, 68–81 (2004)
20. Alami, D., Rodríguez, M., Jansen, S.: Relating health to platform success. In: Proceedings of the 2015 European Conference on Software Architecture Workshops - ECSAW 2015, pp. 1–6 (2015)
21. van Lingen, S., Palomba, A., Lucassen, G.: On the software ecosystem health of open source content management systems. In: Proceedings of the 5th International Workshop on Software Ecosystems, vol. 987, pp. 45–56 (2013)
22. van Vulpen, P., Menkveld, A., Jansen, S.: Health measurement of data-scarce software ecosystems: a case study of Apple's ResearchKit. In: Ojala, A., Holmström Olsson, H., Werder, K. (eds.) ICSOB 2017. LNBIP, vol. 304, pp. 131–145. Springer, Cham (2017). https://doi.org/10.1007/978-3-319-69191-6_9

23. Seichter, D., Dhungana, D., Pleuss, A., Hauptmann, B.: Knowledge management in software ecosystems: software artefacts as first-class citizens. In: Proceedings of the 4th European Conference on Software Architecture: Companion Volume (ECSA 2010), pp. 119–126 (2010)
24. Hoving, R., Slot, G., Jansen, S.: Python: characteristics identification of a free open source software ecosystem. In: 2013 7th IEEE International Conference on Digital Ecosystems and Technologies (DEST), pp. 13–18. IEEE (2013)
25. Gousios, G.: The GHTorrent dataset and tool suite. In: Proceedings of the 10th Working Conference on Mining Software Repositories, pp. 233–236 (2013)

Benchmarking Privacy Policies in the Mobile Application Ecosystem

Sharif Adel Kandil[✉], Micha van den Akker, Koen van Baarsen,
Slinger Jansen, and Paul van Vulpen

Utrecht University,, Budapestlaan 4 3584 CD Utrecht, The Netherlands
{s.a.kandil,m.j.t.vandenakker,k.j.baarsen}@students.uu.nl,
{slinger.jansen,p.n.vanvulpen}@uu.nl

Abstract. Mobile app providers have access to, and gather, large amounts of personal data. The exact data varies by app provider and is described in lengthy privacy policies with varying levels of transparency. Privacy policies with a low level of transparency hamper users from making educated decisions about the data that they want to share with third parties. In this paper, the Privacy Policy Benchmark Model is presented based on existing literature and applied to a selection of 20 mobile applications and their privacy policies. The Privacy Policy Benchmark Model is used for evaluating the transparency and quantity of data that is collected. The model consists of two aspects: the amount of data mobile app provides collect and the transparency of those privacy policies. The examined providers are transparent about what they collected and how they use it. They are less transparent about other topics such as the location of the stored information and how information is processed after removal, making privacy and usage considerations more difficult for users on those specific matters.

Keywords: Transparency · Personal data · Mobile app store
Privacy policies

1 Introduction

Consumers have an intimate connection with their mobile devices and these devices contain sensitive information about the user. The sensitive information is used for personalizing advertisements. Personal advertisements make the advertisement space more valuable to the advertisers, and therefore it allows the mobile application (from now on: "app") providers to sell the advertisement space for a higher price [8]. App providers can also use gathered personal data in other ways, for instance to improve their application and provide services or identifying new potential users of the app and services.

The data collection and business models of the providers lead to a conflict of interest between the users and the developers of an app [1]. On the one hand, it makes sense for a user to protect his or her privacy. On the other hand,

© Springer Nature Switzerland AG 2018
K. Wnuk and S. Brinkkemper (Eds.): ICSOB 2018, LNBIP 336, pp. 43–55, 2018.
https://doi.org/10.1007/978-3-030-04840-2_4

personal information is used to improve customer satisfaction and to generate revenue for the application provider. The conflict of interest is validated by prior research which showed concerns of app users [17,18]. Another research showed that 57% of the worries of application users reached the height in which they either deleted applications or refused to install them in the first place [4]. The application providers use privacy policies to communicate about what personal data they gather and how this data is used. Unfortunately, the privacy policies typically do not address the concerns of end-users [12] and those policies are too much of a burden to be practical and effective [11]. The privacy concerns and the criticism on polices led to the following research question:

- **How can the transparency of privacy polices be measured in a standardized way?**

In this study, a benchmark is done on the privacy policies of the leading app providers. The benchmark helps shed light onto *the data that is collected by the app providers*, and *how transparent they are with regards to this collection of personal data*. There has been no previous research in this domain, resulting in a severe lack of knowledge with regards to the contents and transparency of the privacy policies of the leading app providers. Generating more knowledge about these privacy policies is of value, because it helps consumers to make educated decisions about which apps they could use without sharing more personal information then they would like. Using this information, consumers can determine whether the privacy cost of using apps is worth it to them. In order to give users a quick overview of the collected data and privacy policy the Privacy Policy Benchmark Model was created, which can be used to decrease the effort for users to reason about applications and personal information.

The next section of the paper contains a literature study that provides the context in which this research is framed. Section 3 explains the research methods used when executing this study. In Sect. 4, the gathered data is analysed, and the results, which give a benchmark of the examined companies, are displayed. The paper ends with a discussion about the results in Sect. 5.

2   Literature Study

In order to create a deeper understanding of the context of this study, a few related topics from prior research that explore privacy in mobile ecosystems are discussed. These cover mobile applications (Sect. 2.1); privacy sensitivity of those mobile applications (Sect. 2.2) and privacy policies (Sect. 2.3).

2.1   Mobile Applications

The growth of the use of smartphones over the last few decades is remarkable. The main drivers for this growth are the computation, communication and sensing capabilities they provide [2]. These capabilities are used by (third party) developers in order to create a large variety of applications. Google Play, the Android app store, provides Android users with over 3.300.000 applications (September 2017), and is still growing [3]. The user habits concerning mobile apps shift from a consuming role to a more participative role, which usually involves user-generated content like photos (e.g. Instagram, Snapchat), texts (e.g. Whatsapp, Messenger) and personal experiences (e.g. Facebook, LinkedIn) [9]. Due to the decreasing costs of data storage there is no to little necessity to delete this data [15]. These trends, in combination with the growing number of app providers, nourish privacy concerns amongst users. It raises questions about what personal data is stored and how personal data is handled within such ecosystems.

2.2 Privacy Concerns and Regulations

A survey held in 2012 amongst 2.254 US adults, showed that 57% of the people have either uninstalled an application or declined to install it because of concerns about sharing personal information [4]. Privacy of user data is a much discussed topic [4–6], and many related works show the concerns of users [17–19].

In order to facilitate a secure IT environment the EU Parliament approved of new regulations concerning data protection (April 14th 2016). This law, starting at the 25th of 2018, is called the General Data Protection Regulation (GDPR) and replaces the Data Protection Directive 95/46/EC from 1995. It's main goal is to protect and empower all EU citizens data privacy. Two changes have huge impact related to this research. (A) the new law increased the territorial scope, which means that all companies processing the personal data of data subjects residing in the Union, need to comply; and (B) the conditions for consent have been strengthened and companies are obligated to give the request for consent in an intelligible and easy accessible form [7].

To be clear about what is being collected and how this information is used, companies create privacy policies. These policies state terms, which, in most cases must be accepted before (all functions of) applications can be used. These terms are, for example, about what type of information they collect or with what third parties they share this information.

2.3 Privacy Policies

Prior research on privacy policies criticizes about the way they are set up. The research of Jensen and Potts [11] focused on privacy policies of websites and determined that significant changes needed to be made to the practices in order to meet regulatory and usability requirements. In this research the privacy policies were measured with policy accessibility (are the privacy policies easy to find) readability (is the privacy policy easy to understand) and content (what does the privacy policy show). The primary finding was stated as: *"Too much of a burden is put on the end-user by failing to provide adequate notification of changes, or presenting privacy policies in language the user can understand."* [11]. Another research in this area, analyzing fifty privacy policies, resulted in two general improvements. First, privacy policies must focus more on the privacy concerns of the public instead of only covering their own practices; and second, they have to avoid vague language and present the content in a more suitable and readable format [12].

Applications differ in the data they collect of users. The NSTIC (a US governmental cybersecurity department) distinguished ten types of personal data: identity, relationships, communication, context, content, governmental records, financial, health, activity and ePortfolio [13].

Although much research has focused on privacy policies there is a lack in literature available about how to benchmark privacy policies. This research tries to fill this gap by creating a model which can be used in order to analyse two variables: the data collection and the transparency of privacy policies. The model is tested on the privacy policies of the app-provider of the top 20 apps from the iTunes store in 2017.

3   Research Methods

In this paper, a benchmark model for analyzing the transparency of privacy policies in the mobile app ecosystem is proposed. The benchmark was created using Jetmarová's benchmarking cycle [14]. According to her research, a benchmark consists of four distinct phases: a planning phase, where internal data is analysed in order to determine what should be benchmarked; a data collection phase, where data from external sources is collected; a data analysis phase, in which the results are analysed; and an adaptation phase, in which the results from the benchmark are applied in context.

3.1   Planning

The purpose of the planning phase of the benchmarking cycle is to determine what should be benchmarked. While the domain of the study has already been established (the transparency of privacy policies in the mobile ecosystem), the exact focus of the research had to be clarified in more detail.

The goal of the proposed benchmark is to analyse the privacy policies of apps, and classify them into different categories. These categories had to be based on the transparency about, and the quantity of personal information gathered by mobile app providers. Summarized, the benchmark needed to answer two questions about the analysed companies:

- *How much personal information are mobile app-providers gathering?*
- *How transparent are mobile app-providers about the types of personal information they are collecting, how this information is processed, and how it is used throughout the mobile ecosystem?*

Based on these questions, it was observed that the benchmark needs to have two main variables: a score for the transparency of an app provider's privacy policy, and a score for the quantity of data that is collected by an app provider.

Assigning a Score to the Transparency Variable. The transparency score of the privacy policies focused on grading the completeness of a privacy policy. The privacy policies of the 20 most popular apps in 2017 on the iOS ecosystem [16] were analysed to create objective grading criteria for said completeness. Based on this analysis, we identified different subjects that app providers could provide information about in their privacy policies. These subjects that app providers can discuss in their privacy policies are referred to as "transparency categories" in the rest of this paper.

Each previously transparency category has different topics that need to be described. A transparency point is added to the transparency score for each category topic that is discussed in the privacy policy. All topics in the transparency category are weighed the same. By measuring the sum of the points awarded to each transparency category, it is possible to compare privacy policies to each other.

The categories are briefly described below:

How the Data is Used. The goal of this transparency category is to determine if app-providers tell users what their personal information is used for. App-providers can score transparency points by describing that the data is used for personalized advertisements, identifying users, matching users, or for improving the application.

With Whom the Data is Shared. Thanks to this category, a part of the transparency score stems from how transparent app-providers are about who they share users' personal information with. App providers can score points for describing that the data is shared with nobody, shared with third parties, by listing a partial list of parties, or by listing all parties that the data is shared with.

How the Data is Stored. App-providers can also earn transparency points by describing how their data is stored. Do they tell users in which geographic region the data is stored? Does the privacy policy describe whether the data is stored on an organizations' own infrastructure or the infrastructure of third parties?

How the Data is Secured. Personal information should be secured well because leakage of personal information could have far-reaching consequences. For this reason, app-providers can earn transparency points for describing how their data is protected, and stating why it is stored securely.

Account Removal. Often, deleting an account does not delete the associated information from an organizations servers. App-providers can earn points by describing whether accounts from their services can be deleted, and whether this account deletion will also fully delete the related information from their servers.

Readability. Legal documents like privacy policies can sometimes be hard to read. If consumers cannot understand the privacy policy, this makes it worthless to them. For this reason, a readability score is also assigned to the privacy policies. Readable.io has created an algorithm, that scores the readability of text based on a variety of criteria. Their grade considers factors like how many difficult words a text contains (tested with the New Dale-Chall Score), and how complex the sentences are (using tests like Flesch Reading Ease). Readable.io assigns texts a grade from A to E. In the Privacy Policy Benchmarking Model, an A earns 5 points, a B results in 4 points, a C earns 3 points, a D results in 2 points, and an E gets rewarded with 1 point.

It is important that the score from this category variable only relates to whether an app-provider is transparent about their data collection, not about the quantity of data that is actually collected. Even if the privacy policy does say, for example, that personal information will or will not be used for personalized advertisements they will in both scenarios retrieve a score in our Benchmark Model, because they are transparent about that specific topic.

Assigning a Score to the Amount of Data Gathered Variable. There are many different types of personal information that an organization can gather, and different apps gather different data. As an example, a shopping app might collect credit card information, while a navigation app might primarily store location data.

An existing study by Davis et al. [10], identified the different personal information artefacts that organizations can gather. He classified these artefacts into groups. In our Privacy Policy Benchmarking Model, a score is assigned to the amount of gathered data by searching for the collection of each personal information artefact identified by Davis. The amount of collected artefacts in each personal information type group identified by Davis, provides information about the types of data that is collected by the app providers.

The Privacy Policy Benchmark Model. In order to make the framework easily replicable for other researchers, the grading systems for the two variables were incorporated into an Excel sheet. Using this sheet, researchers can turf which personal information artefacts are collected according to the privacy policies and what topics are discussed in the privacy policy. After making these turfs, scores for the transparency and amount of data collected are automatically generated. The sheet also shows the exact formula and definitions that are used.

3.2   Data Collection

In the second phase of the benchmark cycle, the benchmark is used for analyzing external data sources. In this study, the Benchmarking Model that was described in the previous section is used for analyzing the privacy policies of a small selection of leading mobile apps.

We wanted to do the first data collection process by hand. Manually doing the data collection, and manually applying the benchmark provided more opportunities for evaluation of the model itself. Any errors would be more visible when manually reading privacy policies and calculating scores, then when this would be done in an automated fashion. Because of the considerable time it takes to analyse a privacy policy, and the limited amount of manpower that was available, the number of apps that could be included in the data collection phase of the benchmarking cycle was limited. Therefore only a small sample of apps could be included in the study. Apple recently published a list of most 20 popular apps on the iOS mobile ecosystem in 2017 [16]. All these apps were also released and successful on Android, making this study applicable to mobile ecosystems in general, not just for Apple's iOS.

These 20 most popular apps, were published by 15 app providers. In the data collection stage of the study, the privacy policies of these app providers were saved as PDF documents. All mentions of one of the personal information artefacts or transparency topics were highlighted in these PDF documents. Based on these mentions, the benchmarking framework was filled in.

Whilst and after filling in the Benchmarking Model for the 15 privacy policies, no errors were observed in the benchmark. This means that the data collection can be automated in future research.

4   Data Analysis

During the data analysis process, step three of the benchmark cycle, the previously described benchmarking model was completely filled in. The collected privacy policies have been structurally reviewed, and rated in the Privacy Policy Benchmark Model. The derived Privacy Policy Benchmark Model with example app provider privacy policy data is shown in Fig. 1.

Each privacy policy was saved at the time of reviewing and the topics we relied on are marked through these privacy policies. Due to space constraints, the raw data of the model is not included in this paper. The raw collected and reviewed data[1] is public available. Visualizations of the gathered data in the form of graphs, provide a better overview of the data.

4.1   Categorizing App-Providers

The first artifact that was generated based on the gathered data, is a scatter chart that places the analysed companies in three quadrants. This plot is shown in Fig. 2.

Using this scatter plot, organizations can be placed into different categories depending on the quadrant of the graph that they fall into. The first quadrant, "communicative disposers", refers to organizations that store relatively little user data and communicate about this openly. The second quadrant, "blunt

---

[1] bit.do/PrivacyPoliciesData.

Category	Topics	Company X Described	Category	Topics	Company X Described
Identifiers	Name	Yes	**Communications**	Text	Yes
	Email address	Yes		Speech	No
	Personas	Yes		Social media consumed	No
	Nicknames	Yes		Presence	No
	Phone numbers	No		Score	1
	Score	4	**Context**	Location	Yes
Declared interests	Likes	Yes		People	No
	Favorites	Yes		Objects	No
	Tags	Yes		Events	No
	Preferences	Yes		Score	1
	Settings	Yes	**Content**	Private documents	No
	Score	5		Consumed media	Yes
Personal devices	IMEIs	No		Score	1
	Bluetooth	No	**Goverment records**	Legal names	No
	SSIDs	No		Life events	No
	IP Addresses	Yes		Law enforcement	No
	Device IP	Yes		Military service	No
	Score	2		Score	0
Demographic data	Age	Yes	**Financial**	Income, Expenses, Transactions, etc.	No
	Sex	Yes		Score	0
	Addressess	No	**Health**	Care, Insurance	Yes
	Education	No		Score	1
	Work history	No	**Activity**	Real world	No
	Resume	No		Client application and OS	No
	Score	2		Browser	Yes
Relationships	Address book Contacts	Yes		Score	1
	Communication contacts	Yes	**ePortfolio**	Academic	Yes
	Social network links	Yes		Employment	No
	Family and Genealogy	No		Score	1
	Group Memberships	No			
	Call & Message logs	Yes			
	Score	4			

Fig. 1. Privacy Policy Benchmark Model with example company data

hoarders", contains companies that are collecting a large amount of user data, according to the measured topics elaborated in Sect. 3, but are transparent about this. Finally, organizations in the third quadrant, "silent disposers", do not store a large amount of personal data but have opaque privacy policies.

Organizations in the bottom right quadrant are, from a theoretical point of view, rare, and none are found in this research. The value for the amount of data that is collected, is based on what data is stored by the organization according to their privacy policy. If a company is so nontransparent that they secretly collect a large amount of personal information without describing this in their privacy policy, it is likely that they also score low on the transparency score.

These categories provide a valuable addition to the scientific community. They can be used for classifying organizations in further research. Furthermore, these app-provider categories could also be useful for consumers, providing them with a brief overview of how installing a mobile app would impact their privacy.

4.2 Types of Collected Data

The gathered data also shows what types of data organizations tend to collect. Based on the data from the model, a crosstab was generated that show how much data was collected in each of the previously identified personal information categories. This crosstab is shown in Fig. 3.

Fig. 2. The transparency and quantity of data collection of popular app providers

The cumulative data that app-providers gather, provide more insights into the types of personal information that are flowing around in mobile app ecosystems. The results clearly show that app-providers gather a large amount of data on how users can be identified, which devices they are using the apps from, what real-life relationships users have, and what their interests are. By contrast, little data is collected about the health of users, their governmental records, or their professional history.

This information might tell users more about what aspects of their lives they are sharing when using their favorite apps. As an example, the authors of this paper do not expect users to know that they have shared their phone contacts with numerous app-providers.

The results of the analysis showed that most app-providers use the data that they are gathering in a similar manner. Almost all app-providers use the gathered data for personalized advertisements, identifying users, and improving the application. Furthermore, a large proportion of the app-providers also used the data for matching users.

Category	Google	Amazone	Whatsapp	Facebook	Twitter	Snap inc.	Instagram	Netflix	Spotify	Soundcloud	Pandora Music	Uber	Lyft	Waze Navigation	Wish
Identifiers	4	4	3	4	5	4	4	5	3	3	4	5	4	5	4
Declared interests	3	0	1	4	1	2	4	4	3	4	1	2	0	0	0
Personal devices	4	2	2	5	3	3	2	2	3	2	3	2	3	2	0
Demographic data	0	1	0	1	1	1	0	3	3	4	3	3	2	2	1
Relationships	3	1	4	4	1	4	3	4	2	4	0	2	3	3	0
Communications	2	0	2	3	1	0	0	0	0	1	2	2	1	0	0
Context	2	2	2	2	1	3	1	1	1	3	2	4	2	1	0
Content	0	1	0	2	0	1	0	0	0	1	1	1	0	0	0
Goverment records	1	1	0	0	0	0	0	0	0	0	0	2	0	0	0
Financial	0	1	0	1	0	1	0	0	0	0	1	1	1	0	0
Health	0	0	0	0	0	0	0	0	0	0	0	1	0	0	0
Activity	2	2	0	2	2	3	0	2	2	2	2	3	3	2	0
ePortfolio	0	0	0	0	0	0	0	0	0	0	0	1	0	0	0

Fig. 3. Crosstab collected personal information per category

5 Discussion

Based on the results of the study that is described above, multiple observations were made. These observations are discussed in this section of the paper.

The first observation is that few app providers are transparent in their privacy policies about where personal information is stored. Only Instagram, Facebook, Pandora Music and Twitter mentioned anything about the geographical location where data is stored. Scores for the other variables that determine data storage transparency are also low across all analysed app providers. No app provider earned a high score for information storage transparency.

The majority of app providers also had a low result on the user's rights transparency score, which is measured by how accounts and data can be removed. Few app provides made it easy for users to look into the data that was stored about them. Furthermore, the majority of app providers did not guarantee that a user could fully delete personal information after it was collected.

Luckily, the app providers were more transparent about the data that they are gathering in the other personal information categories.

Another observation that can be made based on the results of the study, is that the usage of personal information is similar for each app provider. Almost all app providers use the personal data that they have gathered for personalized advertisements, identification, and application and service improvements.

Finally it was possible to observe that the personal relations of users are one of the most common types of personal information that are gathered by app providers. App providers are even more likely to collect this information then the interests of their users. The authors of this paper are curious to learn more about why this information is so valuable to app providers.

5.1   Limitations

The first point of discussion is the method used for the research. The method is, due to limited timespan, purely focused on privacy policies. No arguments can be made on what app providers actually collect. This research does not audit the examined app providers.

Another limitation that arose from the use of the privacy policies, was that the interval of data retrieval was not considered in the benchmark model. The privacy policies only describe that certain data is collected, not how often this happens. However, collecting a certain information artifact every hour can have a larger privacy impact then collecting it once.

A final point of discussion is the generalizability of the model outside of the mobile app landscape. During this research the model is only used to go through the privacy policies in this one branch. Beside these limitations it is also worth mentioning that this model is only tested on 20 app privacy policies and not validated outside this scope.

5.2   Future Research

A future research topic, would be finding out whether any companies secretly belong to the "undercover hoarders" fourth quadrant. This can be researched by requesting the personal data that companies have gathered, and determining whether all this data collection is also stated in their privacy policies. Due to the limited time this was not an option for this research, but requesting this, and comparing this data to the privacy policy, would give insights in the honesty of the policies and the companies.

It would also be valuable to see more research on why app providers gather the data that they are gathering. This study has shed light on what information the organizations are gathering, however it would be valuable to learn more about the reasoning behind these decisions. This would provide users with the knowledge that is required to make educated decisions about the data that they want to share. If users do not know why their personal information is used, this makes it more difficult to choose whether to share this personal information or not.

Based on the research results we would like to do some suggestions to improve the way privacy policies are presented. The content of the policies is clear, but hard to read. We suggest a score, derived from the number of personal data, that will give a better and faster insight for end users to review if they accept how much personal information will be stored and processed when using that particular application. Beside this number we would also like to suggest an additional score, which could be presented as a color, for the transparency based on our Benchmark Model. Such a score could be added in app stores to provide a quick review of the privacy scheme of the provider.

6   Conclusion

The goal of this research was to create a benchmark model to analyse privacy policies in the context of the mobile app ecosystem. This goal was realized by developing a Privacy Policy Benchmark Model based on current literature and the reviewed top 20 applications privacy policies (provided by 15 app providers). The model consists of two main aspects: (a) the amount of data the app provides state to collect; and (b) the transparency of those policies.

YeWe succeeded in reaching this goal, with the creation of the Privacy Policy Benchmark Model. Using this benchmark model, the amount of data that app-providers gather, and their transparency about this data collection can be analysed. It also categorizes app-providers in three groups: communicative disposers, which store relatively little user data and communicate about openly; blunt hoarder, collecting a large amount of user data and are transparent; and silent disposers, who do not store a large amount of personal data and have opaque privacy policies.

The Privacy Policy Benchmark Model gave a few insights on the examined applications providers. Most of the application providers were not transparent about where they store data, how personal information can be removed and what happens with personal data after asking for account removal. On the other hand are the companies transparent about what information they store and how they use it. Almost all application use data for personal advertisements, identification and application improvements. The most gathered data is about personal relationships with other users.

References

1. Ngai, E.W., Gunasekaran, A.: A review for mobile commerce research and applications. Decis. Support Syst. **43**(1), 3–15 (2007)
2. Chitkara, S., Gothoskar, N., Harish, S., Hong, J.I., Agarwal, Y.: Does this app really need my location? Context-aware privacy management for smartphones. Proc. ACM Interact. Mob. Wearable Ubiquitous Technol. **1**(3), 22 p. (2017). Article no. 42
3. Statista: Trends in consumer stats, December 2017. https://www.statista.com/statistics/266210/number-of-available-applications-in-the-google-play-store/
4. Boyles, J.L., Smith, A., Madden, M.: Privacy and data management on mobile devices. Pew Internet and American Life Project (2012)
5. Almuhimedi, H., et al.: Your location has been shared 5,398 times!: A field study on mobile app privacy nudging. In: Proceedings of the 33rd Annual ACM Conference on Human Factors in Computing Systems, CHI 2015, pp. 787–796. ACM, New York (2015)
6. Felt, A., Chin, E., Hanna, S., Song, D., Wagner, D.: Android permissions demystified. In Proceedings of the 18th ACM Conference on Computer and Communications Security, pp. 627—638. ACM (2011)
7. EUGDPR, March 2018. https://www.eugdpr.org/key-changes.html
8. Dhar, S., Varshney, U.: Challenges and business models for mobile location-based services and advertising. Commun. ACM **54**(5), 121–128 (2011)

9. Cuadrado, F., Dueñas, J.C.: Mobile application stores: success factors, existing approaches, and future developments. IEEE Commun. Mag. **50**(11), 160–167 (2012)
10. Davis, M.: Rethinking personal data pre-read document. World Economic Forum (2010)
11. Jensen, C., Potts, C.: Privacy policies as decision-making tools: an evaluation of online privacy notices. In: Proceedings of the SIGCHI Conference on Human Factors in Computing Systems, pp. 471–478. ACM, April 2004
12. Pollach, I.: What's wrong with online privacy policies? Commun. ACM **50**(9), 103–108 (2007)
13. Hamlin, K., Gallagher, D.P., Grant, J.: Response by Kaliya Hamlin, Identity Woman (2011). https://identitywoman.net/wp-content/uploads/2011/08/NSTIC-NOI-Kaliya.pdf
14. Jetmarová, B.: The value position of the role of knowledge management and its benefits for benchmarking application. J. Organ. Knowl. Manag. **2012**, 1 (2012)
15. Stajano, F.: Will your digital butlers betray you?. In: Proceedings of the 2004 ACM Workshop on Privacy in the Electronic Society, pp. 37–38. ACM (2004)
16. iTunes, December, 2017. https://itunes.apple.com/story/id1297105905
17. Malhotra, N.K., Kim, S.S., Agarwal, J.: Internet users' information privacy concerns (IUIPC): the construct, the scale, and a causal model. Inf. Syst. Res. **15**(4), 336–355 (2004)
18. Phelps, J., Nowak, G., Ferrell, E.: Privacy concerns and consumer willingness to provide personal information. J. Public Policy Mark. **19**(1), 27–41 (2000)
19. Wang, H., Lee, M.K., Wang, C.: Consumer privacy concerns about Internet marketing. Commun. ACM **41**(3), 63–70 (1998)

Artifact Compatibility for Enabling Collaboration in the Artificial Intelligence Ecosystem

Yuliyan V. Maksimov[1,3]([×]), Samuel A. Fricker[1,2], and Kurt Tutschku[3]

[1] Institute for Interactive Technologies, FHNW University of Applied Sciences and Arts Northwestern Switzerland, Windisch, Switzerland
{yuliyan.maksimov, samuel.fricker}@fhnw.ch
[2] Software Engineering Research Laboratory (SERL-Sweden), Blekinge Institute of Technology, Karlskrona, Sweden
[3] Department of Computer Science and Engineering (DIDD), Blekinge Institute of Technology, Karlskrona, Sweden
kurt.tutschku@bth.se

Abstract. Different types of software components and data have to be combined to solve an artificial intelligence challenge. An emerging marketplace for these components will allow for their exchange and distribution. To facilitate and boost the collaboration on the marketplace a solution for finding compatible artifacts is needed. We propose a concept to define compatibility on such a marketplace and suggest appropriate scenarios on how users can interact with it to support the different types of required compatibility. We also propose an initial architecture that derives from and implements the compatibility principles and makes the scenarios feasible. We matured our concept in focus group workshops and interviews with potential marketplace users from industry and academia. The results demonstrate the applicability of the concept in a real-world scenario.

Keywords: Compatibility · Licensing · Marketplace · Artificial intelligence Machine learning · Deep learning

1 Introduction

Despite the amount of available and rapidly increasing tools to manage data and cloud infrastructure offerings which can be used for collaboration purposes, Artificial Intelligence (AI) systems are still developed as "monolithic systems," where a single company owns the entire development chain [1]. This end-to-end control implies an unnecessarily large cost of ownership and a long time to market creating an investment obstacle which might result in unexploited innovation potential and competitive advantage, particularly for SMEs. There are different reasons for the lack of collaboration between organizations like missing a trustful way to access and share data [1], and technical issues of having incompatible data formats [2].

© Springer Nature Switzerland AG 2018
K. Wnuk and S. Brinkkemper (Eds.): ICSOB 2018, LNBIP 336, pp. 56–71, 2018.
https://doi.org/10.1007/978-3-030-04840-2_5

The Bonseyes AI marketplace is an emerging concept that addresses the challenge of cross-organizational collaboration in the field of AI [1]. One of its main purposes is to facilitate and foster the exchange of AI artifacts like data and AI models being used in the process of AI system development. Bonseyes facilitates the exchange through a digital marketplace. It is a place where companies or organizations that need specific AI solutions, state needs in the form of AI challenges, and where others solve or collaboratively solve challenges by developing and trading or exchanging artifacts. The marketplace allows for specialization in the process of implementing AI solutions. Companies can specialize in solving a particular type of challenges, e.g., object detection or face recognition or they can specialize on offering a particular type of artifacts, e.g., data in the form of images of objects or faces, needed to solve the challenges.

Critical for the marketplace to become established is to facilitate efficient access and exchange of artifacts, ensuring their compatibility, and at the same time to offer a reliable system that protects the rights of the artifact vendors. Companies and organizations not having access to the vast amount of resources and expertise required to collect and process data would profit from the marketplace in that they would be able to more efficiently find partners who are willing to work on their challenges. Others specialized in delivering particular services in the process of AI systems development will be able to target customers and develop solutions more efficiently. A typical case of collaboration and a business case is a company that possesses data and requests expertise from data scientists to build AI models and algorithms that utilize the models.

In this article, we address the topic of compatibility of artifacts offered in the marketplace. In the next Sect. 2, we provide some background on the topic and define terms that we further use. In Sect. 3 we state our method and validation procedure. In Sect. 4 we present our compatibility concept. In Sect. 5 we discuss our contribution by connecting the concept to related work. Section 6 concludes.

2 Background

The AI marketplace is a meeting place for the AI community. There, organizations or individuals can exchange and trade artifacts like data and models that are used in the process of AI system development. Data, for example, can be numbers, text, images or sound. Video data is a sequence of images or frames.

Data can be static or dynamic. Depending on the context, e.g., in the case of a video, the dynamic data can also be called live or stream data. There are also other classifications of data types possible to differentiate continuous, discrete, binary, and categorical data. Static data is offered as datasets or archives. For example, images may be offered as a set of JPEG or PNG files. When a data set is too large to be handled with standard software, e.g., statistical tools like SPSS, the data is termed as big data [3].

Models are machine learning (ML) algorithms designed to work and learn from the data, and in supervised machine learning from the knowledge associated with the data for example in the form of labels. The labels are sometimes also called annotations. Humans can classify data, and the class associated with the data will be its annotation. The so enriched data can be as well an artifact and be registered in the marketplace. The procedure of learning is being called training, and the trained model is used to make predictions for the labels of yet for the model unseen data records. The procedure of predicting the annotations is being called inference.

Some examples of other AI products that can be offered in the marketplace are the tools that create and process the artifacts. For example, software solutions that convert one data type into another or one model type into another. Also, software that cleans the data by automatically dealing with missing values, or tools that benchmark the models also classify as AI products that can be offered on the marketplace, since they increase the efficiency of the AI systems development process.

The artifacts and the tools can be combined and become parts of a so-called AI pipeline. A pipeline is used to solve a given challenge from the marketplace, e.g., find all the faces in an image and draw a bounding box around them.

We refer to organizations or individuals providing the challenges as challenge providers, and those who provide data as data providers. Humans who are working with the artifacts we refer to as data scientists. The same organization or individual can have different roles. Thus, the marketplace is a meeting place for these different roles, which offers them a platform to work collaboratively on a specific AI challenge.

3   Methodology

In our work, we follow the technology transfer model of Gorschek et al. [4]. The model suggests to (1) identify the problem or issue, (2) study state of the art, (3) to create a candidate solution, (4) validate the solution in academia, (5) validate the solution statically for example through interviews, (6) validate the solution dynamically for instance through pilot projects, and (7) release the solution. They stress that the model can and should be adapted according to the industry needs.

Aims. The work at hand describes the outcome of the first two steps in the model namely identifying the issue, studying state of the art, and the beginning of the third step which is formulating a candidate solution. It aims to report our findings and to outline the candidate solution. Section 4.1 presents the compatibility model. The scenarios for the usage of the marketplace and the enabling system architecture we describe in Sects. 4.2 and 4.3 respectively.

Method. We identified the challenge for compatibility in a pipeline in the course of the Bonseyes Project while conducting interviews and workshops with members of the AI community in industry and academia who participate in the project and are part of the Bonseyes consortium. We used these meetings to elicit the requirements for the marketplace. We also studied the literature on collaboration and licensing that can be relevant for a pipeline where distinct organizations are creating artifacts. Our initial thoughts resulted in a flow of actions and a system architecture similar to the ones presented in Figs. 2 and 3 but focused on licensing.

To obtain feedback on our ideas, we decided for a focus group workshop which is a suitable method to fulfill the aim [5, pp. 9–13]. We used the work of Kontio et al. [6] for further guidance on preparing and conducting the workshop. We held an online workshop with seven practitioners and researchers from industry and academia in

March 2018 where one of them was the first author of this paper who moderated the session, and another one was the third author who is responsible for the system architecture of the marketplace. A researcher working on privacy and security concepts for the marketplace was also present. The industry was represented by a senior developer working on AI pipelines, a research manager, and a developer both working on the concepts concerning the front-end of the marketplace, and the last participant was a senior project manager on the consortium level. All industry participants were working in SMEs.

After the feedback, we matured the concepts in interviews. However, we saw the need for a second focus group workshop to validate the changes. It took place one week after the first workshop and had the same setup as the first one except that two of the participants changed. Instead of the third author and the senior project manager, we had two researchers from different universities working on AI pipelines.

To validate and mature the new concepts the first author also conducted five semi-structured one on one interviews, three interviews between the focus group workshops and two interviews shortly after these workshops. He was guided by the recommendations of Hove and Anda in [7]. The first and fourth interviews were conducted in person while the rest were online. The first author discussed the new concept by presenting it and having similar questions like the ones stated below (see Data Collection), but now they were adapted towards the more general topic of artifact compatibility. The interviews, except the fourth one where exact definitions of terms were discussed, were not recorded. Instead, notes of the obtained feedback and hints for improvement were taken.

The first of the interviews was with a researcher outside of the Bonseyes consortium, who later become part of it. He was working in the field of tool support for sharing AI artifacts. The rest of the improvement and validation activities, like the focus group meetings, the following written correspondence, and four of the interviews, were within the Bonseyes consortium.

Data Collection. In the first workshop, we presented our ideas in the form of the diagrams shown in Figs. 2 and 3 and discussed the following questions: *1. Have you experienced licensing compatibility problems in your AI projects? 2. Which artifacts cause them? 3. How did you solve them? 4. Does the suggested concept for checking license incompatibility support you in the process of managing license compatibility? 5. What would you change in this concept?*

The session lasted one hour and was recorded. The discussion was continued after the session in an e-mail thread for open questions. As suggested by [5, pp. 13–15], we used the focus group to elicit inputs on how to mature our concept. We took notes during the session and listened to the recording afterward extracting additional feedback that was not noted in the first place. The notes were shared with the participants to ensure correctness. We did not receive any objections.

We used the feedback from the focus group to create the concept of compatibility (see Sect. 4.1). In the first interviews following the focus group, the first author discussed the new concept by presenting it with questions like the ones stated above but adapted towards the topic of artifact compatibility. The session lasted one hour.

The second interview was between the first and the third author who was also part of the first focus group. It lasted 1.5 h. During the interviewee, the marketplace system architecture (see Sect. 4.3) was discussed intensively. The discussion also continued in an e-mail thread after the interview.

The third interview was with a researcher who works in the field of applied AI in a medical research institute and uses the deep learning technology to create applications for a hospital attached to his institute. The interview lasted an hour discussing questions like the ones above. He was part of the second focus group.

The feedback from the interviews was considered, and changes to the concepts were applied. In the second focus group workshop, the updated concepts were presented and validation questions were stated. The session lasted one hour. We took notes and recorded the session. The notes were again shared without receiving objections. However, we received additional feedback on the compatibility concept from the researcher manager in the SME responsible for the front-end of the marketplace.

In addition, two more interviews were conducted. The first with the CEO of an SME, who is at the same time a project manager of the consortium, and the second one with a senior developer in the same SME, who was part of both workshops. These additional interviews focused on the overall AI pipeline concept and the definition of terms used in it. The first interview lasted one hour and the second 1.5 h. These discussions continued in e-mail and messaging threads.

The participants in the focus groups and the interview partners were selected so that they represent the developers of the marketplace as well as its future users. All of them were familiar with the context since all were or now are part of the consortium.

Analyses and Results. We aimed at maturing the concepts to the extent they could be implemented in the marketplace and validated empirically. In the first focus group workshop, we discussed usage scenarios and architecture of the marketplace. In the second, we discussed the updated version of marketplace and the compatibility model (see Sect. 4.1). We analyzed the results of the workshops and the interviews by going through our notes and the recordings and updated the concepts iteratively.

Overall in the first workshop, we got positive feedback on our concept. For example, the senior developer of the feedback-providing SME stated: "*Overall I think the architecture you presented is going match well our intended usages.*" During the workshop, he also noticed that licensing is an issue, and one license of an artifact can influence how another artifact is used, e.g., models trained with a specific dataset are not allowed to be used with another dataset.

While discussing the last two questions meant to gather feedback on the concept, which was at that time centered on licensing, we noticed that it was not addressing the full needs of the practitioners present at the workshop. For example, not only the dependency between licenses where discussed, but also how these dependencies relate to different types of artifacts and also dependencies between an AI challenge and artifacts were mentioned. In retrospection, we realized that we need to zoom out and look at the whole range of dependencies to have compatible artifacts in a pipeline to solve a challenge, and the licensing was a part of the bigger picture of compatibility. These thoughts resulted in the compatibility concept described in Sect. 4.

In the first ensuing interview, the compatibility model was presented (see Sect. 4.1). The interviewed researcher gave positive feedback and stressed the need for artifact interoperability and the issues connected to it. The result from the second interview is captured in Sect. 4.3. The third interview confirmed the compatibility concept and offered input on the variety of AI challenges. In the second workshop, the participants confirmed the improvements and suggested additional improvement possibilities. In the following two interviews, the pipeline, tools, and artifacts needed to solve the AI challenge were discussed and terms were defined. Here are some of these definitions, for the terms used in the next section:

- AI Challenge: *"A challenge specifies the requirements for a detection, location, classification, or regression capability offered by a target platform."*
- AI Tool: *"A software component that creates or processes an artifact."*
- AI Artifact: *"The product of the execution of a tool. It can be an output of the pipeline or an intermediate result that is processed by other tools."*

Threats to Validity. We realize that we discussed the concept with a small group of people and will need to involve larger groups in the discussion in the feature to account for conclusion validity. Nevertheless, the participants in the focus groups and the interviews were chosen because of their expertise in the corresponding parts of the concept. We as well tried to account for external validity through involving different groups of data scientists in our research, people from industry and academia. We also interviewed a representative of the community at the time outside the consortium.

4 Compatibility Concept

We first present our compatibility model that is a general conceptual model of what kinds of compatibility are required for distinct organizations to collaboratively create a pipeline of AI artifacts. We then present a scenario for the usage of the AI marketplace that will be implemented. For that, we derive on the principles of the introduced model. The principles in that sense are the different compatibility types. Afterword we present the system architecture of the marketplace that allows for such scenarios.

4.1 AI Artifact Compatibility Model

We take a closer look at three key elements that from a data scientist's perspective have to be compatible so that a pipeline of artifacts is formed (Fig. 1): challenges, artifacts, and licenses. There is twofold compatibility between these elements: vertical and horizontal. Vertical compatibility addresses compatibility between a task and artifacts, and between artifacts and licenses. Horizontal compatibility ensures the compatibility between artifacts, and between licenses.

Challenge Category-Artifact Compatibility. A pipeline aims to solve a specific AI Challenge. That means that artifacts are combined and modified to match the specific challenge. The artifacts can be easily discovered, if they belong to the same category of challenges. Just like for data there are different possibilities to categorize AI challenges:

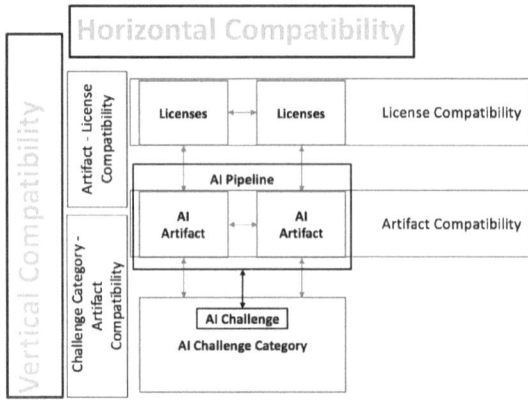

Fig. 1. AI artifact compatibility model

depending on, if the data is labeled or not, the challenges can relate to supervised and unsupervised ML problems respectively, or if the output of the prediction should be classes or a real number the problems are classification and regression problems respectively [8, pp. 14–18]. Or one can go further and differentiate between different types of classification depending on the data, e.g., image and text classification; or be even more specific by dividing the image classification into object or scene detection problems. The workshop participants preferred the latest categorization type. From the data scientist's perspective, it makes sense to have this type of compatibility since this would be one of the ways to search and filter the artifacts on the marketplace.

Artifact-License Compatibility. We adapt Ferrante's definition of software licensing [9] to artifact licensing and define it as any procedure that lets an enterprise or user acquire and use the artifact on a machine or network according to the artifact owners licensing agreement. Not any license is compatible with any artifact. Models for example, if they are intended for the public, can be licensed under one of the GNU licenses. And data, if it is available as open data, can be licensed with one of the Creative Commons (CC) licenses. However, Creative Commons does not recommend the use of CC licenses for software since they miss specific terms for the distribution of source code [10]. This would mean that models especially the ones with open source code should not be licensed under a CC license. The licensing of an artifact depends on what exactly it consists of. If for example a dataset consists of a mix of scientist's proprietary data and open data under the CC BY-SA 4.0 license and the data scientist would like to use his license to distribute it, this would not be possible. The ShareAlike term of the license obligates him to use the same license for the entire data set. He will either need to use the CC license or remove the part of the data licensed under that particular CC license to be able to utilize his own license for his proprietary data.

License Compatibility. The difficulties bound to the compatibility between licenses in one artifact has already being mentioned. There is also plenty of literature concerned with the compatibility of free and open source licenses [11–13]. It gets even more challenging when the artifacts are connected in a cross-organizational pipeline.

A typical example of how proprietary licenses affect the distribution of the pipeline results are models that are trained on a proprietary set of data. In that case, the data would be the one artifact provided by one company, and it will be connected to another artifact a model from another company. Depending on the terms specified in the proprietary license of the data the compiled versions of the model might not be eligible for inference on other data sets. The marketplace would need to detect such incompatibilities between artifacts and give notice to the data scientist that they are about to connect artifacts under incompatible licensing. In certain cases, it would even need to enforce restrictions defined by the licenses, e.g., when having a license bound to time limitations for the usage of an artifact.

Artifact Compatibility. Here we refer to the more technical compatibility between artifacts, e.g., can a certain model work with a particular dataset. Thus, if artifacts are compatible also depends on the tools that create and process them. Tools have to actively collaborate with one another, which is why in terms of the tools we speak of interoperability instead of compatibility. In that sense, we adapt Wiliden and Kaplan's definition of Software interoperability [14] and define tool interoperability as the ability for multiple tools to communicate and interact with one another exchanging compatible artifacts. The aim here is to synchronize the inputs and the outputs of the tools. Interfaces need to be defined, for example by utilizing the REST or SOAP standards. And because the ML community is spread between many different domains of research especially when it comes to applied ML, it will be essential to have not only syntactic but also semantic interoperability between the tools. For that purpose, an ontology would need to emerge. Ontologies allow for encoding of knowledge in a computer-processable way and thus making it transferable within and across domains [15]. With our work, we aim to contribute to this goal.

In our research, we thematize the licensing of artifacts. We define tools as software components, and their licensing would be in accordance with the licensing of software. Being a part of an AI pipeline poses some specific requirements on the licensing of tools, this is further discussed in Sect. 5.1 Related Work.

4.2   AI Marketplace Scenarios

There are many different utilization scenarios possible for the AI Marketplace. The scenarios are a sequence of combinations of atomic use cases offered or rather implemented by the system. Such atomic use cases are for example: register an artifact, access an artifact, search for an artifact, register a custom license, etc. The scenarios depend on the intention of the marketplace users, which most likely will be data scientists, and the possibilities or use cases that the marketplace system implements.

Figure 2 displays a flowchart diagram for the registration of an artifact on the marketplace. Following the steps on the diagram, we demonstrate the realization of the scenario where a data scientist registers an artifact under its own license.

In the illustrated procedure, a data scientist decides to register an artifact on the marketplace. He selects the appropriate "Register Artifact" function depending on the type of artifact he wants to register, e.g., data or model at the UI of the marketplace and so initiates the process illustrated in Fig. 2. Then he needs to enter the description of

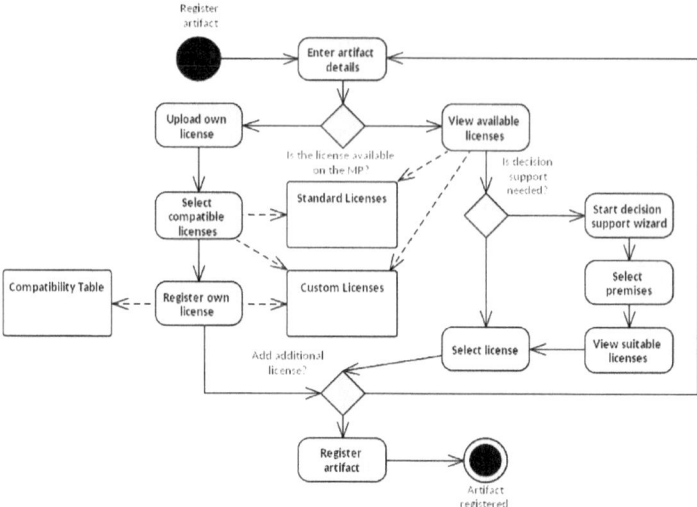

Fig. 2. Flowchart diagram for the registration of an artifact on the AI marketplace

the artifact which will usually include what the artifact is about and how to use it. Afterward, he needs to select an appropriate license for the artifact to account for Artifact-License compatibility. If he decides for a standard license like any CC license for data or one of the GNU licenses for a model, he can get support from the marketplace for the decision which license might be appropriate for his artifact. Based on the example of how CC licenses are selected on the page of Creative Commons: creativecommons.org the marketplace will offer support by asking questions like what features of the license are important for the data scientist. If he, however, decides to use his own license like the scenario in Fig. 2 supposes, he can upload it and will then need to select licenses that are compatible with his own license. This step is intended to support the license compatibility discussed in the previous chapter. He will explicitly need to enter into this step, and this is why we did not model it like a decision point, he can, of course, skip it by selecting an appropriate "skip" option.

The license selection procedure can be iterated through several times if the data scientist would like to license the artifact at the same time under different licenses so that better artifact compatibility for the ones who will later be working with the artifact is achieved. After all information about the artifact is entered, the user can finish the process by for example hitting an appropriate "Register artifact" button at the UI.

4.3   AI Marketplace System Architecture

Figure 3 illustrates the system architecture that will assure the different types of compatibility described in Sect. 4.1 and will allow for scenarios like the one discussed in Sect. 4.2. To understand the need for the different systems and components and their interoperability in the System Architecture of the marketplace we first look at the context of a pipeline in Table 1. A pipeline of tools and artifacts is meant to fulfill an

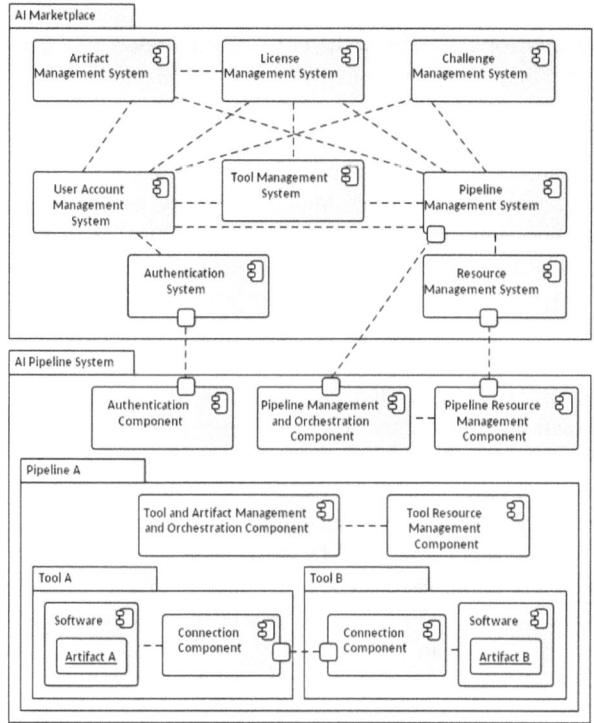

Fig. 3. System architecture for the elements needed to realize the compatibility concept between the AI marketplace and a single pipeline of tools and artifacts

Table 1. Single pipeline context

Context element	Description
The AI challenge	The AI challenge that the pipeline is meant for
Set of users	The users accounted to access the pipeline
Set of licenses	The licenses for the artifacts and tools
Set of artifacts	The artifacts in the pipeline
Set of tools	The tools in the pipeline
Set of resources	The physical resources allocated to the pipeline

AI challenge and will have a predefined and editable set of users, licenses, artifacts, tools, and resources.

These different context elements need to be managed. This is done through the Challenge-, User Account-, License-, Artifact-, Tools- and Resource Management Systems. They will be interconnected by the illustrated schema (see Fig. 3) and will have the possibility to pull and push information from and to the associated systems. They can also be seen as services that exchange information whenever needed to realize use cases and ensure the compatibility and interoperability between the different artifacts and tools of a pipeline.

The Pipeline itself is meant to run on an external system. The system will be installed either locally for example on the hardware provided by a data scientist or in a cloud environment that will allow for an inter-organizational collaboration in the development of a pipeline.

The AI Pipeline System will manage different pipelines through the Pipeline Management and Orchestration Component. This component has its counterpart at the AI Marketplace that is the Pipeline Management System. Through the interplay between these components, different scenarios are possible, e.g., defining a pipeline already in the marketplace and so ensuring tool interoperability between the tools even before downloading or accessing them. Another scenario could be the enforcement of licenses. The Pipeline Management and Orchestration Component will in regular intervals connect to the Pipeline Management System and check for license compatibility. If a license is expired, that tool would not be started, and the user will get an appropriate notification to renew the license.

The data scientist will also be able to allocate system resources for the pipeline through the Pipeline Resource Management Component or the Resource Management System. We intend to offer possibilities for the data scientists to allocate cloud infrastructure resources attached to the Marketplace directly in it for example through a specially designed UI component that will connect to the Resource Management System, which will, in turn, be connected to a third-party infrastructure provider. In such scenario data scientists do not need to organize cloud infrastructure services by themselves.

The interactions between the AI Pipeline System and the AI Marketplace are possible and secured through the interplay between the Authentication System and the Authentication Component on the AI Marketplace and the AI Pipeline System respectively. This is a small part of the security concept for the marketplace, which is being currently discussed and developed.

While the Pipeline Management and Orchestration- and the Pipeline Resource Management Components manage entire pipelines and their resources, their counterparts at the single pipeline level the Tool and Artifact Management and Orchestration- and the Tool Resource Components manage tools and artifacts and their resource allocations. The Tool and Artifact Resource Management Component can thereby only allocate resources to the tools that were allocated to the pipeline.

The tools contain software components, which depending on the artifact type that they create and process, can differ significantly. These can be systems to access big data, can be systems to compile models or any other software tools that can be useful in an AI pipeline. The Connection Components are part of the tool interoperability and the artifact compatibility concept.

5   Discussion

The overall aim is to develop a marketplace system that will enhance the collaboration between different organizations regarding efficiency of pipeline development that addresses a specific AI Challenge. These organizations and the data scientists, in particular, should be facilitated to start sharing their achievements in a proprietary or non-proprietary way. The sharing and acquiring of tools and artifacts should be enabled in an easy to use and understandable way, however not compromising on security and copyright limitations. Having such a largely heterogeneous field of technologies like the ones in the ML domain and at the same time, the variety of privacy and security requirements bound to the AI artifacts makes the task extremely challenging.

In countless projects meetings within the Bonseyes consortium in smaller and bigger circles as well through our findings in the literature [16, 17] we figured out that there are two major challenges that we need to address if we strive to develop a system that is perceived as useful. On the one hand, tools and artifacts need to be technically compatible and on the other trust between the collaborators has to be established. Licensing contracts are meant to protect intellectual property rights and deal with issues arising in conflict situations [18, pp. 101–112]. Therefore we started by focusing on licensing issues. In the first focus group workshop, we realized that we have to broaden our view and address more of the needs of industry. We, however, found ourselves in the difficult situation of being confronted with many interrelated compatibility issues. We developed the AI artifact compatibility model to distinguish between different problem areas that we are going to encounter in the process of the AI marketplace development.

Having the model allowed us to much easier develop usage scenarios for the marketplace that address and offer solutions to the encountered compatibility problems. An example there is the scenario of a data scientist selecting licenses compatible to his proprietary model and so supporting the license compatibility of artifacts in a pipeline.

Having the model and the scenarios made it then again easier to develop a system architecture that supports the development of a marketplace which aims to ease the burdens of data scientists who collaboratively develop artifacts in a pipeline.

With our concept of the marketplace and the exchange of artifacts and tools, we aim to enable a cross-domain collaboration. E.g., a specific tool for annotation from one domain can be used in another one, or a particular dataset can be utilized in two different ways. Data scientists and data science applications, in general, can thus profit from the AI Marketplace.

However, we also realize that there are potential limitations of the concept. For example, there is certain expertise needed to work with specific artifacts and tools. Or there is a need to install a particular environment be able to automatically interact with the marketplace, e.g., the Docker Engine to be able to pull and push dockerized tools. Other than mentioning that an environment needs to be installed there was no discussion on the limitation in the workshops or the interviews. However, it will be important to elaborate and validate these concerns in the future.

5.1   Related Work

Software ecosystems are composed of different software components that can be supplied by different software vendors and have different licenses [19]. Scacchi and Alspaugh [19] work on how software niches, which they define as networks of software producers, integrators, and consumers of specific components, are better defined by software component licenses and the architectural composition of the system. They state that if licenses change customers might decide to change to a more desirable product in the ecosystem. Our concept of the marketplace can also be seen as a software ecosystem where data scientists are enabled to pick the best tool or artifact that they need for their pipelines. An earlier version of Scacchi and Alspaugh's work can be found in [20].

Van Angeren et al. [21] published results about the strategies that software vendors use to select suppliers in software ecosystems and the factors influencing the decisions. The research shows that many software vendors would appreciate minimal dependence. This is also something from which the AI community might benefit utilizing the AI marketplace.

Research that combines the topics of AI, eco-systems, and IP is scarce, and we only came across the work of Keisner et al. [22]. They focus on robotics ecosystems and the IP bound to these. It is not a technical paper proposing a new eco-system. They analyze, among other robotics and IP bound topics, what the role of patents for IP in robotics is, mention some open source eco-system platforms, and raise the question to whom belongs the IP that robots create. These topics will also be important for the AI marketplace in the near future and will need further investigation. We can also analyze the existing platforms in the field of robotics.

Despite the scarcity of combined research, there is specialized literature for particular compatibility issues identified by the AI Artifact compatibility model. Thereof we can derive ideas on how to solve specific compatibility issues related to compatibility of artifacts.

How vital licensing is and what kind of primary licensing models exist can be found in [9]. These issues arise as application developers often try to find suitable algorithms for a task on the Internet, and there are no indicators as to why AI developers would behave differently. AI developers combine different services and software packages. The combination of these elements can increase the risk of license incompatibility [11] already at this experimental phase. If these algorithms reach production stages in the project, this might cause license incompatibilities with the intended license for the final solution.

Even if developers are careful, licenses can change over time and cause incompatibility issues. Di Penta et al. [12] collect five different famous cases in the field of free and open source software (FOSS) related to license incompatibility issues after license evolution. They also analyze some widely-spread FOSS systems and find out that a large proportion of the source code file changes is due to changes in the licensing statements and develop a method to track the evolution of licenses in files.

By the time of writing, we count 83 approved licenses only by the Open Source Initiative: https://opensource.org/. The plethora of legal issues related to contrasting licenses in open source and free software is discussed for example by Nimmer in [13].

Thompson and Jena in [23] provide an overview of different digital services needed for an electronic license. In [24] Raekow et al. provide a license management architecture for distributed environments. Cacciari look et al. provide in [25] SLA based licensing services for the cloud. A formal way of expressing formal licensing clauses is mentioned by Gangadharan and D'Andrea in [26].

We also looked at literature that concerns software interoperability where we could derive ideas for how AI tools interoperability and artifact compatibility should work. Componend based software development is discussed for example by Medvidovic et al. in [27]. Chapman et al. provide a service management framework for on-demand cloud provisioning [28].

6   Summary and Conclusions

We developed and described an AI compatibility concept consisting of three parts: An AI artifact compatibility model, scenarios for the usage of the AI marketplace that comply with and implement the principles of the model, and a system architecture that is aligned and derives its structure from the compatibility model and enables the scenarios. We matured the concept through focus group workshops and interviews. The overall feedback on the concept was positive, and we were encouraged to continue our research. Some of the discussions especially the interviews went deep into the concepts and many questions for further investigation were raised. For example, concerning the license compatibility, and because there is a large variety of different artifacts which standard licenses are suitable for which artifacts? Which rights of the license owner should be enforced in what way? Or concerning tools interoperability, how exactly should the interfaces between the tools supporting the exchange of artifacts or how should the components of the pipeline environment in the AI Pipeline System be specified so that they can exchange data in a standard manner? What will be the limitations of these approaches?

Establishing trust in the marketplace by addressing privacy and security concerns and raising the attention of the machine learning community as well as getting the attention of SMEs by offering attractive business models are additional fields where further research is required.

Acknowledgments. We express our gratitude to our colleagues from SYNYO GmbH in Austria and nViso SA in Switzerland for the fruitful collaboration, as well as to all participants in our focus group workshops and interviews for their invaluable input. This project has received funding from the European Union's Horizon 2020 research and innovation programme under grant agreement No 732204 (Bonseyes). This work is supported by the Swiss State Secretariat for Education, Research and Innovation (SERI) under contract number 16.0159. The opinions expressed and arguments employed herein do not necessarily reflect the official views of these funding bodies.

References

1. Llewellynn, T., et al.: BONSEYES: platform for open development of systems of artificial intelligence. In: Proceedings of the Computing Frontiers Conference. ACM (2017)
2. Herbsleb, J.D., Moitra, D.: Global software development. IEEE Softw. **18**(2), 16–20 (2001)
3. Snijders, C., Matzat, U., Reips, U.-D.: "Big Data": big gaps of knowledge in the field of internet science. Int. J. Internet Sci. **7**(1), 1–5 (2012)

4. Gorschek, T., et al.: A model for technology transfer in practice. IEEE Softw. **23**(6), 88–95 (2006)
5. Greenbaum, T.L.: The Handbook for Focus Group Research. Sage Publications, Thousand Oaks (1998)
6. Kontio, J., Lehtola, L., Bragge, J.: Using the focus group method in software engineering: obtaining practitioner and user experiences. In: 2004 Proceedings of the International Symposium on Empirical Software Engineering, ISESE 2004. IEEE (2004)
7. Hove, S.E., Anda, B.: Experiences from conducting semi-structured interviews in empirical software engineering research. In: 2005 11th IEEE International Symposium Software Metrics. IEEE (2005)
8. Flach, P.: Machine Learning: the Art and Science of Algorithms that Make Sense of Data. Cambridge University Press, Cambridge (2012)
9. Ferrante, D.: Software licensing models: what's out there? IT Prof. **8**(6), 24–29 (2006)
10. Creative Commons FAQ: Can I apply a Creative Commons license to software? (2018). https://creativecommons.org/faq/#can-i-apply-a-creative-commons-license-to-software. Accessed 17 Mar 2018
11. German, D.M., Di Penta, M., Davies, J.: Understanding and auditing the licensing of open source software distributions. In: 2010 IEEE 18th International Conference on Program Comprehension (ICPC). IEEE (2010)
12. Di Penta, M., et al.: An exploratory study of the evolution of software licensing. In: Proceedings of the 32nd ACM/IEEE International Conference on Software Engineering, vol. 1. ACM (2010)
13. Nimmer, R.T.: Legal issues in open source and free software distribution. Open Source Software Fall, pp. 43–48 (2006)
14. Wileden, J.C., Kaplan, A.: Software interoperability: principles and practice. In: Proceedings of the 21st International Conference on Software Engineering. ACM (1999)
15. Heflin, J.: OWL Web Ontology Language use cases and requirements. W3C Recommendation **10**, 24 (2004)
16. Ahmadi Mehri, V., Tutschku, K.: Flexible privacy and high trust in the next generation internet-the use case of a cloud-based marketplace for AI. In: Swedish National Computer Networking Workshop (2017)
17. Khan, K.M., Malluhi, Q.: Establishing trust in cloud computing. IT Prof. **12**(5), 20–27 (2010)
18. Fricker, S.A.: Software product management. In: Maedche, A., Botzenhardt, A., Neer, L. (eds.) Software for People. Management for Professionals. Springer, Heidelberg (2012). https://doi.org/10.1007/978-3-642-31371-4_4
19. Scacchi, W., Alspaugh, T.A.: Understanding the role of licenses and evolution in open architecture software ecosystems. J. Syst. Softw. **85**(7), 1479–1494 (2012)
20. Alspaugh, T.A., Asuncion, H.U., Scacchi, W.: The role of software licenses in open architecture ecosystems. In: IWSECO@ ICSR (2009)
21. Van Angeren, J., Blijleven, V., Jansen, S.: Relationship intimacy in software ecosystems: a survey of the Dutch software industry. In: Proceedings of the International Conference on Management of Emergent Digital EcoSystems. ACM (2011)
22. Keisner, A., Raffo, J., Wunsch-Vincent, S.: Robotics: Breakthrough technologies, innovation, intellectual property. Форсайт **10**(2(eng)) (2011)
23. Thompson, C.W., Jena, R.: Digital licensing [software reuse]. IEEE Internet Comput. **9**(4), 85–88 (2005)
24. Raekow, Y., Simmendinger, C., Jenz, D., Grabowski, P.: On-demand software licence provisioning in grid and cloud computing. Int. J. Grid Util. Comput. 5, **4**(1), 10–20 (2013)

25. Cacciari, C., et al.: SLA-based management of software licenses as web service resources in distributed computing infrastructures. Fut. Gener. Comput. Syst. **28**(8), 1340–1349 (2012)
26. Gangadharan, G.R., D'Andrea, V.: Service licensing: conceptualization, formalization, and expression. Serv. Orient. Comput. Appl. **5**(1), 37–59 (2011)
27. Medvidovic, N., Gamble, R., Rosenblum, D.: Towards software multioperability: bridging heterogeneous software interoperability platforms. In: Proceedings, Fourth International Software Architecture Workshop, June 2000
28. Chapman, C., et al.: Software architecture definition for on-demand cloud provisioning. Cluster Comput. **15**(2), 79–100 (2012)

Software Product Management and Business Models

Continuous Software Portfolio Performance Management

Paul van Vulpen(⊠), Sjaak Brinkkemper, Slinger Jansen, and Garm Lucassen

Utrecht University, Utrecht, The Netherlands
p.n.vanvulpen@students.uu.nl,
{s.brinkkemper,slinger.jansen,g.Lucassen}@uu.nl

Abstract. Product portfolio decision making is the process of coming to decisions regarding resource division along multiple software products. This process is part of portfolio management, and is an essential task in managing a software company. However, product portfolio decision making is an implicit process, and product managers are too occupied with tactical and operational decision making to execute strategic decisions regarding portfolio management. Academic research has not yet provided a model to adapt intuitive and opportunistic portfolio decision making to an explicit and data-driven cycle. The goal of this research is to make portfolio decision making explicit by modeling this process in the Dutch software industry. Case studies at 6 small to medium-size software companies in the Netherlands evaluate the initial Software Portfolio Decision Making (SPDM) model. We present the SPDM model after adaptation to the findings in the case studies. Using this model enables software companies to move from an intuitive decision making process towards data-driven explicit decision making.

Keywords: Software product management
Portfolio management · Strategic decision making

1 Introduction

Software product management is the discipline and role that governs a product from its inception to market/customer delivery to generate biggest possible value to the business, stated by Ebert [1]. The product manager operates at varying levels, ranging from the smallest abstraction level, requirements management, to the largest abstraction level, portfolio management [2]. Software portfolio management, the perspective of dividing resources among several software products, is vital to business operations. Academia has already investigated management of a single product, such as Lehtola [3], Weiss [4] and Bosch [5]. However, need arises for theory about portfolio decision making across software products.

Portfolio management is part of strategic decision making and is beyond the day-to-day business operations. Jansen et al. recognize that companies lack abilities in portfolio decision making, regarding sunsetting software products [6].

© Springer Nature Switzerland AG 2018
K. Wnuk and S. Brinkkemper (Eds.): ICSOB 2018, LNBIP 336, pp. 75–89, 2018.
https://doi.org/10.1007/978-3-030-04840-2_6

We find that in practice, portfolio management is overlooked by product managers as they are occupied with operational and tactical decision making. The act of focusing on operational and tactical decisions without clearly defining strategic goals can lead to missed opportunities, and the downfall of a software firm. This emphasizes the business need of portfolio management and explicit portfolio decision making.

Portfolio management is one of the business functions of the SPM competence model created by Bekkers et al. [7]. For the business function of portfolio management, this paper investigates decision making. Decision making is defined for this research as "the entire cycle of findings inputs for decision making, making the decision and executing the outputs of this decision." Software portfolio decision making in the context of this paper does not focus on what the optimal software portfolio is, as this question is too large to answer. Instead, we focus on making optimal portfolio management decisions, given the circumstances of the firm. The business need and absence of academic guidance in portfolio decision making lead to the following research question:

How can decision making regarding the software portfolio be conducted?

Answering this question provides initial steps in the guidance of software firms in selecting software products and maintaining a competitive software product portfolio. Employing a cyclic process for software product portfolio decision making creates the opportunity to make data-driven decisions. Olsson [8] finds that data-driven decisions that use post-deployment data as input lead to more effective product development. Incorporating the use of data from products in the field is a practice that companies need to be establish as central to their work, stated by Bosch [9].

This paper starts with the current research on portfolio management in Sect. 2. Section 3 describes the research method of theoretical model creation and case study evaluation. By applying the process model of benefits management described by Ward [16] to software product management, this research creates a cyclic model of portfolio decision making in Sect. 4. The Software Portfolio Decision Making (SPDM) model is then tested and evaluated by case studies in the Dutch software industry. The case studies are conducted to investigate the used software portfolio decision making method, the formalization of the process, and the models used. Sections 5 and 6 reveal the case study results and lessons learned. In the discussion, we present the SPDM model and we end with the conclusion about the SPDM model and software portfolio management in practice.

2   Portfolio Management in Theory

Software portfolio management is an under-investigated topic when compared to product portfolio management in general. This section discusses portfolio management for non-software products and the applicability of this theory to the software industry. McNally [10] has investigated decision making in product portfolio management. His research finds that balancing new radical products and proven concepts is crucial in successful firm performance. Furthermore, firms hinder innovation when they solely focus on aligning products with their strategic plan. Lastly, McNalley concludes that personality traits of managers are relevant in managing the product portfolio.

Cooper [11] analyzes 200 firms to discover how production firms manage their portfolio. Firms are clustered into four groups according to management's view of portfolio management. Benchmark businesses, firms that employ a formal, explicit method for managing their portfolio are most effective at portfolio management. These businesses rely on clear, well-defined portfolio procedures, consistently apply their portfolio method to every project, and management is involved in the approach.

Both McNally [10] and Cooper [11] reveal how firms use portfolio management to meet their business goals. However, both articles discuss portfolio management in production firms, and software production is different than producing non-software products. As Cusumano [12], states, producing software is different than other products. Software products have high development costs, but the cost of manufacturing and distributing extra copies is low. Furthermore, van de Weerd [2] explains that software products change or update easily by using patches or release updates. Therefore, the existing theories of portfolio management are not applicable to software portfolios, and software firms may take different approach than non-software firms.

3   Research Method

The first step in investigating software product portfolio management is the creation of an initial framework by applying the Process Model of Benefits Management described by Ward [16] to portfolio decision making. This research evaluates the software portfolio decision making (SPDM) model by using a case study theory testing approach. The case study contribution is two-fold. The case studies allow this research to investigate software portfolio management in practice. Afterwards, we adapt the SPDM model to the case study findings and present the final model. This leads to a theory based and empirically tested model of software portfolio decision making.

This paper takes a case study approach to investigate portfolio decision making. This approach provides in-depth explanations, as stated by Yin [13]. The case studies consist of an initial interview that investigates software portfolio management. The interview approach is semi-structured, to allow for follow-up questions. We abstained from a grounded theory approach because software portfolio management is implicitly embedded in the company's processes. Software portfolio decision making is not formalized or written down in protocols. Instead, managers make portfolio decisions according to their insights. Conducting case studies without a previously defined model may miss essential aspects of portfolio decision making because of a lacking interview structure. After the initial interview, we invited the interviewees for a follow-up meeting. The goal of the follow-up meeting was to present the initial results and cross-validate these findings.

As this research has an exploratory aim, the case studies are not used to fully understand portfolio decision making of a certain group of companies. Instead, we focus on globally understanding portfolio decision making throughout the software industry at every level of maturity and size. Therefore, the case studies focus on six Dutch software companies of varying size and expertise. For exploring software portfolio management, six case studies is deemed sufficient.

Out of the 250 firms that are closely related to the department, we have selected ten medium-sized product software firms with multiple products with an email request. Out of these ten, six agreed to participate in this research. One of the case studies subjects is a venture capitalist specialized in investing in software companies. The interviewees are involved in decision making for the software portfolio, to ensure the relevance of the results. Table 1 shows the overview of the interviewees and interviewed companies. The interviewees are coded with an interview number.

To structure the interviews, an interview protocol is created based on the activities that are described in the initial model[1]. Every process is broken down into multiple questions. In this way, the interview protocol covers every process of the SPDM model. The interviews are conducted by two interviewers similar to Bechhofer [14]. Having two researchers conducting the interview enhances the validity of the results [14]. Furthermore, the researchers have a varying background. The follow-up questions were asked from multiple backgrounds, which provides more information.

The transcribed interviews are taken together per question in result tables, which is based on the EA technique tables of van Steenbergen [15]. The result tables are structured per question, and in the columns, the interviewees' answers are given[2]. Additional results which are not captured in the questions and the result table are noted elsewhere and are discussed in the lessons learned section, or provided as a quote at a relevant question or process in the results.

4   Initial Model Creation

Ward [16] defines Benefits Management as the identification, definition, planning, tracking and realization of business benefits. A benefit is "an advantage on behalf of an individual or group of individuals" [17]. The Process Model of Benefits Management assists in organizing and managing potential benefits arising from the use of IT [16]. Using this model creates a rationale for strategic applications, by clarifying the trade-off between benefits [17].

We propose the initial Software Portfolio Decision Making (SPDM) model by applying the Process Model of Benefits Management to software product portfolio decision making. The application of the Process Model of Benefits Management to create strategic decisions based on the trade-off between benefits make this model relevant to portfolio decision making. Portfolio decision making also

---

[1] The interview protocol is available at: http://bit.ly/2FTBSd5.
[2] The transcriptions and result tables are available upon request.

Table 1. Case studies' context

Company nickname, Interviewee number	AgriComp, i1	VentComp, i2	ERPComp, i3	CEComp, i4	RetailComp, i5	DataComp, i6
Market of operation	Agricultural software	B2B Software focused venture capitalist	ERP software	Customer experience	Several different markets	Data analytics
Gross yearly revenue (Million Euros)	2	0	122	9	460	5
Position of interviewee	Commercial director	Partner	CTO	CMO	Strategic product manager	Business manager
Time in IT sector (Years)	33	7	19	22	11	5
Time at current profession (Years)	18	1	6.5	1	3	5

concerns strategic decision making where multiple stakeholders and products are considered.

The SPDM model describes decision making practices for the portfolio of an organization. This model focuses on using product data for supported decision making. We assume that the quality of portfolio decision making increases by data-driven decisions. This is based on the hypothesis that rational, data-driven decisions, where the product manager excogitates the effects, lead to better outcomes than intuitive decision making.

We describe the phases of the SPDM model below. The model has changed context from benefits management to portfolio decision making, which requires adaptation of several phases. The phases of the SPDM model are:

- In aiding and supporting a company's next decision, the product manager should access the historical performance of products and decisions, similar to the *Review and Evaluate Results Stage* of the Process Model of Benefits Management. In the **Data Gathering** process, the product manager retrieves information about the products from the data sources. The product manager brings the information together to create an overview of the products.
- The **Data Reduction** process is the act of reviewing what is important for the next cycle of portfolio management. This is based on the *Potential for further Benefits Stage* of the Process Model of Benefits Management. The product manager selects key indicators based on the strategy and vision, to guide the portfolio to the company's long-term goals. Key indicators are product properties, used to based the next decision upon, such as forecasted revenue or market opportunities. The strategy and vision of the company are used as it is the path that the company presumes to be most successful.
- **Modelling** is the process where models are created from key indicators. Models can be any visualization that attempts to clarify the comparison between products, such as graphs, presentations, SWOT's or matrices. To compare products or features, The firm should use a model that compares on multiple

key indicators. Modelling can be performed with or without tool support, and with varying tools such as an excel data comparison, or more extensive models such as the BCG Matrix [18], Gartner's Wave [19] or Porter's five forces model [20].

- In the **Pattern Recognition** process the product manager interprets the models, and compares the product's characteristics. He focuses on recognizing a pattern in the models. A pattern is a phenomenon that affects business results. Examples of patterns are: this product's sales are lower than expected this month, or the recurring revenue stream is rising.
- In the **Insight**, the product manager finds the cause for the recognized pattern. The Insights process generates concrete advice for decision making. In this way, finding the cause of a certain pattern allows a firm to steer away or towards this pattern with decisions. For example, when a product manager recognizes a decline in sales of a product caused by a cut in marketing budget, the root of the revenue loss is found and he can take steps to increase the revenue.
- The most important phase in the SPDM model is the **Decision Making**. In the decision making process, the company decides which investments in the portfolio are made in the next period. This is in the form of a long-term roadmap, or short-term accepted projects. Decision making is a process done by the management board to steer the portfolio in the next period. The product manager has already decided the direction in the Insights process.
- The final process in the SPDM model is the **execution**. The management applies the decisions to the operations of the company. For example, the firm carries out additional investments in a development team or the merge of two software products. This process provides new data for the Data Gathering phase, allowing for a new decision making cycle. The execution is an extensive step which requires a vastly different approach, depending on the decision made. Therefore, this step is out of scope for this research.

The SPDM model structures the activities performed by forms to make portfolio management decisions. The next section describes how the phases of the SPDM model are carried out in practice. We adapt and evaluate the SPDM model in the discussion section, based on the case study findings.

5   Results

In this section, we link the results of the case studies to the goal of this research. The interviews have taken place in October-December, 2017 and each interview lasted approximately 90 min. The "reunion" meeting took place in January 2018.

Decision Making - In the decision making process, decisions reshape and focus the product portfolio. One of the leading questions in this process is what an optimal portfolio looks like. The interviewees reveal three visions:

- The **ad hoc view**, in which every product is adapted to its own market. Focusing the entire product portfolio is impossible as *"you should focus every product in its own way"*, stated by i1 and i6.

– The **complementary view**, where the optimal portfolio consists of complementary products. Customers should understand the distinction between products. When products do not overlap, there is no redundant development and no competition between products. Every product has its own salescycle and marketing team. i2 and i4: *"customer understanding of your product portfolio is a bellwether of the optimization of your product portfolio."*
– The **product line view**, where the complete portfolio is considered as one product consisting of components that are independently managed. This product line is adaptable to varying markets. In this way, development will never have to do develop an overlapping feature twice. i3 and i5 have this vision. ERPComp uses their optimal product portfolio vision in their own product, as ERPComp has a single product line used in every market where the company participates.

The yearly planning cycle is a part of the decision making process. In the yearly planning cycle, the company determines the choices and opportunities across its products. This is done product portfolio-wide, and not per product. The planning meeting frequency differs in the case studies, and is performed yearly, half-yearly, or whenever a major decision has to be made. For the interviewed companies, several stakeholders have a voice in the decision making process. In every case study, the CEO and CTO play an important role in decision making. The companies that have the function of the product manager and product owner also involve these actors in decision making. The role of sales and marketing was unclear in decision making. Some companies involve representatives of sales and marketing in the yearly planning cycle and some companies don't. i3 explicitly states: *"Sales must not be involved in the planning, as the company can not be sales oriented."*

The management boards make decisions in multiple ways. In the case studies, two different strategies have been found. Data-driven decision making goes through the steps of gathering data about the products, formalizing models about the products' performance, interpreting the models and creating a strategy based on these models. The other strategy is entrepreneurial intuition-driven decision making, where the management makes decisions based on entrepreneurial intuition, gut feeling or instinctive feeling. The interviewed companies employ both strategies simultaneously.

Data Gathering - In the Data Gathering process, the product manager gathers product information for measuring performance. Companies measure performance of products differently. i1: *"We measure product performance by revenue, recurring revenue and percentage recurring revenue of total revenue."* ERPComp also focuses on customer usage of the products. RetailComp measures the strategic relevancy of products to both the company and the clients.

Companies use varying sources to retrieve data from. Table 2 lists data sources used for retrieving product data. Internal data sources are within the sphere of influence of the company. There are three kinds of internal data sources. First, operational sources are sources that are company wide and required to keep the firm operational, such as the accounting system. A firm has project sources that are created for a specific product or project, such as the Business case or the market analysis. Finally, the human internal data source is the input of employees of the firm. The external data sources column consists of data sources that are out sphere of influence of the company.

Table 2. Data gathering sources

Internal data sources		External data sources
Operational sources	ERP-system	Competitors
	Accounting system	Customers
	Budget	External market research
Project sources	Project management system	Research from financial institutions
	Market analysis	Market standards
	Product database	
	Business case	
Human sources	Entrepreneurial intuition	
	Employee's opinion	

Data Reduction - The product manager defines concrete properties and indicators before he decides what is most important for the next update. Product performance should be in line with the company's strategy and vision. Therefore, the product manager uses the strategy and vision as a primary source of guidance for products. In practice, decisions are rarely fully aligned with the strategy and vision of the company. Therefore, the data reduction is not based solely on the strategy and vision.

Key indicators are product properties, used to base the next decision upon. The product manager collects these indicators from the data sources. Every company uses different indicators. Table 3 lists the key indicators found in the case studies. The indicators are split in internal and external indicators. The internal indicator list consists of economic, technical, human and market indicators, depending on the nature of the indicator. Economic indicators are related to the cash flows of the product. Technical indicators are related to the development of the product. Human indicators are indicators that have the employees as a source. Market indicators reflect on the own share of the market.

Companies base a distribution key on entrepreneurial intuition and past performance. Firms measure customer satisfaction in multiple ways, depending on the branch, company size, budget and time constraints. Customer satisfaction is measured by questionnaires, workshops with key customers and other feedback methods.

In selecting key indicators for data reduction, the relevance of the company's strategy and vision is questioned. i4: *"the key indicators are only aligned with the CEO's vision and strategy, as the CEO is the final authority in the decision making process."* The vision of i5 is that product portfolio management starts with formulating a strategy and vision. *"Alignment with the firm's strategy and vision is then essential in managing your product portfolio"*.

Companies perform the data reduction in two ways. Managers that apply data-driven decision making select key indicators to make decisions. Data reduction for entrepreneurial intuition-driven decision making does not formally select key indicators to reduce the data.

Table 3. Key indicators found in case studies

Internal indicators		External indicators
Economic indicators	Profit	Market size
	Profit forecast	Market growth
	Revenue	Number of competitors
	Forecasted revenue	Products specifications when compared to competing products
	Budgeted revenue	Market saturation
	Revenue growth	Customer satisfaction
	Revenue split	
	Costs	
Technical indicators	Number of issue tickets	
	Response time on tickets	
	Number of lines of code	
	Number of developed scrum features	
Human indicators	Number of FTE's	
	Number of absence days through illness	
	CEO's affection for certain product lines	
Market indicators	Market opportunities	
	Number of features used per branch	
	Number of customers	
	Number of end users	
	Position of the customer	
	Profit for the customer	

Modelling - Companies employ several different modelling techniques. Both industry-wide and in-house developed models find their application in understanding product performance. Often, firms use multiple models. AgriComp, VentComp and CEComp apply an in-house created model. The advantages of in-house models are that it is adapted to the situation at the company, and that the interviewee is more familiar with the model than an industry-wide model. The industry-wide models are divided into two categories. The first category is structured models, where the product manager creates a comparison between products with a limited number of key indicators. Examples of structured models are the BCG Matrix or a SWOT analysis. Unstructured models have limitless input of key indicators, but require more input from the product manager. Examples of these models are the Five Forces Model or the Gartner Wave and Hypecycle.

Pattern Recognition and Insights - After creating models of the products' performance, the manager finds the pattern and insight in this model. i1 uses entrepreneurial intuition in the Pattern Recognition and Insights processes. This

CFO interprets the in-house created model, to recognize patterns of interest. He compares this to his own experiences to create insight to share to the rest of the board. For example, from previous experience, the CFO knows that the revenue per co-worker should be between 100.000 and 120.000, and the declarability of consultants should be 70−75%. Deviation from these numbers is a cause for making decisions to change business performance. ERPComp applies Pattern Recognition and Insights by using a tool that reviews product portfolio performance. The tool compares the products' performance against business as usual or a predefined forecast and brings focus on key indicators that are not performing as expected. Other firms apply the Pattern Recognition and Insights processes in an intuitive and more implicit practice.

6   Lessons Learned

In this section, we compare the results to previous knowledge to reflect on the impact of the findings. Several findings were unexpected, or contradictory findings that require further attention. These findings influence the decisions that a software company makes about their portfolio, and are not directly related to a process of the SPDM model.

A Mixture of Data-Driven and Entrepreneurial Intuition - The companies in the case studies employ data-driven mixed with entrepreneurial intuition. Data-driven decision making creates data-supported decisions based on product performance. This approach leads to clear rational decisions. However, modeling imperfections result in suboptimal decisions. Furthermore, models have a limited number of inputs.

La Pira [21] defines entrepreneurial intuition as creating opportunities and exploiting these opportunities without regard to resources currently controlled. an entrepreneurial intuition-driven decision making strategy leaves room for out-of-the-box opportunities that are not found in models, and this strategy improves decision making speed. However, a product manager that does not use model support can misestimate product performance. Furthermore, a biased opinion or a specific product affection leads to suboptimal results. For example, when the founder and CEO makes portfolio decisions, the results tend to align with the products that he founded the company with. The CEO gives other products with potential a lower priority, as he has a bias towards his own products and favors them over other products.

Furthermore, i4: *"You use models in an attempt to convince the CEO that his founded products do not fit the market anymore. The CEO loves his products so much, that he will only use the pattern when it aligns with his own vision"*, which indicates the bias of stakeholders in the decision making process. Even when models are used, their effectiveness is not without question.

Tools support Parts of Portfolio Decision Making - AgriComp and ERPComp are applying integrated tools in product portfolio management. These tools assist in or automate parts of the Data Gathering, Data Reduction, Modelling, Pattern Recognition and Insights. For example, ERPComp utilizes a tool that retrieves data from the data sources. After entering the key indicators, the tool visualizes the data in models and assists in the Pattern Recognition and Insights.

Opportunism in Smaller Software Companies - Smaller software companies may take an opportunistic approach, as their existing customer base provides insufficient funds for a steady income stream. The company falls back on an opportunistic approach, where the manager accepts projects for their short-term profitability over the contribution to long-term goals. i6: *"We do realize that aligning your development to your roadmap is better for long-term performance, but we also have to keep the lights on."* Focusing on customer-driven products or features over aligning the products with the company's strategy and vision leads to a smaller focus on the strategy and vision. However, this may be crucial for the firm's short-term survival. Choosing for alignment of the portfolio with the company's strategy and vision, may result in a lower short-term revenue, because the firm develops projects without a paying customer. Still, focusing on aligning the portfolio with the company goals is vital to a firms long-term survival, to avoid a fragmented and opportunistic product portfolio. This indicates that organization maturity is a major determinant for portfolio decision making.

Partnering with Launching customers for Major Products Enhancements - One way of overcoming the difficulty of having to choose between customer-driven requirements and strategy and vision-driven requirements is by using launching customers. In the interviews, the concept of a customer helping in creating an entrance in a new market became clear. A launching customer is an agreement between the company in focus and one of their customers. The customer has a specific wish which is also on the roadmap for the company. The presence of the wish of the customer enables possibilities and market entrances that were not present without this collaboration. This is in a market or niche where the developing company is not yet familiar in, and gives a new direction to the product portfolio. The trust of the other company allows the developing company to use opportunities that were not possible without the collaboration. This collaboration is beneficial for the developing company. On one side, the company is implementing a feature for a customer and is being paid for this customer-specific request. On the other side, the implementation of the request also satisfies the other customers, or opens up a new market. This satisfies other (potential) customers. In this way, three stakeholders, the company, the launching customer, and other customers are benefiters. Therefore, projects initiated by a launching customer increase both the alignment with customer-specific requests, and market wide requests. Figure 1 shows how partnering with launching customers leads to an increased alignment with both customer specific requests and market wide requests. At ERPComp, managers give Projects with a launching customer priority over other projects. i5: *"projects with a feature that is currently not on the planning are added when a customer is willing to invest to create this opportunity."*

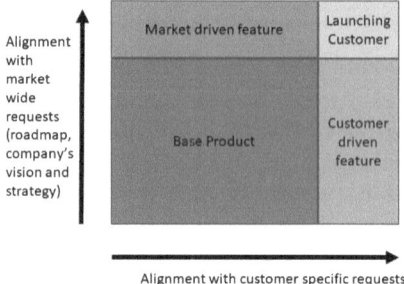

Fig. 1. Collaboration with a launching customer improves both alignment with customer-specific requests and alignment with market wide requests

7 Discussion

This section reflects on the results and lessons learned. We start this discussion with the adaptation of the SPDM model to the case study findings. Afterwards, the impact of the research method is discussed.

SPDM Model Adaptation - The case studies provide a partial confirmation of the SPDM model. Figure 2 shows the final SPDM model. Companies apply the Decision making, Execution, Data Gathering and Data Reduction similar to the expectations based on theory. However, the processes are simpler and less distinct. Furthermore, the product portfolio decision making process is a bi-cyclic process. The case studies show a yearly cycle for long-term planning and companies simultaneously make decisions for short-term adaptations.

Recognizing a pattern and finding a cause for this pattern are intertwined processes in the case studies. None of the interviewees made a difference between the processes. For example, realizing that revenue is declining due to a reduction in one-off sales may start with the recognized pattern that revenue is declining, or with the insight that the one-off sale reduction causes a revenue decrease. The Insight and Pattern processes are intertwined and unsequenced. Therefore, we combine these steps in a process called Interpretation. In the Interpretation, the product manager interprets models to form advice for decision making.

Every firm balances between data-driven decision making and entrepreneurial intuition-driven decision making. In data-driven decision making, the manager performs the Modelling and Interpretation to create and interpret the data models. In entrepreneurial intuition-driven decision making, the Modelling and Interpretation are not performed, and the Data Reduction is a more informal process. We visualized this in the SPDM model by drawing an arrow from Data Reduction to Decision making, indicating that product portfolio management is possible without Modelling and Interpretation.

The SPDM model assumes a structured cyclic process, which may not be the case in practice. When making product portfolio decisions, a company may loop between SPDM processes. For instance, a manager that is selecting key indicators decides that he needs another data source. This suggests a loop between Data

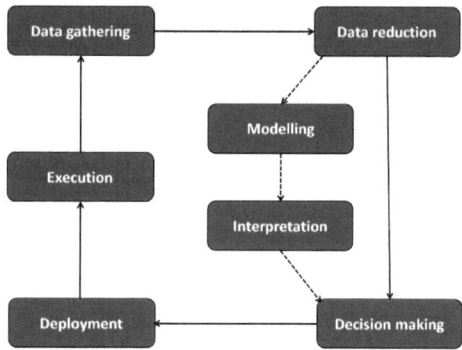

Fig. 2. The software portfolio decision making (SPDM) model

Gathering and Data Reduction. However, this was not confirmed in the case studies and requires further confirmation.

Applicability of the SPDM Model - This research proposes the SPDM model, usable by software firms to formalize their portfolio management. The SPDM model is worked out to a greater or lesser extent. Data Gathering, Data Reduction, Modelling en Decision Making are processes that are covered in the case studies. On the other hand, the Interpretation has remained implicit in the case studies. The Execution stands beyond the scope of this research but is described in literature already.

Reliability and Validity Considerations - The method of applying a predefined model based on researchers' previous portfolio decision making experience has both advantages and drawbacks. This enables investigation in an implicit and vague process. The downside of using this method is the subjective nature of using a predefined method. Conducting interviews related to a predefined method may lead to confirmation of the method, regardless of the validity of the method. The internal validity is preserved by critically reviewing the SPDM model and reviewing model relevancy for the case studies.

The case studies provide a similar execution of portfolio management. Every case study subject has a limited degree of formality in portfolio decision making. This leads to the hypothesis that the entire Dutch software industry executes portfolio decision making in an implicit manner. If this is true, then the entire Dutch software industry may benefit in using the SPDM model to make portfolio decision making more explicit.

The reliability of the data collection method is guaranteed by limiting the variation in interviews. For every interview, the same interview protocol is used. Furthermore, every interviewee is a key actor in portfolio decision making.

Effectiveness of Data-Driven Decision Making - In this paper, one of the research goals was to investigate the degree of formalization of product portfolio management. Formalization is supporting decisions with data and models about the products. A hypothesis that flows from this research goal is that firms that collect and model data, make better decisions. However, testing this assumption is beyond the scope, because this research does not focus on portfolio management effectiveness.

i5 was not interested in formalizing decision making. Data focuses on short-term profit. i5: *"product management should focus on aligning the product port-folio with the vision and strategy, to ensure long-term performance"*.

8   Conclusion

By utilizing a case study approach, this research investigated product portfolio decision making in the Dutch software industry. This research makes this process explicit by answering the research question: How can decision making regarding the software portfolio be conducted?

The SPDM model created in this paper describes the continuous decision making cycle that enables software companies to make portfolio management decisions explicit. With the application of the process model of benefits management to SPM, this paper hopes to change portfolio decision making from an implicit and intuition-driven process towards an iterative and data-driven cycle. Implementing the SPDM model in the company's operations enables the product manager to escape the operational decision making and focus on strategic decision making for the product portfolio.

The SPDM model reveals the mixture of data-driven and entrepreneurial intuition decision making. When using the SPDM model for portfolio decision making, the role of the manager as a visionary is supplemented with models, leading to better supported decisions. Furthermore, this research hopes to stimulate software portfolio management as a research topic. Aspects of software portfolio management need further investigation and we state some below.

The scope of this research was too large to sufficiently cover the process of entrepreneurial intuition. Using managers' experience to influence future decisions is essential in decision making. The exact role of entrepreneurial intuition remains unclear. Further research could cover how entrepreneurial intuition can improve decision making.

Every company combines entrepreneurial intuition-driven decision making and data-driven decision making in portfolio management. Combining the decision making methods leads to optimal business results. Academic research can focus on finding the balance between these methods, or creating a model to combine these approaches. This will extend the SPDM model and aid software companies in portfolio management.

References

1. Ebert, C.: The impacts of software product management. J. Syst. Softw. **80**(6), 850–861 (2007)
2. Van De Weerd, I., Brinkkemper, S., Nieuwenhuis, R., Versendaal, J., Bijlsma, L.: Towards a reference framework for software product management. In: 14th IEEE International Conference Requirements Engineering, pp. 319–322. IEEE (2006)

3. Lehtola, L., Kauppinen, M., Kujala, S.: Linking the business view to requirements engineering: long-term product planning by roadmapping. In: 2005 Proceedings 13th IEEE International Conference on Requirements Engineering, pp. 439-443. IEEE (2005)
4. Weiss, D.M., Lai, C.T.R.: Software Product-line Engineering: A Family-based Software Development Process, vol. 12. Addison-Wesley, Reading (1999)
5. Bosch, J.: Design and Use of Software Architectures: Adopting and Evolving a Product-Line Approach. Pearson Education, London (2000)
6. Jansen, S., Popp, K.M., Buxmann, P.: The sun also sets: ending the life of a software product. In: Regnell, B., van de Weerd, I., De Troyer, O. (eds.) ICSOB 2011. LNBIP, vol. 80, pp. 154–167. Springer, Heidelberg (2011). https://doi.org/10.1007/978-3-642-21544-5_13
7. Bekkers, W., van de Weerd, I., Spruit, M., Brinkkemper, S.: A framework for process improvement in software product management. In: Riel, A., O'Connor, R., Tichkiewitch, S., Messnarz, R. (eds.) EuroSPI 2010. Communications in Computer and Information Science, vol. 99, pp. 1–12. Springer, Heidelberg (2010). https://doi.org/10.1007/978-3-642-15666-3_1
8. Holmström Olsson, H., Bosch, J.: Towards data-driven product development: a multiple case study on post-deployment data usage in software-intensive embedded systems. In: Fitzgerald, B., Conboy, K., Power, K., Valerdi, R., Morgan, L., Stol, K.-J. (eds.) LESS 2013. LNBIP, vol. 167, pp. 152–164. Springer, Heidelberg (2013). https://doi.org/10.1007/978-3-642-44930-7_10
9. Bosch, J.: Speed, data, and ecosystems: the future of software engineering. IEEE Softw. **33**(1), 82–88 (2016)
10. McNally, R.C., Durmuolu, S.S., Calantone, R.J.: New product portfolio management decisions: antecedents and consequences. J. Prod. Innov. Manag. **30**(2), 245–261 (2013)
11. Cooper, R.G., Edgett, S.J., Kleinschmidt, E.J.: New product portfolio management: practices and performance. J. Prod. Innov. Manag. **16**(4), 333–351 (1999)
12. Cusumano, M.A.: The Business of Software. Free Press, New York (2004)
13. Yin, R.K.: Case Study Research and Applications Design and Methods. Sage publications, Thousand Oaks (2017)
14. Bechhofer, F., Elliott, B., McCrone, D.: Safety in numbers: on the use of multiple interviewers. Sociology **18**(1), 97–100 (1984)
15. Steenbergen, M.V.: Maturity and effectiveness of enterprise architecture (Doctoral dissertation), Utrecht University, p. 245 (2011)
16. Ward, J., Daniel, E.: Benefits Management: Delivering Value from IS and IT Investments, p. 418. Wiley, Chichester (2006)
17. Ward, J., Murray, P., Daniel, E.: Benefits management best practice guidelines. In: Information Systems Research Center, Cranfield School of Management, Cranfield (2004)
18. Udo-Imeh, P.T., Edet, W.E., Anani, R.B.: Portfolio analysis models: a review. Eur. J. Bus. Manage. **4**(18), 101–117 (2012)
19. Linden, A., Fenn, J.: Understanding Gartner's hype cycles. Strategic Analysis Report N R-20-1971. Gartner, Inc. (2003)
20. Porter, M.E.: The five competitive forces that shape strategy. Harvard Bus. Rev. **86**(1), 25–40 (2008)
21. La Pira, F.: Entrepreneurial intuition, an empirical approach. J. Manage. Mark. Res. **6**, 1 (2011)

Generating Win-Win Strategies for Software Businesses Under Coopetition: A Strategic Modeling Approach

Vik Pant[1(✉)] and Eric Yu[1,2]

[1] Faculty of Information, University of Toronto, Toronto, Canada
vik.pant@mail.utoronto.ca, eric.yu@utoronto.ca
[2] Department of Computer Science, University of Toronto, Toronto, Canada

Abstract. Interorganizational coopetition describes a phenomenon in which businesses cooperate and compete simultaneously. Such behavior is common-place among software firms wherein vendors concomitantly deal with each other both as partners and as rivals. Sustainable coopetitive relationships are predicated on the logic of win-win strategies. Conversely, win-lose or lose-lose strategies do not lead to durable coopetitive relationships. This aspect of coopetition requires decision-makers in coopeting software businesses to generate and analyze win-win strategies. This paper proposes a strategic modeling approach to systematically search for alternatives and generate win-win strategies. This approach synergistically combines *i** goal-modeling to analyze the distributed intentional structures of actors and Game Tree decision-modeling to reason about the moves and countermoves of actors. An illustrative example of a published case study is presented to demonstrate the strengths and weaknesses of this methodology.

Keywords: Strategic modeling · Coopetition · Win-win · Positive-sum

1 Introduction

Many software businesses join ecosystems (SECOs) to benefit from open innovation [1] as well as to access: shared market, common technological platform, and opportunities for information/resource/artifact exchange [2]. Each SECO comprises an intricate network of multifaceted relationships among software vendors. Coopetition, which refers to simultaneous cooperation and competition among two or more actors [3], is commonplace within SECOs [4].

The need for analyzing strategic relationships in and among SECOs has been by emphasized by several researchers [2, 5, 6]. Many researchers have proposed SECO modeling techniques to explain structures and processes of SECOs [7–11]. However, none of these SECO modeling techniques focus directly on coopetition in and among SECOs.

Decision-makers require insight into the intentions of coopeting actors to discern the motives behind their actions and responses. They also require foresight to predict the moves and countermoves of actors under coopetition. Game Trees (i.e., multi-actor Decision Trees) are commonly used to analyze multi-actor decisioning scenarios.

© Springer Nature Switzerland AG 2018
K. Wnuk and S. Brinkkemper (Eds.): ICSOB 2018, LNBIP 336, pp. 90–107, 2018.
https://doi.org/10.1007/978-3-030-04840-2_7

However, Pant and Yu note, "Game trees elide the intentional structure of the players" [12]. This is because while Game Trees encode the motivations of actors into *payoffs* implicitly they do not express those motivations explicitly. Therefore, Game Trees do not provide a systematic method for exploring the space of potential strategic alternatives to generate new win-win strategies.

*i** Strategic Rationale (SR) models can be used to show the internal intentional structures of actors overtly and can be used to complement Game Trees. A novel methodology for the synergistic use of actor goal modeling (with *i**) and decision modeling (with Game Trees) was introduced by Pant and Yu [12]. The present paper extends that work by proposing a systematic method for generating win-win strategies.

The remainder of this paper is organized as follows. In the next section we discuss strategic outcomes in coopetitive relationships including the notions of win-win, win-lose, and lose-lose strategies. The third section presents a modeling-based methodology for generating and evaluating win-win strategies among actors by building upon a novel approach introduced in [12]. In the fourth section we instantiate this method-ology by applying it to a published case study about SECOs under coopetition. In the fifth section we review related work while in the sixth section we discuss our con-clusions and future work.

2 Strategic Outcomes in Coopetitive Relationships

Simultaneous cooperation and competition is characterized by the partially congruent interest structures of coopeting actors [13]. Actors in such relationships "cooperate to grow the pie and compete to split it up" [14]. According to Game Theory (e.g., [3]), a multi-actor relationship can be classified as: positive-sum, zero-sum, or negative-sum.

In positive-sum scenarios, each actor gains by participating in the relationship; in zero-sum scenarios, some actors are better off while some actors are worse off by participating in the relationship; and in negative-sum scenarios all actors are harmed by participating in the relationship. In zero-sum scenarios, the magnitude of gain for some of the actors equals the degree of pain for the other actors in that relationship.

It is definitional and logical that rational and self-interested actors are likely to voluntarily take part only in those relationships that are beneficial for themselves (i.e., zero-sum but only where they are advantaged, or positive-sum) [15].

Coopetitive relationship are regarded as strategic because the actions of any actor can impact the actions of any other actor(s) and, similarly, the decisions of any actor can inhibit or impel the decisions of any other actor(s). Therefore, actors in such relationships are codependent on each other for the achievement of their common goals as well as individual objectives.

A win-win strategy is the sole practical choice for an actor under coopetition because only it is likely to yield an equilibrium condition under which all actors are willing to remain in that relationship voluntarily [3]. Therefore, decision-makers in coopetitive organizations must search for win-win strategies by: (1) analyzing existing alternatives, and (2) generating new alternatives. This can be done by using *i** to search for new alternatives and Game Trees to evaluate those alternatives. Complementary usage of *i** and Game Trees is demonstrated in Sects. 3 and 4 where these techniques are used to search for new alter-natives. The process for modeling, evaluating, and exploring the space of alternatives is depicted in Fig. 1.

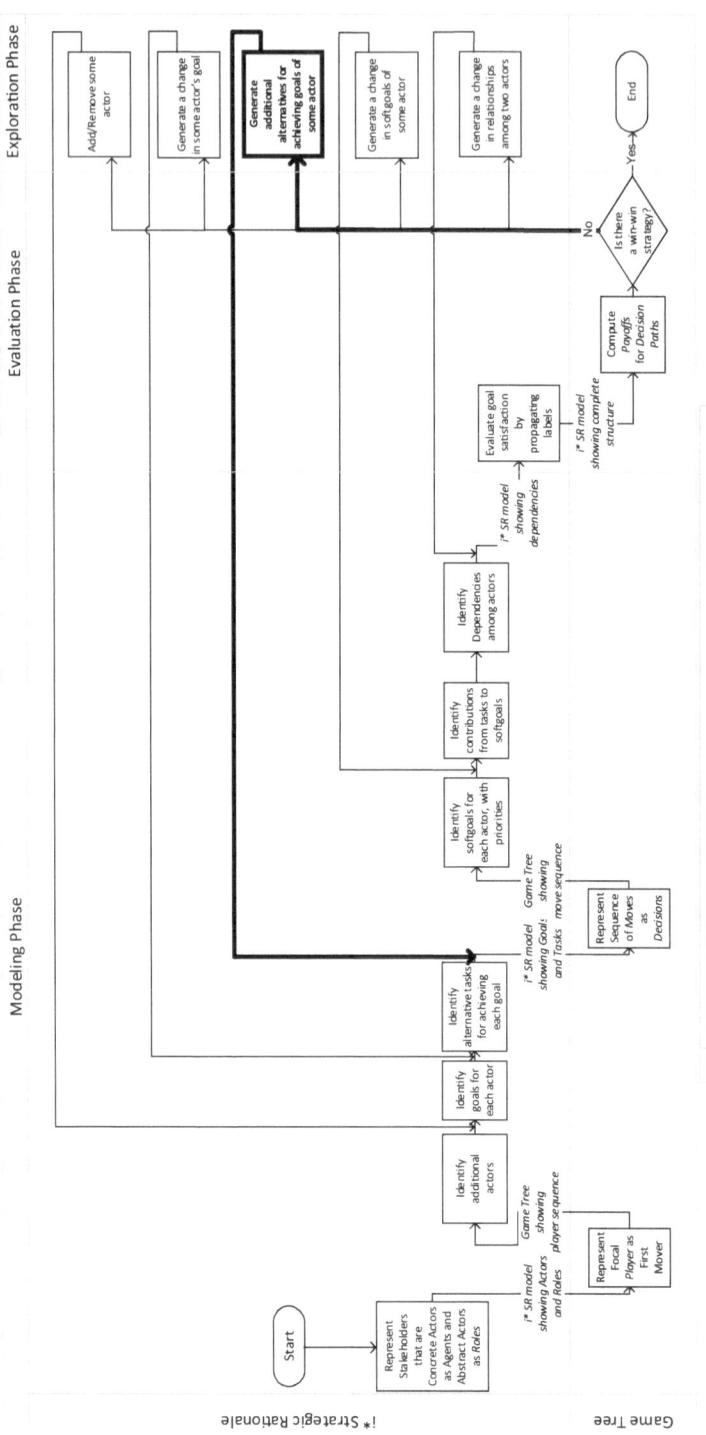

Fig. 1. Process to develop *i** SR diagram and its corresponding Game Tree [**emphasis** on introduction of new task] (adapted from [12])

3   Methodology for Generating Win-Win Strategies with *i** and Game Trees

We explain a methodology for generating win-win Strategies with *i** and Game Trees by using a simple example from Game Theory. Let us assume that two siblings, namely Cake Cutter (CC) and Slice Selector (SS), wish to divide a cake among themselves. The only rule that governs their sharing of a cake is that one sibling cuts the cake (CC) into two slices and the other sibling distributes each of those slices (SS). Researchers from myriad disciplines have contemplated concepts such as fairness and reciprocity using variations of this basic scenario [16–20].

Suppose that both CC and SS wish to obtain the larger share of cake for themselves and that CC has only one alternative available to it which is of cutting the cake into two unequal slices. Consequently, SS has two alternatives available to it which are that it can either take the larger slice or the smaller slice for itself and give the remaining slice to CC.

If SS takes the larger slice then its goal is satisfied but the goal of CC is denied. Alternatively, if SS takes the smaller slice then its goal is denied but the goal of CC is satisfied. Therefore, cutting the cake into unequal slices by CC does not lead to a positive-sum outcome. Moreover, if a decision by CC to cut the cake into unequal slices can lead to SS winning and CC losing then these alternatives represent a win-lose strategy.

CC must generate one or more new alternatives for achieving its goal since the existing alternative does not represent a win-win strategy. CC can generate a win-win strategy by analyzing its own alternatives and goals as well as those of SS. A new alternative that CC can generate is to cut the cake into equal slices. This new alternative for CC necessitates SS to generate a new alternative as well. This is because there is no such thing as a larger or a smaller slice when the cake is cut into equal slices. Therefore, the new alternative for SS is to take either of the equal slices. This allows both CC and SS to obtain equal slices. Considering the rules of their arrangement this allows both to satisfy their goals.

Formal solutions to such fair-division problems (e.g., "I cut, you choose") have been proven via minimax and maximin theorems [21]. Game Trees are commonly used to analyze such scenarios because they support the notion of *payoffs*. However, Game Trees do not allow a systematic search for new alternatives—which is a necessary step for generating win-win strategies.

Figure 1 presents a structured and systematic methodology for generating win-win strategies among actors. This proposal complements the Game Tree method with a strategic goal-modeling approach. It is explained in this section with reference to this example of cake sharing. Figure 2a is an *i** Strategic Rationale (SR) diagram that depicts the application of the Modeling and Evaluation phases of Fig. 1. *i** (denoting "distributed intentionality") is a goal- and actor-modeling language that supports strategic reasoning [22].

In the Modeling phase, Fig. 2a portrays the relationship between two actors—CC and SS. Figure 2a shows that the primary objective of the two parties is to get the larger share of the cake for itself. Each actor uses this as a quality criterion to evaluate and compare alternatives. They assess each option by estimating the impact of an option on their obtaining the larger share of the cake. This quality criterion is depicted as a *softgoal*. The relative importance of each *softgoal* is depicted with one or more exclamation mark(s) to indicate lower (!) and higher (!!) priorities.

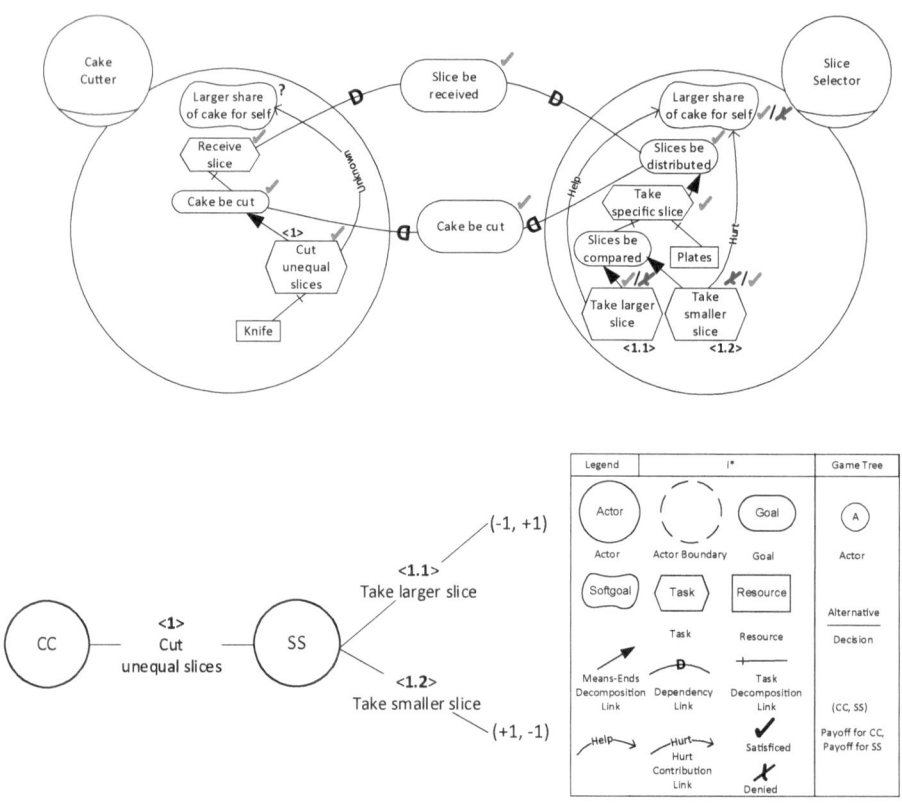

Fig. 2. (a) *i** SR model depicting As-Is relationship among CC and SS. (b) Game Tree depicting As-Is decision alternatives with resulting payoffs

A *task* is an activity that can be used to achieve a *goal*. In the As-Is scenario, CC has one way of achieving the *goal* "Cake be cut", by cutting into unequal slices. We extend the *i** notation slightly to depict multiple options as well as moves and countermoves in the same *i** model. Each option is designated a number which is enclosed within angle brackets. For example, "Cut unequal slices" is identified as <1>. Countermoves corresponding to this option are denoted as <1.x> where x denotes a possible response to "Cut unequal slices". Therefore, "Take larger slice" is denoted as <1.1> and "Take smaller slice" is denoted as <1.2>. Countermoves in response to <1.1> and <1.2> can be depicted as <1.1.x> or <1.2.x> (not shown). This allows a sequence of moves and countermoves of any length to be represented in the *i** model.

Tasks can be refined into lower-level *goals, tasks, softgoals*, and *resources*. These subsidiary *goals, tasks, softgoals*, and *resources* are related to a higher-level *task* using a *task decomposition link* such that each of the lower level elements must be satisfied in order for their associated higher-level *task* to be fulfilled. A *resource* (e.g., knife, plate) is a physical or informational entity required to perform a *task*.

A task is related to a goal using a *means-ends link* (with solid arrowhead) such that the completion of any *task* leads to the fulfilment of its associated *goal*. A *goal* represents a state of affairs that an actor wishes to achieve in the world.

Contribution links (e.g., *help, hurt, unknown*) (curved arrows with open arrowheads) are used to show the impact of *tasks* and *softgoals* on one or more *softgoals*. *Labels* (such as *satisfied, denied*) are propagated along contribution links to derive the impact of model elements on other elements. In this example, it is *unknown* whether cutting the cake into unequal slices will help or hurt CC's *softgoal* of obtaining the larger share of the cake. This is because, per the rules of their arrangement, it is SS that decides the distribution of cake slices. Therefore, if SS keeps the larger piece for itself (e.g., exhibiting opportunism) then CC's *softgoal* will not be satisfied but if SS keeps the smaller piece for itself (e.g., demonstrating altruism) then CC's *softgoal* will be satisfied.

Figure 2a shows that SS can choose either the larger or the smaller slice for itself and give the other slice to CC. This choice is shown as two alternative *tasks* leading towards the same *goal* via *means-ends* links. SS compares unequally sized slices to decide whether to keep or give the larger or smaller sized slice. This is shown as a *sub-goal*. SS judges an alternative by reckoning its ability to help SS obtain the larger share of cake for itself. This is depicted as a *softgoal*.

CC and SS are inter-reliant on each other for the sharing of cake to take place among themselves. In the As-Is scenario, SS needs CC to cut the cake and CC needs SS to obtain a slice of the cake. This inter-dependency among CC and SS is shown via *dependency links*. A *depender* is an actor that depends on a *dependee* (i.e., another actor) for a *dependum* (i.e., something such as a *task* to be completed, a *goal* to be satisfied, a *resource* to be provided, or a *softgoal* to be fulfilled). The curved side on the D in the *dependency link* faces the *dependee* while the flat side faces the *depender*.

We complement *i** means-ends modeling with Game Tree modeling to show the gain or loss associated with various strategies for each *actor/player*. Figure 2b depicts a Game Tree representing sequential *actions/decisions* by CC and SS as well as the *payoffs* associated with each *action/decision path*. Dixit and Nalebuff present an overview of Game Trees in [15].

In the Modeling phase, Fig. 2b shows the sequence of *actions/decisions* by the actors. In the Evaluation phase, the *payoffs* for each configuration of move and countermove for every actor are calculated by assessing *softgoal* satisfaction/denial in Fig. 2a. Figure 2b shows that CC moves first since it is necessary for it to cut the cake before SS can distribute the cake slices. CC has only one strategy available to it in the As-Is configuration. Therefore, CC decides to adopt the strategy of cutting the cake into unequal slices. SS makes the next move by deciding whether to give the larger or smaller of the cake slices to CC. SS can act opportunistically (larger slice for SS) or altruistically (larger slice for CC).

Let us suppose that if SS decides to keep the larger slice of cake for itself then it earns a payoff of +1 while CC earns a payoff of −1. This is because, in this situation, SS is able to satisfy its *softgoal* while CC is unable to fulfil its *softgoal*. Conversely, If SS decides to keep the smaller slice of cake for itself then it earns a payoff of −1 while CC earns a payoff of +1. This is because, in this situation, SS is unable to satisfy its *softgoal* while CC is able to fulfil its *softgoal*.

This integrated analysis, of the $i*$ SR model and Game Tree, indicates that the As-Is relationship between CC and SS only comprises win-lose strategies and not any win-win strategies. This is because in one outcome CC ("+1") is advantaged but SS ("−1") is disadvantaged while in the other outcome SS ("+1") is advantaged but CC ("−1") is disadvantaged. This aspect of the As-Is relationship between CC and SS motivates the need for generating win-win strategies by applying the steps recommended in the Exploration phase.

In the Exploration phase, one or more subject matter experts (SME) or domain specialists contemplate ideas for generating win-win strategies. They follow an iterative and incremental process for enlarging and pruning the $i*$ models and their associated Game Trees.

The Exploration phase consists of five steps that are arranged in a non-deterministic manner. SMEs can choose to start with any of the steps in the Exploration phase. Each step in the Exploration phase loops back to a corresponding step in the Modeling phase. This allows SMEs to make one change at a time to the intentional ($i*$) model and assess its impact on the decision-support (Game Tree) model in an incremental fashion. SMEs iterate through the Exploration, Modeling, and Evaluation phases until they successfully generate one or more win-win strategies.

In the Exploration phase, SMEs apply their knowledge of the motivations of the actors as well as of their shared context to select any of the steps in that phase. They can change the relationship among two actors by changing the object of their dependency on each other (i.e., *dependum*). Alternatively, they can change a quality criterion (i.e., *softgoal*) by which some actor compares alternate means for achieving their desired ends. Else, they can develop a new alternative (i.e., *task*) for achieving the objectives (i.e., *goal*) of some actor. Or, they can change an actor's objective (i.e., *goal*). Otherwise, they can Add/Remove an actor from the relationship. After making one change at a time the SMEs can repeat the process (Modeling and Evaluation phases) to check whether any win-win strategy is generated from that change.

In our example, we suppose that CC (i.e., a SME of cake sharing) performs the steps in the Evaluation phase to extend and refine Fig. 2a and b. CC does this because the As-Is scenario does not consist of any win-win strategies. To generate a new win-win strategy (i.e., To-Be scenario), CC can begin by selecting any of the steps in the Exploration phase.

Figure 3a (To-Be) is an $i*$ Strategic Rationale (SR) diagram that extends Fig. 2a (As-Is) by applying steps from the Exploration phase. Figure 3b depicts a Game Tree that extends Fig. 2b to show new *payoffs* associated with an additional strategy that is depicted in Fig. 3a. Model elements with black color represent existing model elements from Fig. 2a and b while model elements with blue color represent new model elements in Fig. 3a and b.

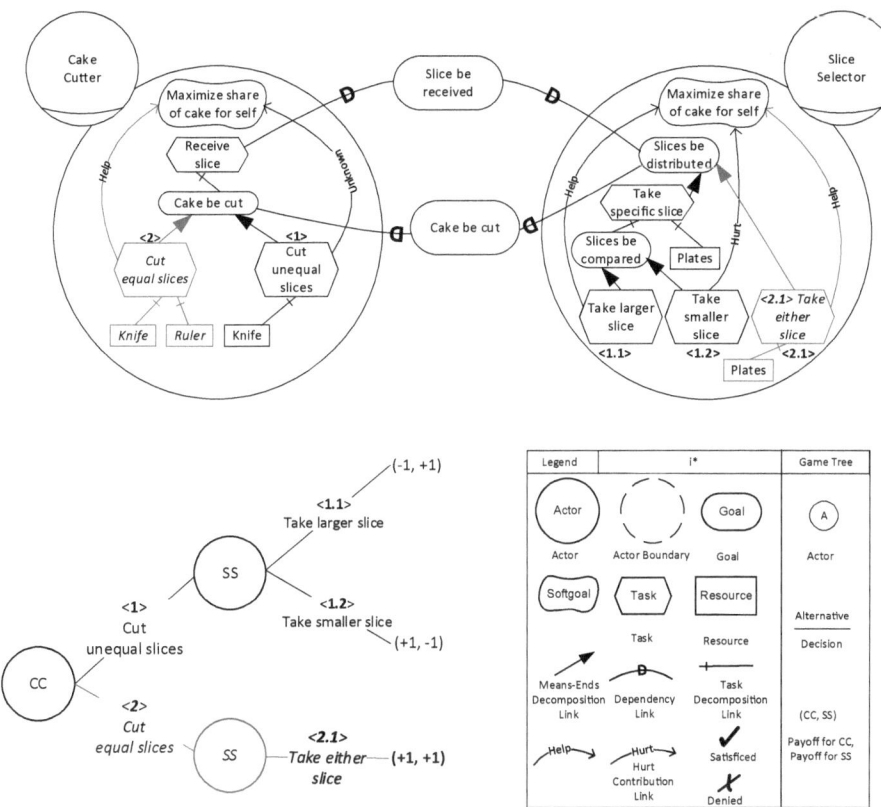

Fig. 3. (a) *i** SR model depicting To-Be relationship among CC and SS. (b) *i** Game Tree depicting To-Be decision alternatives with resulting payoffs

CC evaluates Fig. 2a and b to understand the reasons for the absence of any win-win strategy in the As-Is scenario. CC recognizes that its As-Is strategy of cutting the cake into unequal slices can be disadvantageous for itself. This is because SS has a *softgoal* of maximizing its (SS's) own share of the cake which can only be satisfied if SS selects the larger slice for itself and gives the smaller slice to CC. CC realizes that it is improbable for SS to act altruistically by selecting the smaller slice for itself and giving the larger slice to CC since the *i** model does not contain any *softgoal* to justify such behavior from SS.

CC starts the Exploration phase by contemplating a new alternative that can help it to achieve its sole *softgoal*. However, this alternative must also help SS to satisfy its only *softgoal*. This new strategy (To-Be) can only exist if CC cuts the cake into equal slices. This new alternative for CC will also change the space of alternatives available to SS. This is because by cutting the cake into equal slices CC will require SS to generate a new alternative of taking either slice. This new strategy (To-Be) will bring the interest structures of CC and SS into congruence because it will allow both of them to satisfy their respective *softgoals*.

Figure 3b represents the updated *payoffs* for CC and SS considering this new strategy (To-Be). If CC cuts the cake into equal slices then both CC and SS earn a payoff of +1. This is because the To-Be strategy allows SS to maximize its own share of the cake while also permitting CC to obtain the largest possible share of the cake considering the terms of their arrangement. By generating this new strategy, CC eliminates the possibility for SS to act either opportunistically or altruistically. This new alternative represents a win-win strategy for both CC and SS.

The next section demonstrates the application of this methodology to a real-life historic case. It clarifies the systematic structure of the reasoning steps via instantiations of goal-models (*i** SR diagrams) and complementary decision-models (Game Trees). The following example draws upon multiple published sources [see 23–27]. It is presented as an interpretive reconstruction that interleaves ground truth (i.e., historical fact) and creative conjecture (e.g., new alternatives). It is presented in this way to accommodate and reflect factual and counterfactual aspects of this case.

4   A Case Example of Coopetition: Apple and Adobe SECOs

A widely studied case of industrial coopetition among SECOs pertains to the relationship between Apple and Adobe [see 23–27]. Apple and Adobe operated as partners because Adobe's Flash-based web-applications added value to Apple's web browser (Safari) on its desktop operating system (macOS). Similarly, Adobe generated acceptance and adoption of its Flash technology from Apple's customer base that accessed Flash-based web-applications on their Apple computers. However, Apple and Adobe also behaved as rivals since they operated competing SECOs for mobile apps (i.e., Apple iOS app store and Adobe Flash Gallery).

Figure 4a depicts an *i** SR model of Apple's "walled garden" strategy and Adobe participation. In the Modeling phase, we use *i** to show the internal intentional structures of Adobe and Apple. This model is based on details from [23–27] and is adapted from [12]. The left side of Fig. 4a shows a condensed model of Apple's strategy. Apple's objective was to drive the adoption of its proprietary OS (i.e., iOS) in the mobile device market ("iOS be adopted in smart mobile device market"). The success of iOS was tied to higher sales of iPhone, iPod, and iPad devices because Apple's iOS and its mobile devices were only compatible with each other (not shown).

We extend the notation of *i** slightly to depict the impact of multiple options on *softgoals* in the same *i** model. A *softgoal* satisfaction/denial label is preceded by a number which represents the option that leads to the satisfaction/denial of that *softgoal*. For example, "Reference Objective-C API" is shown as option <2>, which satisfies the *softgoal* titled "Apps be optimized for iOS".

Apple's SECO was a core component of its iOS proliferation strategy. A mobile OS requires a complementary catalog of third-party apps to boost its acceptance and adoption by users ("External innovation be encouraged"). Third-party apps bring new capabilities to a mobile OS and make that mobile OS more useful for its users. Hence, a relatively large catalog of apps ostensibly affords greater choice to the users of a SECO compared to a relatively small catalog.

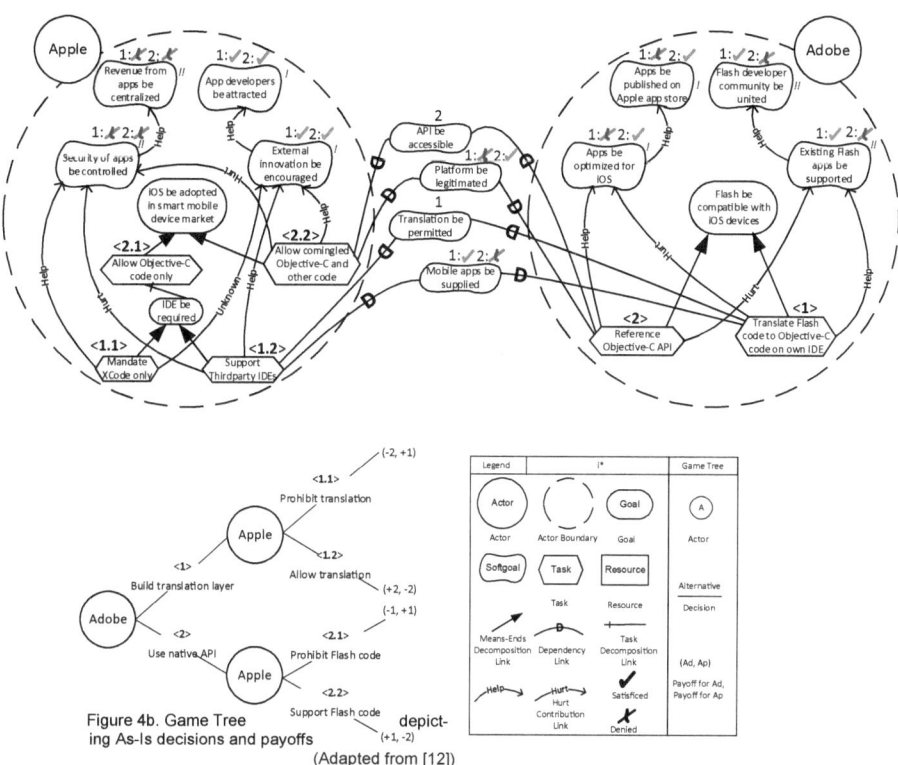

Figure 4b. Game Tree depicting As-Is decisions and payoffs (Adapted from [12])

Fig. 4. (a) *i** SR model depicting As-Is actor relationships. (b) Game Tree depicting As-Is decisions and payoffs (Adapted from [12])

Moreover, positive cross-side network effects synergistically correlate the user base and developer community on a SECO [34] such that growth in the numbers of apps (and their developers) on a SECO attracts more users to that SECO while growth in the number of users on a SECO incents more developers to develop apps for that SECO ("App developers be attracted").

Apple coupled its mobile hardware and software tightly so that it could exert maximal control on the security of apps that were used on iPhone, iPod, and iPad devices ("Security of apps be controlled"). App developers could generate revenues by charging users for downloading their apps in addition to building in-app purchases and value-added offers into their mobile apps (not shown). Apple protected its commissions from these income streams by forcing users to purchase apps from its iOS app store (i.e., prevent revenue flight) as well as requiring developers to use its IDE and programming language (i.e., prevent revenue obfuscation). This "walled garden" strategy helped Apple to safeguard its commissions ("Revenue from apps be centralized").

Apple had two strategic options ("Allow Objective-C code only" and "Allow comingled Objective-C and other code"). Objective-C is Apple's proprietary programming language that is supported by iOS. Each of these options impacted Apple's *softgoals* differently. The option to "Allow comingled Objective-C and other code" (e.g., Adobe Flash code) afforded app developers the opportunity to hide forbidden or malicious functionality outside the purview of Apple security reviews (*Hurts* softgoal "Security of apps be controlled").

The option to "Allow Objective-C code only" had two sub-options. Objective-C code could be developed using Apple XCode ("Mandate XCode only") or generated using a third-party IDE ("Support Third-party IDEs"). XCode is Apple's native integrated development environment (IDE) for iOS. Third-party IDEs afforded app developers the opportunity to bypass security policies implemented by Apple in its XCode IDE (*Hurts* softgoal "security of apps be controlled").

The "Mandate XCode only" option could have positive or negative impact ("Unknown") on the *softgoal* "External innovation be encouraged". The outcome of this option depended upon the perceived difficulty of using Apple's XCode IDE by an app developer that was unfamiliar with Objective-C. If usage of XCode was perceived as being simple then it would Help that *softgoal* but if it was perceived as being complex then it would Hurt that *softgoal* (not shown).

Now consider Adobe's strategic options. Adobe intended for its Flash technology to be supported on Apple iOS devices ("Flash be compatible with iOS devices"). A plethora of Flash-based web-apps could be accessed on the Internet and Adobe's goal was to make these apps available on popular mobile devices such as iPhones, iPods, and iPads. To achieve this objective Adobe had two alternatives which were: "Reference Objective-C API" and "Translate Flash code to Objective-C code on own IDE". Each of these strategies had different pros and cons for Adobe.

The first alternative involved translating Flash code into Objective-C code directly within Adobe's IDE for developing Flash applications (Adobe Flash Builder). Under this option, developers of Adobe Flash apps did not need to use any Apple tools or technologies. This translation option is depicted as scenario <1> in Fig. 4a. This option allowed reuse of Flash code (*Helps* softgoal "Existing Flash apps be supported"). It also allowed cohesion to be maintained in the Flash developer community (*Helps* softgoal "Flash developer community be united").

The second alternative involved referencing Objective-C API from Flash code directly within Adobe's IDE for developing Flash applications (Adobe Flash Builder). This commingling option is depicted as scenario <2> in Fig. 4a. This option allowed developers to optimize apps for iOS (*Helps* softgoal "Apps be optimized for iOS") and for those apps to be publishable on Apple iOS app store (*Helps* softgoal "Apps be published on Apple app store").

Adobe depended on Apple for the operationalization of both options under its consideration (i.e., "Translate Flash code to Objective-C code on own IDE" and "Reference Objective-C API"). This reliance is shown via outbound *dependency links* from Adobe to Apple ("Translation be permitted" and "API be accessible" respectively for the two options).

Figure 4b depicts the *payoffs* for Adobe and Apple for each of these scenarios. In the Evaluation phase, we use a Game Tree to compare various alternatives. Adobe was the first-mover since it had the choice of selecting either the translation (<1>) or the commingling (<2>) option. Apple was the second mover since it controlled the iOS platform and could permit or prohibit actions by third-parties that depended on it for some decision or action. Therefore, Apple could respond to Adobe either by supporting its first-move or blocking it.

If Adobe selected the translation option (<1>) and Apple supported it then Adobe obtained a payoff of +2 while Apple obtained a payoff of −2. This is because the high priority *softgoals* of Adobe were achieved but the high priority *softgoals* of Apple were denied (comparing softgoals priorities and achievements associated with <1> in Fig. 4a). However, if Adobe selected the translation option (<1>) and Apple blocked it then Adobe obtained a payoff of −2 while Apple obtained a payoff of +1. This is because Apple was able to avoid the countermanding of its high priority *softgoals* but the high priority *softgoals* of Adobe were not fulfilled (<1> in Fig. 4a). For the purpose of illustration, we use simple representative values for the payoffs.

Alternatively, if Adobe selected the commingling option (<2>) and Apple supported it then Adobe obtained a payoff of +1 while Apple obtained a payoff of −2. This is because some *softgoals* of Adobe, albeit of lower priority, were satisfied but the high priority *softgoals* of Apple were denied (<2> in Fig. 4a). However, if Adobe selected the commingling option (<2>) and Apple blocked it then Adobe obtained a payoff of −1 while Apple obtained a payoff of +2. This is because high priority *softgoals* of Adobe were unfulfilled but Apple was able to avoid the denial of its high priority *softgoals* (<2> in Fig. 4a).

This analysis of Fig. 4b, following the Evaluation phase of Fig. 1, shows that the relationship between Adobe and Apple did not comprise of any win-win strategies. Rather their relationship characterized only win-lose strategies wherein if one party wins then the other party loses. We now illustrate the methodology depicted in Fig. 1 by applying the Exploration phase to generate a win-win strategy for Adobe and Apple. In the Evaluation phase, we use *i** to contemplate and create new strategic options.

Figure 5a presents an extended actor model showing the *goals* of Adobe and Apple. Existing model elements are denoted by black color while new model elements are denoted by blue color. It is possible that SMEs at Adobe predicted that Apple was unlikely to greenlight either of Adobe's As-Is strategies (of translation or commingling) because each of these strategies would result in the denial of Apple's *softgoals*. Moreover, Adobe SME's probably recognized the asymmetry in the bargaining power between Apple and Adobe because Apple governed and controlled the iOS platform at its own sole discretion. Therefore, Adobe needed to generate new strategies that could help it to satisfy its own *goals* while enabling Apple to meet its objectives as well.

The Exploration phase offers five possible activities for generating new win-win strategies. These pertain to adding, removing, or changing *goals*, *dependencies*, *softgoals*, *actors*, and *tasks*. In terms of *goals*, Adobe wanted to bring support for Flash to popular mobile devices. It could have changed its *goal* to making Flash apps compatible with Android devices (not shown). With respect to *dependencies*, Adobe could have tried to change its relationship with Apple purely at the interface level. It could have paid fees to Apple to induce Apple to support its chosen option (not shown). In terms of *softgoals*, Adobe could influence Apple to modify its *softgoals*. Adobe could mount a public relations campaign to encourage Apple to support Flash (not shown).

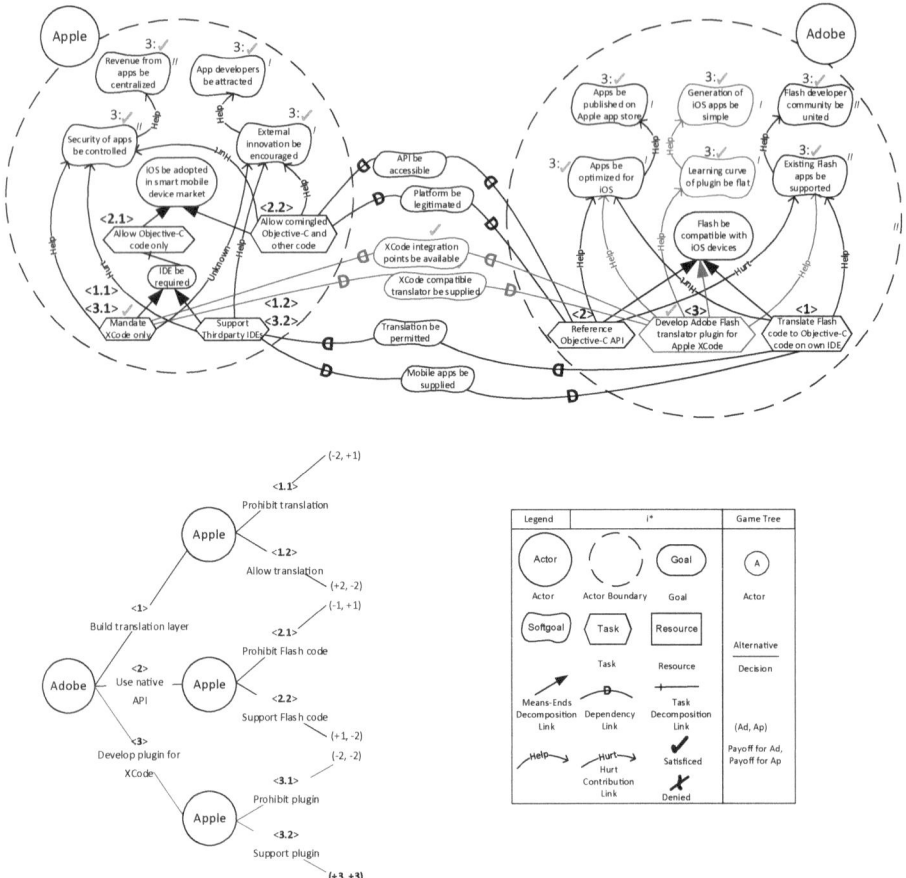

Fig. 5. (a) *i** SR model depicting To-Be actor relationships. (b) Game Tree depicting To-Be decisions and payoffs (Adapted from [12])

With respect to *actors*, Apple or Adobe were in a dyadic relationship. Adobe could have incented Apple to add support for Flash into iOS by bringing a new *actor* (e.g., its community of Flash app developers) into this relationship. Access to a large developer community that was willing to embrace iOS app development could be persuasive and compelling for Apple (not shown).

In terms of *tasks*, Adobe SMEs might have reasoned that Adobe needed to generate new alternatives in its search for a win-win strategy. Adobe SMEs likely recognized that Flash support on iOS could help Apple to satisfy its *softgoals* of "encouraging external innovation" and "attracting App developers". However, Adobe might also have understood that Apple would not support Flash on iOS if it meant that its more important *softgoals* (i.e., "Security of apps be controlled" and "Revenue from apps be centralized") were denied. Therefore, Adobe would have needed to create a new alternative that would be helpful for Apple to achieve its higher priority *softgoals*.

Starting with existing options to create new options is useful because the impact of existing options on extant intentional elements of *actors* is likely to be well understood in the Evaluation phase. As shown in Fig. 4a, translation option (<1>) was preferable to Adobe over commingling option (<2>) since the former satisfied its higher priority *softgoals* while the latter satisfied its lower priority *softgoals* (comparing <1> and <2> in Fig. 4a). However, Adobe's operationalization of the translation option (<1>) via its own IDE (Adobe Flash Builder) made it unacceptable for Apple. This is because it countermanded Apple's higher priority *softgoal* of "security of apps be controlled" and its related higher priority *softgoal* of "Revenue from apps be centralized".

However, a different implementation of the translation option might have helped Adobe and Apple to achieve their higher priority *softgoals*. For example, Adobe could have developed "Adobe Flash translator plugin for Apple XCode". Such a plugin could be embedded within XCode and could automatically inherit and apply the security policies implemented by Apple in its IDE. In such an implementation, app developers would have been able to convert Flash code into Objective-C code using XCode rather than Flash Builder. Developers of Flash apps would have had a minimal learning curve ("Learning curve of plugin be flat") which would have been limited to learning the usage of the Adobe supplied translator plugin inside XCode ("Generation of iOS apps be simple"). Apple would have been satisfied knowing that the output of this translator plugin would be Objective-C code generated inside XCode. Likewise, Adobe would have been contented knowing that its Flash apps would be supported on Apple iOS devices. Eaton et al. [25] have noted that various blogs and online news articles about Apple's service system discussed an Adobe Flash Plug-in option that was not realized. The systematic method proposed in this paper can be used to generate such a novel solution. However, it cannot replace creative thinking and deep domain knowledge but rather support and supplement it.

Figure 5b presents an extended game tree showing the payoffs for Adobe and Apple. Two decision paths at the top of this game tree are the same as those in Fig. 4b. The decision path on the bottom of this game tree reflects the new alternative that is present in Fig. 5a. This decision path is shown in blue color to differentiate it from the others. If Adobe were to select the plugin option and Apple supported it then both Adobe and Apple would have obtained payoffs of +3 each. This is because both actors could have satisfied each of their *softgoals*. Additionally, this new *task* would have unlocked additional *softgoals* for Adobe. However, if Adobe were to select the plugin option and Apple blocked it then both Adobe and Apple would have obtained payoffs of −2. This is because neither of the actors would have been able to fulfil any of their *softgoals* and would have missed out on a promising business opportunity. Therefore, this plugin option represents a win-win strategy for Adobe and Apple wherein both actors would be better off if they operationalize it as partners.

In this example, a win-win strategy was arrived at in one iteration. In the general case, one may need to go through various paths in the exploratory phase multiple times to arrive at a win-win strategy. For instance, in this example, Adobe was able to generate a new alternative ("Develop Adobe Flash translator plugin for Apple XCode") that was compatible with an element of Apple's internal intentional structure ("Mandate XCode only"). However, generation of win-win strategies in other cases may require changes to be made to the internal intentional structures of multiple actors. Such cases will necessitate multiple iterations over different paths of this process.

Similarly, additional iterations of this process would yield other win-win strategies. For instance, in this example, Adobe could have performed additional exploration to generate other alternatives that resulted in win-win. It could have developed a translator that converted Flash code to HTML5 code since iOS supported HTML5 (not shown). Alternatively, it could have developed a translator that converted Flash code to Java-Script since iOS supported JavaScript (not shown). It is conceivable that each of these options might have led to better *payoffs* for Adobe and Apple.

5   Related Work

A number of researchers have contributed to research in these areas: (1) game-theoretic analysis of coopetition, and (2) model-based analysis of SECOs. Brandenburger and Nalebuff [3] introduced the idea of coopetition based on game theory. They also explicated facets of coopetition such as players, added value, roles, tactics, and scope [14]. Nalebuff and Brandenburger [28] defined the roles of complementors and substitutors in coopetition. Brandenburger and Stuart [29] applied cooperative game theory for strategy development. They also introduced a model of biform games to explain noncooperative-cooperative games [30]. These works do not provide a systematic method for exploring the space of strategic moves to generate new win-win strategies.

Fricker [31] developed a framework for analyzing SECO requirements using ideas from negotiation and network theories. Handoyo et al. [8] developed value chains to identify key actors and roles in SECOs. Jansen et al. [32] proposed a set of universal requirements and understandings about SECO modeling. Santos [33] developed Power Models for assessing power in SECOs.

Yu and Deng [11] were the first to use $i*$ strategic modeling to analyze SECOs. Pant and Yu [12] introduced a methodology for modeling strategic moves and reciprocity among actors. This methodology introduced synergistic links between Game Trees and $i*$ models. It was accompanied with a set of guidelines for, "instantiating an $i*$ SR model and its complementary game tree in a consistent manner" [12]. Key assumptions of this methodology included: (i) focal-actor orientation; (ii) distinctive preference profiles and idiosyncratic interest structures of actors; and (iii) information imperfection, incompleteness, and asymmetry [12]. The present paper extends that work by offering a systematic method for generating win-win strategies.

6   Conclusions and Future Work

This paper contributed to a line of research that links strategic modeling ($i*$) with decision analysis (Game Tree). The primary contribution in this paper was in the Exploration phase of this methodology. This phase is crucial for incremental and iterative generation of win-win strategies. This phase of the methodology was explicated using a simple example predicated on minimax and maximin theorems from

Game Theory. This paper illustrated this methodology by applying it to instantiate models of SECOs under coopetition based on a published case study.

The next step in this research area is to accommodate additional facets of complexity in two-person zero-sum games within Game Trees [35]. A following step to this concerns empirical validation of this methodology in a real-life case study. Progression from validation using a published case study to validation using an empirical case study will surface the strengths and weaknesses of applying this methodology in the field. Another advancement in this research area will come from further elaboration and explication of the Exploration phase. More structured and systematic guidelines for selecting among the five steps in that phase will support practitioner efforts to use this methodology in industrial settings.

Additional areas for exploration include adding support in $i*$ for: (i) temporal reasoning, (ii) expressing negative dependencies, and (iii) conditional logic. The notions of time and sequence are relevant for analyzing coopetition since path dependent phenomena such as reciprocity and trust impact the moves and counter-moves of actors. The depiction of negative dependencies is necessary for analyzing coopetition because the coincidental absence of dependencies and the intentional independence between actors can impel or impede coopetitive strategies. Support for conditional logic is relevant for representing cause and effect relationships such as those between the actions and responses of coopeting actors. These additions to the expressiveness of $i*$ can support a practitioner to more fully portray and understand the motivations behind the decisions and actions of actors in coopetitive relationships.

References

1. Chesbrough, H.: Open innovation: a new paradigm for understanding industrial innovation. In: Open Innovation: Researching a New Paradigm, pp. 0–19, 400 p. (2006)
2. Jansen, S., Finkelstein, A., Brinkkemper, S.: A sense of community: a research agenda for software ecosystems. In: 31st International Conference on Software Engineering Companion Volume, pp. 187–190. IEEE, May 2009
3. Brandenburger, A.M., Nalebuff, B.J.: Co-opetition. Doubleday, New York (1996)
4. Duc, A.N., Cruzes, D.S., Hanssen, G.K., Snarby, T., Abrahamsson, P.: Coopetition of software firms in open source software ecosystems. In: Ojala, A., Holmström Olsson, H., Werder, K. (eds.) ICSOB 2017. LNBIP, vol. 304, pp. 146–160. Springer, Cham (2017). https://doi.org/10.1007/978-3-319-69191-6_10
5. Coutinho, E.F., Viana, D., dos Santos, R.P.: An exploratory study on the need for modeling software ecosystems: the case of SOLAR SECO. In: Proceedings of the 9th International Workshop on Modelling in Software Engineering, pp. 47–53. IEEE Press, May 2017
6. Rausch, A., Bartelt, C., Herold, S., Klus, H., Niebuhr, D.: From software systems to complex software ecosystems: model- and constraint-based engineering of ecosystems. In: Münch, J., Schmid, K. (eds.) Perspectives on the Future of Software Engineering, pp. 61–80. Springer, Heidelberg (2013). https://doi.org/10.1007/978-3-642-37395-4_5
7. Boucharas, V., Jansen, S., Brinkkemper, S.: Formalizing software ecosystem modeling. In: Proceedings of the 1st International Workshop on Open Component Ecosystems, pp. 41–50. ACM, August 2009

8. Handoyo, E., Jansen, S., Brinkkemper, S.: Software ecosystem modeling: the value chains. In: Proceedings of the Fifth International Conference on Management of Emergent Digital Ecosystems, pp. 17–24. ACM, October 2013

9. Handoyo, E.: Software ecosystem modeling. In: Herzwurm, G., Margaria, T. (eds.) ICSOB 2013. LNBIP, vol. 150, pp. 227–228. Springer, Heidelberg (2013). https://doi.org/10.1007/978-3-642-39336-5_25

10. Alves, A.M., Pessoa, M., Salviano, C.F.: Towards a systemic maturity model for public software ecosystems. In: O'Connor, R.V., Rout, T., McCaffery, F., Dorling, A. (eds.) SPICE 2011. CCIS, vol. 155, pp. 145–156. Springer, Heidelberg (2011). https://doi.org/10.1007/978-3-642-21233-8_13

11. Yu, E., Deng, S.: Understanding software ecosystems: a strategic modeling approach. In: Proceedings of the Third International Workshop on Software Ecosystems, Brussels, Belgium, pp. 65–76, June 2011

12. Pant, V., Yu, E.: Understanding strategic moves and reciprocity on software ecosystems: a strategic modeling approach. In: 9th International Workshop on Software Ecosystems (IWSECO 2017) (2017)

13. Padula, G., Dagnino, G.B.: Untangling the rise of coopetition: the intrusion of competition in a cooperative game structure. Int. Stud. Manag. Organ. **37**(2), 32–52 (2007)

14. Brandenburger, A.M., Nalebuff, B.J.: The Right Game: Use Game Theory to Shape Strategy. Harvard Business Review, pp. 57–71 (1995)

15. Dixit, A.K., Nalebuff, B.: The Art of Strategy: A Game Theorist's Guide to Success in Business & Life. WW Norton & Company, New York (2008)

16. Magdon-Ismail, M., Busch, C., Krishnamoorthy, M.S.: Cake-cutting is not a piece of cake. In: Alt, H., Habib, M. (eds.) STACS 2003. LNCS, vol. 2607, pp. 596–607. Springer, Heidelberg (2003). https://doi.org/10.1007/3-540-36494-3_52

17. Barbanel, J.B., Brams, S.J., Stromquist, W.: Cutting a pie is not a piece of cake. Am. Math. Mon. **116**(6), 496–514 (2009)

18. Chen, Y., Lai, J.K., Parkes, D.C., Procaccia, A.D.: Truth, justice, and cake cutting. Games Econ. Behav. **77**(1), 284–297 (2013)

19. Deng, X., Qi, Q., Saberi, A.: Algorithmic solutions for envy-free cake cutting. Oper. Res. **60**(6), 1461–1476 (2012)

20. Aziz, H., Mackenzie, S.: A discrete and bounded envy-free cake cutting protocol for any number of agents. In: 57th Annual Symposium on Foundations of Computer Science, pp. 416–427. IEEE, October 2016

21. Dall'Aglio, M., Hill, T.P.: Maximin share and minimax envy in fair-division problems. J. Math. Anal. Appl. **281**(1), 346–361 (2003)

22. Yu, E., Giorgini, P., Maiden, N., Mylopoulos, J.: Social Modeling for Requirements Engineering. MIT Press, Cambridge (2011)

23. Ghazawneh, A., Henfridsson, O.: Governing third-party development through platform boundary resources. In: Proceedings of the 31st International Conference of Information Systems (ICIS), St. Louis (2010)

24. Ghazawneh, A., Henfridsson, O.: Micro-strategizing in platform ecosystems: a multiple case study. In: Proceedings of the 32nd International Conference on Information Systems (ICIS) 2011, Shanghai, China (2011)

25. Eaton, B., Elaluf-Calderwood, S., Sorensen, C., Yoo, Y.: Distributed tuning of boundary resources: the case of Apple's iOS service system. MIS Q.: Manag. Inf. Syst. **39**(1), 217–243 (2015)

26. Prince, J.D.: HTML5: not just a substitute for flash. J. Electron. Resour. Med. Libr. **10**(2), 108–112 (2013)

27. Elaluf-Calderwood, S.M., Eaton, B.D., Sørensen, C., Yoo, Y.: Control as a strategy for the development of generativity in business models for mobile platforms. In: 15th International Conference on Intelligence in Next Generation Networks (ICIN), pp. 271–276. IEEE, October 2011
28. Nalebuff, B.J., Brandenburger, A.M.: Co-opetition: competitive and cooperative business strategies for the digital economy. Strategy Leadersh. **25**(6), 28–33 (1997)
29. Brandenburger, A.M., Stuart, H.W.: Value-based business strategy. J. Econ. Manag. Strategy **5**(1), 5–24 (1996)
30. Brandenburger, A., Stuart, H.: Biform games. Manage. Sci. **53**(4), 537–549 (2007)
31. Fricker, S.: Specification and analysis of requirements negotiation strategy in software ecosystems. In: Proceedings of International Workshop on Software Ecosystems (2009)
32. Jansen, S., Handoyo, E., Alves, C.: Scientists' needs in software ecosystem modeling. In: Proceedings of the International Workshop on Software Ecosystems (2015)
33. Santos, G.A.V.: A theory of power in software ecosystems formed by small-to-medium enterprises. Ph.D. thesis (2016)
34. Boudreau, K.J.: Let a thousand flowers bloom? An early look at large numbers of software app developers and patterns of innovation. Organ. Sci. **23**(5), 1409–1427 (2012)
35. Koller, D., Megiddo, N.: The complexity of two-person zero-sum games in extensive form. Games Econ. Behav. **4**(4), 528–552 (1992)

Exploring Business Model Changes in Software-as-a-Service Firms

Eetu Luoma[(✉)], Gabriella Laatikainen, and Oleksiy Mazhelis

Faculty of Information Technology, University of Jyväskylä,
P.O. Box 35 Agora, 40014 Jyväskylä, Finland
{eetu.luoma,gabriella.laatikainen,
oleksiy.mazhelis}@jyu.fi

Abstract. This paper reports the findings from research on the changes in the business models of Software-as-a-Service (SaaS) firms. The extant literature defines these firms through the use of cloud computing technologies as part of their products and service. However, current literature is missing consideration of the effects of adopting these technologies on the elements of business model, including value proposition, activities, structure and revenue logic. This paper presents findings from 324 responses to a questionnaire survey on how these business model elements of software firms have changed as a result of adopting cloud computing technologies and competitive pressures, and identifies the differences in changes between the SaaS firms originating from software product and software services business. The findings suggest that the SaaS firms are generally unifying their core product offering and pricing across customers and increasing their sales efforts. Besides, the two types of SaaS firms are different in terms of their software-related activities. The present study therefore provides insights into development of the software market, where SaaS firms are claimed to challenge the proprietary software vendors. The findings also imply that the conceptualization of SaaS in IS adoption and IT outsourcing studies can be improved.

Keywords: Software-as-a-Service · SaaS · Cloud computing
Business models · Changes · Software firms

1 Introduction

This paper contributes to the growing body of literature on Software-as-a-Service (SaaS). SaaS is one of the layers of cloud computing services [3, 28] and the term is used to designate standard applications delivered over the Internet [20, 37]. Choudary [10] submits that the SaaS model is associated with subscription-based revenue logic and, on that account, SaaS would entail different means of software licensing and way of charging customers compared to the traditional software business models.

The Software-as-a-Service (SaaS) firms are claimed to radically change the software business setting, by breaking down the positions of big proprietary software vendors [2]. It is therefore surprising that the consideration of SaaS firms business model in the extant literature is mostly limited to their core product offering and their

© Springer Nature Switzerland AG 2018
K. Wnuk and S. Brinkkemper (Eds.): ICSOB 2018, LNBIP 336, pp. 108–124, 2018.
https://doi.org/10.1007/978-3-030-04840-2_8

revenue logic. Beyond this point, the contemporary literature does not provide much more empirical evidence about how the software firms have organized their business model to develop and deliver the SaaS offerings. Specifically, the absence of empirical research on SaaS firms' business models suggests a gap in understanding the changes in software firms' business model to encompass the possibilities of cloud computing technologies and perils of the competitive environment.

In this research, the authors investigated the changes in software firms' business models and a set of possible explanations for the changes. A business model is understood as a coherent configuration of the four key elements [1, 16, 19, 31, 42]: value proposition, activities, structure and revenue logic. The authors considered (1) what are the changes in software firms' business model induced by cloud computing technologies, (2) have the changes occurred because of availability of new technology or because of competitive pressures and (3) whether there are differences in changes caused by adoption of cloud computing technologies between software product firms and software services firms. These research questions were addressed by analyzing responses to a survey questionnaire from 324 Finnish software firms.

2 Theoretical Background: Business Models

Basically, a business model is a description or an interpretation of how a company organizes itself, operates and makes money [5, 25, 31]. Being a description, the business model acts as a conceptual tool, which narrates either the state of current business or planned future business [1, 16]. Business model is also a concept used to describe the key elements of a focal firm's business [18] and implies that the elements are interrelated. Individual decisions of business model design affect several aspects of the firm [16, 40]. The discussion on the key elements of a business model seems to be converging and researchers are then able to elaborate the details of individual elements (called parameters). The common elements include value proposition incorporating both the customer segment and product/service portfolio, activities performed by the focal firm to create and appropriate value, internal structure and position in the value network, and revenue logic referring to the structure of income.

Studies of business models of software firms often classify firms into representative groups to allow for statistical inferences. For instance, Rajala et al. [33] identify different characteristics of software firms according to their product strategy, revenue logic, cost structure/pricing strategy and distribution model. The German software industry survey uses a highly detailed classification scheme with five first-order constructs and 25 second-order constructs as parameters [36]. Cusumano [12, 13] alternatively uses two broad categories based on firms' value proposition and source of revenue, namely software product firms and software services firms. He observes the lifecycle dynamics, i.e. a gradual shift in software firms' business models towards increasing service offering and revenues, which is attributable to competitive pressures, but also individual firm's age and lagging sales [12, 13].

Also Teece [40] argues that business models are provisional and likely to be changed. The changes may appear as companies create new business models (in case of start-ups), extend their business model by adding activities, value propositions or partners, revise their business model by modifying or replacing these elements, or terminate an existing business model [21]. An observable sign of business model change is a substantial change in the structure of revenue sources [16], which reflects overall changes in both the value proposition and the revenue logic.

The extant literature suggests that business models may change in response to both external and internal influences. Considering the external factor first, authors widely demonstrate and agree on two external factors for business model changes: Advances in contemporary technology [8, 9, 35, 42] and competitive forces [8, 13, 16, 35]. These external forces have the power to change the value of the firm's product/service portfolio, structure of the value network, and the costs of performing activities and acquiring resources [16], as well as reshape customer demand. In relation to the outcomes, Chesbrough and Rosenbloom [9] contend that the financial performance of a given firm *is* associated with developments in firm's environment, but *only* through changes in the firm's business model. Similarly, adoption of cloud computing technology does not directly improve or worsen financial performance of a software firm, but the business model extensions and revisions are mechanism to achieve such gains. However, adoption of the new technology may be a prerequisite to overcome the limitations of existing business model and adoption of new technologies may results in business model changes of different magnitude [9].

The business model changes also originate from within the company. A business model design, the practical means to create and appropriate value, is a choice of the company's managers and employees, who interpret the changes in the environment and accordingly make decisions about and implement the changes in the business model [4, 9, 16]. As underscored above, elements of the business model are interrelated. Consequently, the extensions and revisions to one element is likely to cause successive determined and emergent changes [16].

3   Prior Research on SaaS

The importance of business aspects of cloud computing has already been recognized and considered in information technology research [26]. To understand the role of cloud computing technologies to software firms' business, we explored the prior research on business aspects of the Software-as-a-Service (SaaS) firms. Our search on the relevant literature revealed that recent empirical studies have examined both demand and supply sides of this SaaS phenomenon. Most common topics looking at the client side include consideration of the opportunities and risks of SaaS adoption [7, 20], studies on service quality and related expectations by SaaS customers [7, 10] and explaining the reasons to outsource in SaaS mode [6, 39]. Software vendors' side has been investigated in studies seeking to find archetypal SaaS business models [38] in comparing SaaS to other business models [14, 37] and in papers examining distinct aspects of SaaS business [23, 41].

Our search of the extant literature reveals that, overall, holistic business models of SaaS firms have received relatively modest attention from researchers, beyond investigating isolated elements of the business model. We find this somewhat surprising, since business models convey several important aspects affecting adoption of software applications, information technology outsourcing and software business. We also found that, to date, empirical examinations of the *changes* in the SaaS firm's business model at large is missing altogether. An article by Stuckenberg et al. [38] addresses this gap through a small set of interviews, but the focus of their article is rather able to identify the current parameters of SaaS firms business model than examining the changes thereof. Moreover, lack of empirical studies of business model changes signifies that we are unsure which changes in business model parameters are attributable to cloud computing technologies and which are related to the present competitive pressures. In the current study we therefore focused on empirically examining how adoption of cloud computing technology affects the business models of software firms.

4   Hypothesis Development

Some researchers see the value proposition of Software-as-a-Service firms as very similar to the traditional model for selling software products, where only a single set of functionalities is provided to all customers with limited possibilities for customer-specific alterations [7]. However, the business model of Software-as-a-Service firms is here argued to be different from preceding software business models, since the delivery of software capabilities using cloud computing technologies changes the business model configuration. Observed differences to software product business model include more direct customer relationship, subscription based pricing logic, and combining both software development and hosting as key activities [24, 38]. SaaS vendors may often provide their prices on their websites [23], indicating more transparent and unified pricing across customers. Consider Dropbox as a contemporary example of a firm with such SaaS business model. SaaS has also been compared to business of supplying customer-specific applications. SaaS firms would target smaller firms with one-to-many model for non-critical applications, as opposed to targeting large firms with customer-specific offering for critical applications [34, 36]. Based on the claimed characteristics of SaaS firms, we hypothesize that the cloud computing technologies has an effect on the business models parameters of software firms:

H1. Adoption of cloud computing technologies by software firms is associated with change toward (a) targeting the segment of smaller customers, (b) offering more standardized product, (c) decreasing customer-specific software development and production activities, (d) increasing the sales activities, (e) decreasing the allocation of employees into customer-specific activities, (e) increasing the allocation of employees into sales activities, (f) committing to shorter subscription periods and (g) unifying the pricing across different customers.

Whereas most authors perceive and conceptualize SaaS offering as described above, few articles [11, 24] introduce possible variations of the assumed pure-play SaaS. An enterprise SaaS business model is suggested, which is a configuration with more complex or bundled application aimed at larger customer firms and requiring support services, a combination of subscription fee and time and materials fee, more high-touch customer relationships and varying marginal costs. The latter business model configuration seems to inherit characteristics of software services firms. It follows that cloud computing may be employed differently by software firms and, thus, adoption of cloud computing technology by a software firm may have varying effect on business model. Some firms use cloud computing to change their value proposition, whereas some deploy cloud computing for internal efficiency [26]. We find it likely that a software product firm revises its business model into being a SaaS firm with highly standardized software and minimal adjacent services. By contrast, software services firms would rather adjust their business model to enjoy the benefit of improved efficiency. Accordingly, we hypothesize that:

H2. Software product firms adopting cloud computing technologies are more likely to change their business model toward (a) targeting the segment of smaller customers, (b) offering more standardized product, (c) decreasing customer-specific software development and production activities, (d) increasing the sales activities, (e) decreasing the allocation of employees into customer-specific activities, (e) increasing the allocation of employees into sales activities, (f) committing to shorter subscription periods and (g) unifying the pricing across different customers, than software service firms adopting cloud computing technologies.

5   Research Method

5.1   Data Collection

Our empirical study is aimed at capturing changes in software firms' business models related to cloud adoption. This study uses data collected as part of the annual Finnish software industry survey, which target most of the software companies in Finland. The survey focuses on firms whose main activities are providing software as either products or services to their customers and follows a modified version of the tailored survey design [18], using postal mail and web-based form with email invitations to collect the data. The survey was developed in Finnish and delivered to respondents either in Finnish, Swedish or English. The mailing list of the survey contained key informants of 4878 software companies. Software firms are identified using their NACE industry classification code (division 62 in rev.2.), and contact persons for each software firm are identified from the Orbis database. After contacting the firms in the sample five times the data collection resulted in 379 complete and 121 partial responses.

For this paper, a subset of the data was used. As our focus is on firms providing Software-as-a- Service, we excluded producers of embedded software and software resellers from the analysis. Further, since the objective of this study is to examine the factors causing changes in the firms' business models that we deem are unclear in case of a start-up software firm, also the software firms younger than two years were excluded from the analysis. In total, 324 software companies matched our inclusion criteria and their complete answers were used for the analysis.

5.2   Concepts and Their Operationalization

The multifaceted business model construct was conceptualized through its constituent elements: value proposition, activities, structure and revenue logic of the firm. Value proposition   combined   the   firm's   choices   of   a   customer   segment   and   of   a product/service offering as parameters [9]. Structure was conceptualized as allocation of firm's employees into customer-facing unit performing customer-specific work, or the back-end unit producing products and services [14]. Activities performed by the software firm are then divided into software-related activities, including development, deployment and maintenance, and those associated with creating and maintaining the customer relationship [34]. Revenue logic incorporated the temporal rights (e.g. perpetual license or subscription) and price discrimination [22, 23].

Ascribed to the nature of the survey, the authors were faced with the choice of examining specific changes in the business models with single-item measures or examining one of the business model elements in detail. While the configuration approach [29] would advocate measuring one aspect and inferring changes to the whole business model, the configurations of SaaS firms business model evidentially vary irrespective of the assumption of cloud technology adoption. The authors therefore preferred the research design to measure and interpret various business model changes with single-item measurements.

Accordingly, the dependent variables of this study measure the changes of software firm's business model – value proposition, activities, revenue logic and structure – during the last three years. They are based on the characteristics of assumed business model of a SaaS firm capturing directly the change of parameters toward targeting firms marketing efforts smaller customers than before (labelled ValuePropSeg), toward offering more standardized product or service than before (ValuePropProd), toward decreasing the amount of customer-specific software development or service production activities (ActivitiesSW), toward increasing in the amount of personal sales activities (ActivitiesSales), toward committing to shorter contracts than before (RevenueSubs), and the change toward more unified pricing across the customers (RevenuePric). With these six dependent variables, the informant was asked "How well these statements describe the change of your company's business model during the last three years?" and response options were anchored ranging from "1 = strongly disagree" to "5 = strongly agree".

Further, the dependent variables reflecting the change in the internal structure directly measure the increase in the number of employees in customer-specific work as compared to the total (StructureCust) and the increase in the number of employees in sales as compared to the total (StructureSales). With these variables, the informant was asked "How has the structure of your company changed during the past three years?" and an ordinal measure was used ranging from "1 = decreased significantly" to "5 = increased significantly".

Cloud platform adoption is the independent variable (labelled isCloudAdopter), which was measured by the question "Which third party software platforms has your firm to a significant degree developed software?", and had four options; "Public cloud, rented computing capacity, e.g. Amazon EC2, Rackspace, Azure", "Public cloud, application platform, e.g. Heroku, App Engine, Azure", "Open-source, e.g. Hadoop, Cloud Foundry" and "Private Cloud". The cloud adoption was reduced to a dummy (binary) variable that describes whether or not firms develop software for private or public cloud platform. For classifying the software firms, the authors use an independent variable obtained from the question where the respondent is asked to describe their business being either a product firm, service firm or not a software firm. For clarity, the authors created a dummy variable that describes whether or not the firm is a software product firm (labelled isProductFirm).

The authors controlled for the competitive forces, company age and company size. The competitive forces factor was operationalized by applying a set of five questions describing the environmental dynamism by Miller and Friesen [30]. The questions capture the competitor, technological and customer components of external forces. Compared to Miller and Friesen's scale, the survey instrument in this study used reverse coded measures (i.e. higher values of EnvDyn indicate less dynamism, hence less pressure from external forces). Using company age as control variable is justified, since the more mature companies are likely to suffer from inertial forces within the organization that obstructs changes. By contrast, a larger company may have better resources to initiate and execute changes compared to smaller firms with limited resources. The following analysis uses a ln(Age) and ln(Size). For the company size variable, the revenue of the firm was used as a proxy.

5.3   Data Analysis

The hypotheses in this study were investigated through the Mann-Whitney U test and multivariate ordinal regression analyses. In particular, the former is used to compare the business model changes of software firms; between adopters of cloud platforms and non-adopters, and between software product firms and software services firms that have adopted cloud platforms. The ordinal regression analyses were employed to assess whether the business model changes are attributable to adoption of cloud platforms or competitive forces in the software firms' environment. Ordinal regressions treat each ordinal value as an independent variable. It is therefore possible to examine parameter estimates for a certain range of values within an independent variable [27].

The checks prior to the data analysis affected the informed choice among different possible statistics. Specifically, the authors noticed that the dependent variables were negatively skewed and applied the Shapiro-Wilk's test of normality. The test was significant meaning that the sample did not come from normally distributed population. This advised use of non-parametric statistics. The other concerns were related to the potential presence of outliers, common method variance as a typical problem with the survey research [32], multicollinearity of the independent variables and the proportional odds assumption of the ordinal regression To avoid these concerns the authors first explored the data and detected four influential responses visually using box plots and removed them from the analysis. Next, the authors applied Harman's single-factor test to assess common method variance. The unrotated factor solution did not reveal a single factor, which would account for the majority of the variance in the model, suggesting that the method variance would not be a problem in the data. From the correlation statistics presented in the Table 1, the authors did not detect high correlations between the two independent variables. This suggested that multicollinearity would not impede the results, permitting the use of regression analysis. Finally, to test the proportional odds assumption the authors ran tests of parallel lines in SPSS. Within all the models, the Chi-Square statistics were insignificant, indicating that the assumption was not violated.

Table 1. Non-parametric correlations between the variables

Spearman rtio		1	2	3	4	5	6	7	8	9	10	11	12	13
ValueProp Seg	Coefficient	1,000												
	Sig.	.												
ValueProp Prod	Coefficient	-,002	1,000											
	Sig.	,974	.											
Activities SW	Coefficient	-,112	-,269	1,000										
	Sig.	,084	,000	.										
Activities Sales	Coefficient	-,124	,143	,186	1,000									
	Sig.	,057	,028	,004	.									
Revenue Subs	Coefficient	,229	,276	,218	,088	1,000								
	Sig.	,000	,000	,001	,180	.								
Revenue Pric	Coefficient	,019	,261	-,132	,003	,185	1,000							
	Sig.	,771	,000	,044	,959	,005	.							
Structure Cust	Coefficient	-,208	-,029	,262	,221	-,111	-,031	1,000						
	Sig.	,001	,654	,000	,001	,092	,633	.						
Structure Sales	Coefficient	-,152	,083	,044	,332	,052	-,001	,268	1,000					
	Sig.	,020	,206	,508	,000	,426	,984	,000	.					
ln(Age)	Coefficient	,089	,010	,032	-,078	,047	,025	-,039	-,051	1,000				
	Sig.	,168	,876	,622	,232	,475	,697	,547	,434	.				
ln(Size)	Coefficient	-,109	,114	,130	,251	,153	,017	,218	,227	,159	1,000			
	Sig.	,099	,086	,050	,000	,018	,802	,001	,001	,009	.			
EnvDyn	Coefficient	-,066	,070	-,051	-,219	-,065	,122	-,027	-,144	,071	-,077	1,000		
	Sig.	,308	,279	,437	,001	,316		,674	,026	,263	,235	.		
isProductFirm	Coefficient	,072	,234	,446	-,136	,153	,150	-,139	,058	,011	,034	,091	1,000	
	Sig.	,264	,000	,000	,035	,018	,021	,031	,373	,839	,580	,151	.	
isCloudAdopter	Coefficient	,019	,231	-,052	,134	,283	,193	-,045	,092	-,137	,128	-,058	,135	1,000
	Sig.	,765	,000	,427	,038	,000	,003	,483	,156	,025	,044	,357	,027	.

6 Results

Table 1 shows the variables together with their non-parametric correlations. The results show that some variables capturing the changes in software firms' business models are positively (ValuePropProd, ActiviesSales, RevenuePric) correlated with the adoption of cloud platforms. Also, the results demonstrate positive correlations (ValuePropProd, RevenuePric) and negative correlations (ActivitiesSW, ActivitiesSales, StructureCust) between changes in business models and the type of software firm (isProductFirm). Further, the results show negative correlations between environmental dynamism and ActivitiesSales, RevenueSubs and StructureSales variables (note the reverse coded EnvDyn variable). Table 1 also shows correlations between dependent variables. The authors mark the association between unifying the offering and the pricing, and between sales efforts and unifying both offering and pricing.

Table 2 is used to compare the means of variables capturing the business model parameters' change between adopters of cloud platforms and non-adopters and between software product firms and software services firms who have adopted cloud platforms. As can be seen in Table 2, the Mann- Whitney U tests indicate significant ($p < 0.05$) differences between adopters and non-adopters in terms of changes toward offering more standardized product or service, toward increasing in the amount of personal sales activities and toward more unified pricing across the customers, but not in terms of other hypothesized changes in business model parameters. Table 2 also shows significant differences between software product firms and software services firm in changes regarding the product/service offering, the software-related activities and the length of contract with customers. However, the Mann- Whitney U tests show that in relation to the rest of the changes in business model parameters product and services firms are not significantly different.

Results from the ordinal regressions of the eight models are shown in Table 3, which reports the regression parameter estimates for the levels of dependent variables ("threshold"), for the independent variables and controls. The table also reports two pseudo r-squares of Nagelkerke – for the full model and for controls only – which assess the overall goodness of fit of the ordinal regression models. While the values give some indication of the strength of the associations between the dependent and the predictor variables, the authors note that these r-squares should not be interpreted similarly to the OLS regressions. However, comparing the r-squares between a model including only controls and the full model, the higher r-square on each full model indicates better prediction on the outcome. Lastly, the tables include model fitting information for the final models; -2 log-likelihood, Chi-square and significance. The values are statistically acceptable for all models, except for the "DV = ValuePropSeg" model. This means that the rest of the models yield predictions more fitting than the marginal probabilities for the dependent variable categories.

Table 2. Comparing changes in business model parameters between groups

| | All firms | | | | | | | Cloud platform adopters | | | | | | |
| | isCloudAdopter = Q | | | isCloudAdopter = 1 | | | U test | isProductFirm = Q | | | isProductFirm = 1 | | | U test |
	N	Mean	SD	N	Mean	SD	Sig.	N	Mean	SD	N	Mean	SD	Sig.
ValueProp Seg	117	2,69	,995	123	2,76	1,074	,765	60	2,63	1,057	63	2,87	1,085	,219
ValueProp Prod	119	3,17	,986	122	3,59	,907	,000	59	3,24	0,953	63	3,92	0,725	,000
Activities SW	118	2,74	1,025	121	2,84	,983	,426	58	2,36	0,718	63	3,29	0,991	,000
Activities Sales	118	3,25	,924	121	3,49	,932	,038	59	3,54	0,877	62	3,44	0,985	,457
Revenue Subs	118	3,19	,945	121	3,71	,873	,000	60	3,59	0,899	61	3,82	1,015	,039
Revenue Pric	117	3,23	,875	122	3,57	,792	,003	60	3,45	0,79	62	3,69	0,781	,069
Structure Cust	119	3,29	,865	122	3,20	,968	,482	59	3,32	0,797	63	3,08	1,097	,201
Structure Sales	120	3,18	,718	121	3,31	,857	,155	59	3,27	0,784	62	3,35	0,925	,712

Table 3. Ordinal regression models with parameter estimates

	DV = ValueProp Seg			DV = ValueProp Prod			DV = Activities SW			DV = Activities Sales		
	Estimate	StdErr	Sig.	Estimate	StdErr	Sig.	Estimate	StdErr	Sig.	Estimate	StdErr	Sig.
DV ordinal level = 1	-2,804	,913	,002	-1,803	,978	,065	-3,212	,967	,001	-4,499	1,023	,000
DV ordinal level = 2	-,712	,892	,425	,548	,911	,547	-,823	,928	,375	-1,921	,932	,039
DV ordinal level = 3	,341	,891	,702	1,753	,917	,056	,368	,925	,691	-,576	,923	,533
DV ordinal level = 4	3,010	,966	,002	4,555	,965	,000	3,477	,969	,000	2,201	,942	,019
ln(Age)	,256	,173	,140	,026	,178	,883	-,074	,182	,685	-,206	,181	,253
ln(Size)	-,068	,047	,151	,067	,048	,164	-,088	,050	,077	,143	,049	,004
EnvDyn	-,193	,175	,270	,108	,181	,553	,062	,183	,734	-,630	,186	,001
isProductFirm = 1	,331	,246	,179	,731	,259	,005	1,793	,274	,000	-,580	,256	,023
isCloudAdopter = 1	,086	,246	,728	,831	,259	,001	,108	,257	,674	,498	,256	,052
Pseudo R² (Nagelkerke)	,030			,109			,223			,143		
Pseudo R² (Controls only)	,020			,013			,022			,111		
Model fitting information	631,91	6.514	,259	573,28	24.35	,000	552,44	52.72	,000	563,48	32.26	,000

	DV = Revenue Subs			DV = Revenue Pric			DV = Structure Cust			DV = Structure Sales		
	Estimate	StdErr	Sig.	Estimate	StdErr	Sig.	Estimate	StdErr	Sig.	Estimate	StdErr	Sig.
DV ordinal level = 1	-3,091	,966	,001	-1,288	1,024	,209	-2,410	,973	,013	-3,928	1,070	,000
DV ordinal level = 2	-1,822	,930	,050	,837	,947	,377	-,789	,930	,396	-1,944	,969	,045
DV ordinal level = 3	-,102	,919	,911	2,427	,957	,011	1,665	,935	,075	,844	,960	,379
DV ordinal level = 4	2,599	,942	,006	5,720	1,032	,000	3,404	,957	,000	3,221	,996	,001
ln(Age)	,224	,181	,216	,127	,183	,487	-,143	,179	,425	-,180	,185	,330
ln(Size)	-,024	,049	,619	,049	,049	,317	,142	,049	,004	,127	,050	,012
EnvDyn	-,285	,182	,117	,396	,186	,033	-,042	,181	,818	-,394	,189	,037
isProductFirm = 1	,573	,258	,026	,473	,262	,071	-,539	,258	,037	,189	,261	,468
isCloudAdopter = 1	,990	,263	,000	,670	,262	,011	-,208	,256	,416	,143	,263	,585
Pseudo R² (Nagelkerke)	,110			,079			,066			,064		
Pseudo R² (Controls only)	,012			,025			,041			,059		
Model fitting information	562,28	24.37	,000	529,56	16.81	,005	574,05	14.48	,013	511,95	13.47	,019

Focusing on the ordinal regression parameter estimates for this study, the adoption of cloud platform is significant in predicting the change in towards more standardized product or service and more unified pricing (in model "DV = ValuePropProd", Est. = .831, Sig. = .001 and in model "DV = RevenueSubs", Est. = .670, Sig. = 0.11), and to some extent notable in predicting the change towards increasing sales activities ("DV = ActivitiesSales, Est. = .498, Sig. = .052). In other words, the cloud platform adopters are more likely to make such changes in their business model parameters. However, the change toward more standardized product or service is also predicted by the type of the software firm, that is, software product firms are more likely to standardize their products and services ("DV = ValuePropProd", Est. = .731, Sig. = .005). The type of the software firm is also significant predictor of changes towards decreasing the amount of customer-specific activities ("ActivitiesSW", Est. = 1.793, Sig. = .000), *decreasing* the sales activities ("ActivitiesSales", Est. = −.580, Sig. = .023), committing to *longer* contracts ("RevenueSubs", Est. = −.814, Sig. = .001) and *decreasing* the number of employees in customer-specific work as compared to the total ("StructureCust", Est. = −.539, Sig. = .037).

Interestingly, environmental dynamism is a significant predictor for several of the business model parameters changes. The greater the environmental dynamism, the more likely the software firm's change towards increasing its sales activities ("ActivitiesSales", Est. = −.630, Sig. = .001), towards committing to longer contracts ("RevenueSubs", Est. = −.544, Sig. = .002), towards price discrimination ("RevenuePric", Est. = .396, Sig. = .033) and towards increasing its allocation of employees to sales activities as compared to the total ("StructureSales", Est. = −.394, Sig. = .037). Finally, the company size as measured by its revenues is a significant predictor for change towards increasing the sales activities ("ActivitiesSales", Est. = −.143, Sig. = .004), and in allocation of more employees to both customer-specific and sales activities as compared to the total ("StructureCust", Est. = .142, Sig. = .004; "StructureSales", Est. = .127, Sig. = .012).

7   Discussion

The current study identifies several interesting results on the effects of adopting cloud platforms and of environmental dynamism to changes in software firms' business model parameters. First, as the prior literature suggests [7, 38], adoption of cloud computing technology by a software firm is seemingly associated with change towards unifying both the product/service offering and pricing across different customer. The cloud adopters also appear to increase the sales effort, which is associated with offering commodity software, hence with decreasing competitive advantage. These findings confirm the hypotheses H1b, H1d and H1g, and also implicate connectedness of business model elements. However, this study could not find support for the rest of the hypothesized connections between cloud technologies and business model parameters. We find that: *Adoption of cloud computing technologies by software firms is associated with change toward offering more standardized product, increasing the sales activities and unifying the pricing across different customers.*

Instead, the software firms' changes in reducing customer-specific software-related activities, in preferring longer contracts and in decreasing the employees in customer-specific activities seem to be attributed to the software firm type rather than to the adoption of new technology. This can be interpreted through the lifecycle dynamics [13]: all software product firms are striving for efficiency regardless whether they are adopting cloud technology. In addition, the changes in increasing sales efforts, adding more employees to the sales activities and increasing the length of contract period are also associated with increasing competitive pressures for all software companies. The software product firms' aim for longer contracts could be explained by use of perpetual licenses or the required high initial investment in developing the software product; with longer customer relationships the firms secure their return of investments under potentially heavy competition.

By comparing the software product firms and the software services firms adopting cloud computing technologies, this study finds that the two kinds of firms are significantly different in terms of changing their business models towards offering more standardized product or service, towards extending the duration of customer contracts and towards reducing the customer-specific activities. The results lead to confirming the hypotheses H2b and H2c, but to rejecting the rest. Specifically, we find that: *Software product firms adopting cloud computing technologies are more likely to change their business model toward offering more standardized product and decreasing customer-specific software development and production activities, when compared to software service firms adopting cloud computing technologies.*

The observation regarding customer-specific activities is in line of the features of the enterprise SaaS firms [11, 24] and of importance considering the conceptualization of SaaS and SaaS as a form of IT outsourcing. Based on the results, the authors suggest that software product firms are moving towards SaaS offering with commodity application without customer- specific work and the software services firms are moving towards SaaS offering with standardized but more complex applications with required adjacent services such as tailoring, training and integration; both categories of SaaS firms configure their business models accordingly.

The values indicating the strength of associations between variables reflect the complexity of choices related to adjusting a business model. Thus, it possible that the software firm's managers' cognitive processes play an important role in changing the business model, even greater than the technological opportunities or competitive pressures. The authors also consider a possibility that the software firm had already executed the changes before, thus, there have not been changes in the last 3-year period.

The common sources of potential fallacies in survey research are related to the errors in measurements, sampling, coverage, and non-response [18]. To reduce the risk for measurement error we attained guidance on the survey questions from both researchers and practitioners in the field. One of the concerns with the measurements is the use of single-item measures, which is argued to insufficiently capture the conceptual domain. However, this claim has been challenged by DeVellis [17] by arguing that each item of a scale is precisely as good measure as any other of the scale items and that the items' relationship and errors to the variable are presumed identical. Understanding of this perplexity guided the authors not to make claims about the changes in business model elements (e.g. value proposition), but rather about the parameters (e.g. product/service portfolio).

The software industry survey practically covers and contacts all the Finnish software companies. The authors therefore consider coverage and sampling errors irrelevant. The overall sampling rate for the software industry survey nonetheless is roughly 10%, which suggests a potential risk of non-response bias. However, the effective sample contained software firms of all types, ages and sizes, and the concern is principally if there are theoretically relevant differences respondents and non- respondents. The authors note that the effective sample contained almost equal rate between adopters and non-adopters of cloud platforms and sufficient variety in dependent variables to support the analysis of the hypothesis.

Using Finnish software firms in deriving the empirical results implies a geographical limitation of the empirical study. The Finnish software firms serve mainly the local markets, but due to the limited size of the domestic market many software firms also attempt international operations. Most of software firms serve other businesses and organizations in the public sector. Overall, the market conditions are deemed equal to most other European markets in terms of distribution of software firms into large, small and medium-sized and micro-sized firms, in terms of industry consolidation and the effects of globalization, IT outsourcing and offshoring.

8 Conclusions

As a result of the exploration of the extant literature, the authors found a lack of studies focusing on the business models of the Software-as-a-Service firms that would go beyond investigating isolated aspects of SaaS firms' business. Business model concept is principally used to describe a configuration of several elements of business, emerging as choices as a response to the cognitive interpretation of the opportunities of new technologies and of the threats of competitive environment. The authors noticed a convergence of the key elements of a business model in the recent discussion and used conceptualizations of value proposition, activities, structure and revenue logic to investigate changes of software firms' means of conducting business. In particular, the present study examined the changes in business models induced by adoption of cloud computing technology and external pressures. Besides, it compared the business model changes in software product firms and software services firms.

After analyzing an effective sample of 324 software firms, the authors conclude that the software firms adopting cloud computing technologies have generally increased the uniformity of the core offering and pricing across customers and increased their sales activities, in a holistic manner. These findings are in line with the characteristics of SaaS firms in the contemporary literature. With regards to the second research question, the authors conclude that the increased sales efforts of software firms and preferring longer contract are attributed to the increasing environmental dynamism. If present, these forces affect activities and revenue logic for all software firms. The authors also conclude that for all software product firms, the lifecycle dynamics lead to decreasing their customer-specific activities. Finally, the consideration of differences between software product firms and software services firms reveals that both types of firms are adopting cloud computing technologies and standardizing their core offering to transform into SaaS companies. However, these two types of firms are different as to the software-related adjacent activities. The authors therefore conclude that the different customer needs shall be served by two kinds of SaaS firms, those that embrace cost efficiency approach and those that focus on customer intimacy.

Since this study seems to be among the first to examine the business model changes of SaaS firms, the authors suggest these findings to serve as a starting point for future studies. Besides, some of the acclaimed changes related to SaaS firms' business are yet unclear and this calls for further investigations. Detection of the difference between the SaaS firms originating from software product business and the SaaS firms evolving from software services business clearly has implications for the future studies on SaaS provisioning and adoption by the end-users. That is, the authors assert that for studying SaaS adoption or SaaS as a form of IT outsourcing, the conceptualization of SaaS needs to take into account all the software-related activities by the software firm and offerings to the end-user. The practical implication of the present study is an increased under-standing about how the SaaS vendors are changing their business model and conse-quently how the market of software products and services is evolving. Limiting the survey to Finland may fall short of providing a representative illustration on SaaS business model in a global context. The authors therefore welcome insights from similar studies in other countries.

References

1. Al-Debei, M., Avison, D.: Developing a unified framework of the business model concept. Eur. J. Inf. Syst. **19**(3), 359–376 (2010)
2. Andriole, S.: Seven indisputable technology trends that will define 2015. Commun. Assoc. Inf. Syst. **30**, 61–72 (2012)
3. Armbrust, M., et al.: A view of cloud computing. Commun. ACM **53**(4), 50–58 (2010)
4. Aspara, J., Lamberg, J.A., Laukia, A., Tikkanen, H.: Strategic management of business model transformation: lessons from Nokia. Manag. Decis. **49**(4), 622–647 (2011)
5. Baden-Fuller, C., Morgan, M.: Business models as models. Long Range Plan. **43**(2–3), 156–171 (2010)
6. Benlian, A., Hess, T., Buxmann, P.: Drivers of SaaS-adoption – an empirical study of different application types. Bus. Inf. Syst. Eng. **1**(5), 357–369 (2009)
7. Benlian, A., Koufaris, M., Hess, T.: Service quality in software-as-a-service: developing the SaaS-Qual measure and examining its role in usage continuance. J. Manag. Inf. Syst. **28**(3), 85–126 (2011)
8. Casadesus-Masanell, R., Ricart, J.: From strategy to business models and onto tactics. Long Range Plan. **43**(2–3), 195–215 (2010)
9. Chesbrough, H., Rosenbloom, R.S.: The role of the business model in capturing value from innovation: evidence from Xerox Corporation's technology spin-off companies. Ind. Corp. Change **11**(3), 529–555 (2002)
10. Choudhary, V.: Comparison of software quality under perpetual licensing and software as a service. J. Manag. Inf. Syst. **24**(2), 141–165 (2007)
11. Currie, W.L., Desai, B., Khan, N.: Customer evaluation of application services provisioning in five vertical sectors. J. Inf. Technol. **19**(1), 39–58 (2004)
12. Cusumano, M.: Finding your balance in the products and services debate. Commun. ACM **46**(3), 15–17 (2003)

13. Cusumano, M.: The changing software business: moving from products to services. IEEE Comput. **41**(1), 20–27 (2008)
14. Dsouza, A., Kabbedijk, J., Seo, D., Jansen, S., Brinkkemper, S.: Software-as-a-Service: implications for business and technology in product software companies. In: PACIS 2012 (2012)
15. Davies, A., Brady, T., Hobday, M.: Charting a path towards integrated solutions. MIT Sloan Manag. Rev. **47**(3), 39–48 (2006)
16. Demil, B., Lecocq, X.: Business model evolution. in search of dynamic consistency. Long Range Plan. **43**(2–3), 227–246 (2010)
17. DeVellis, R.: Scale Development: Theory and Applications. Sage Publications, London (2003)
18. Dillman, D., Smyth, J., Christian, L.: Mail and Internet Surveys: The Tailored Design Method, 2nd edn. Wiley, Hoboken (2007)
19. Hedman, J., Kalling, T.: The business model concept: theoretical underpinnings and empirical illustrations. Eur. J. Inf. Syst. **12**(1), 49–59 (2003)
20. Kern, T., Willcocks, L., Lacity, M.: Application service provision: risk assessment and mitigation. MIS Q. Exec. **1**(2), 113–126 (2002)
21. Kindström, D.: Towards a service-based business model – key aspects for future competitive advantage. Eur. Manag. J. **28**(6), 479–490 (2010)
22. Laatikainen, G., Ojala, A., Mazhelis, O.: Cloud services pricing models. In: Herzwurm, G., Margaria, T. (eds.) ICSOB 2013. LNBIP, vol. 150, pp. 117–129. Springer, Heidelberg (2013). https://doi.org/10.1007/978-3-642-39336-5_12
23. Lehmann, S., Buxmann, P.: Pricing strategies of software vendors. Bus. Inf. Syst. Eng. **1**(6), 452–462 (2009)
24. Luoma, E., Rönkkö, M., Tyrväinen, P.: Current Software-as-a-Service business models: evidence from finland. In: Cusumano, M.A., Iyer, B., Venkatraman, N. (eds.) ICSOB 2012. LNBIP, vol. 114, pp. 181–194. Springer, Heidelberg (2012). https://doi.org/10.1007/978-3-642-30746-1_15
25. Magretta, J.: Why business models matter. Harvard Bus. Rev. **80**(5), 86–92 (2002)
26. Marston, S., Li, Z., Bandyopadhyay, S., Zhang, J., Ghalsasi, A.: Cloud computing — the business perspective. Decis. Support Syst. **51**(1), 176–189 (2011)
27. McCullagh, P.: Regression Models for Ordinal Data. J. R. Stat. Soc., Ser. B (Methodol.) **42**(2), 109–142 (1980)
28. Mell, P, Grance, T.: The NIST definition of cloud computing. national institute of standards and technology (2011)
29. Miller, D.: Configurations of strategy and structure: towards a synthesis. Strateg. Manag. J. **7**(3), 233–249 (1986)
30. Miller, D., Friesen, P.: Innovation in conservative and entrepreneurial firms: two models of strategic momentum. Strateg. Manag. J. **3**(1), 1–25 (1982)
31. Osterwalder, A., Pigneur, Y., Tucci, C.: Clarifying business models: origins, present, and future of the concept. Commun. Assoc. Inf. Syst. **16**, 1–25 (2005)
32. Podsakoff, P., MacKenzie, S., Lee, J., Podsakoff, N.: Common method biases in behavioral research: a critical review of the literature and recommended remedies. J. Appl. Psychol. **88**(5), 879–903 (2003)
33. Rajala, R., Rossi, M., Tuunainen, V.: A framework for analysing software business models. In: ECIS 2003, pp. 1614–1627 (2003)
34. Rajala, R., Westerlund, M.: Business models – a new perspective on firms' assets and capabilities: observations from the finnish software industry. Entrep. Innov. **8**(2), 115–125 (2007)

35. Rappa, M.: The utility business model and the future of computing services. IBM Syst. J. **43** (1), 32–42 (2004)
36. Schief, M., Buxmann, P.: Business models in the software industry. In: HICSS 2012, pp. 3328–3337. IEEE (2012)
37. Schwarz, A., Jayatilaka, B., Hirschheim, R., Goles, T.: A conjoint approach to understanding IT application services outsourcing. J. Assoc. Inf. Syst. **10**(10), 748–781 (2009)
38. Stuckenberg, S., Fielt, E., Loser, T.: The impact of software-as-a-service on business models of leading software vendors: experiences from three exploratory case studies. In: PACIS 2011. Queensland University of Technology (2011)
39. Susarla, A., Barua, A., Whinston, A.: A transaction cost perspective of the 'Software as a Service' business model. J. Manag. Inf. Syst. **26**(2), 205–240 (2009)
40. Teece, D.: Business models, business strategy and innovation. Long Range Plan. **43**(2–3), 172–194 (2010)
41. Tyrväinen, P., Selin, J.: How to sell SaaS: a model for main factors of marketing and selling Software-as-a-Service. In: Regnell, B., van de Weerd, I., De Troyer, O. (eds.) ICSOB 2011. LNBIP, vol. 80, pp. 2–16. Springer, Heidelberg (2011). https://doi.org/10.1007/978-3-642-21544-5_2
42. Wirtz, B., Schilke, O., Ullrich, S.: Strategic development of business models: implications of the web 2.0 for creating value on the internet. Long Range Plann. **43**(2–3), 272–290 (2010)

Software Start-ups

Determinants for the Success of Software Startups: Insights from a Regional Cluster

Paulo Afonso$^{(\boxtimes)}$ (iD) and João M. Fernandes (iD)

Dept. Produção e Sistemas and Dept. Informática/Centro ALGORITMI
Universidade do Minho, Braga, Portugal
`psafonso@dps.uminho.pt, jmf@di.uminho.pt`

Abstract. In recent years, we have seen a growing interest in technology-based companies and intensive knowledge. Several regional clusters have appeared supported in dynamic entrepreneurial ecosystems which, alongside intrinsic aspects of the business, are important determinants of the success of new companies. However, most startups created in these innovation-oriented spaces do not survive the first years of life, due to the high competitiveness of the technological market, due to deficiencies in the business model, due to the support conditions provided by the surrounding ecosystem, and finally due to a weak adjustment between all these dimensions. Among several models available, the Early-Life Decision Model (ELDM) presents itself as an interesting framework for studying the development and success conditions of software companies. This article discusses the application of the ELDM based on a series of interviews conducted to 15 Portuguese software startups installed in a technological cluster located in the northeast of Portugal. Based on the results obtained, it was appropriate to add a new dimension to the ELDM model (learning) and complementing it with the perspectives of the business type and internal versus external determinants.

Keywords: Software development · Startups
Early-Life Decision Model · Business model · Technology clusters

1 Introduction

There have been proliferating ecosystems to support technological-based startups and intensive knowledge. However, due to the high competitiveness of the technology market and the current global economic crisis, most of these startups do not survive in their first years of life. Indeed, the failure rate of these companies in their first years of life is relatively high. Most software startups (between 50% to 80%) fail during the first five years of their existence [1,2].

According to Ries [3], these companies are created to build a new product or service under conditions of extreme uncertainty and are based on business models that are in a dynamic development process, being constantly changing to adjust to the market. This author adds that a startup needs to be in a constant

© Springer Nature Switzerland AG 2018
K. Wnuk and S. Brinkkemper (Eds.): ICSOB 2018, LNBIP 336, pp. 127–141, 2018.
https://doi.org/10.1007/978-3-030-04840-2_9

learning process that ensures the sustainability of it. This is assured by the build-measure-learn feedback loop of creating and testing solutions and products, used to measure and learn from customers reactions in order to improve the product and achieve a good fit with the market.

The importance of testing and prototyping is also highlighted by Osterwalder and Pigneur [4], who argue that exploring multiple directions allows to learn more and discover better value propositions. Furthermore, Ries argues that innovation is at the heart of the success of these companies and that this innovation can be achieved in a number of ways, notably, reuse of existing technology on the market, planning a business model that unlocks or creates hidden value and direct the value proposition to customers not yet served by existing solutions.

It is therefore essential to understand the differences between startups that fail and those that have success in the market and what are the reasons for such differences. Sutton indicates that these companies face challenges, such as the fact that they have little or no operational history, have limitations in the resources at their disposal, face multiple influences often contradictory, and are highly affected by the dynamism of technologies and markets [5]. In many cases, a major reason for the failure of startups is the lack of skills of their entrepreneurs.

Entrepreneurial ecosystems play an important role in this process of leveraging technological startups. There is a growing technological, entrepreneurial and innovation cluster in the Northwest of Portugal, particularly in the axis Braga-Porto-Aveiro. Given these circumstances, there is an increase demand for software products and services, which greatly encourages the emergence of new startups. Therefore, several entrepreneurs have been motivated to open their own businesses, and increasingly new software startups have been created. According to some studies[1], in Portugal, startups represent 6.5% of the companies and 18% of the new jobs. In this context, several business cooperation initiatives have been launched, with particular importance for the information and communication technologies sector (ICT). For example, in 2014, the Braga Municipality, in partnership with the local agency for the investment promotion, established a strategic plan for the economic development of the Braga cluster, in order to make it more attractive to investors and entrepreneurs. The Braga cluster began between the years 2000 and 2003 with the launching of several initiatives of business cooperation (called "business circles"). Based on the potential of the region, notably the presence of the University of Minho and the consequent supply of qualified human resources, the IT sector has naturally gained a particular importance.

The study reported in this manuscript aims to understand how startups enter the market and what distinguishes those that survive in the market from the remaining ones, through the evaluation of internal and external determinants of success. Thus, this manuscript contributes for understanding the conditions in which entrepreneurs build their startups, increasing the chances of success in

---

[1] Jornal de Negócios (Portuguese business newspaper), 08.nov.2013. http://www.jornaldenegocios.pt/empresas/detalhe/startups-representam-65-do-tecido-empresarial-em-portugal.

the development of software products and services with market viability. Particularly, this manuscript explores the Early-life Decision Model (ELDM), a model composed of several decision types that can be taken by entrepreneurs to ensure business sustainability.

ELDM is a model for supporting the development of startups [6]. It consists of four dimensions presented in the form of a four-leaf clover, in which each leave represents a dimension. These dimensions become crucial for the newly created companies to sustain themselves in the market and to obtain profits that support and leverage the business.

The research methodology adopted was the semi-structured interview, since it presents the most appropriate characteristics for the purpose of this study. CEOs, CTOs, and founders of startups were interviewed, because they have a complete and solid knowledge of the history of the company. Accordingly, a series of interviews in 15 companies were prepared and conducted. The data obtained with these interviews was complemented with additional general information related to the companies (e.g., number of employees, year of foundation, sales volume) providing a rich set of information for analysis.

The organization of this manuscript is the following. Firstly, an introduction about the ELDM (Sect. 2) is presented. The research approach taken during the study, which is based on semi-structured interviews, is explained in Sect. 3. In Sect. 4, the internal and external determinants found throughout this study are used to analyze the type of decisions made by software startups, particularly, the determinants related to the "shaping the company" dimension suggested in the ELDM. This section also presents the results in a four-quadrant matrix that allows a more complete analysis among different types of companies, internal determinants vs. external ones, and the respective impact. Section 5 discusses the main findings of this study, taking into account the four major dimensions of the ELDM. Finally, Sect. 6 discusses the major conclusions of the manuscript and points out some possible ideas for future work.

2 Early-Life Decision Model

Startups in general and software startups in particular are pushed to take several decisions in their early-life. These decisions and related results can be important determinants for the success of these companies. The different decision types have been discussed through several models and categorizations namely, the business model canvas (BMC), proposed in [4], the managerial growth conceptualization for small software firms by Miettinen et al. [7] or the top five management priorities in the product-software market identified by Hoch et al. [8].

These models are related to several management focus areas such as marketing, partnering, globalization, people management and development. van Cann et al. [6] share this general approach and their four decision categories presented in the Early-Life Decision Model (ELDM) correspond to the main focus areas found by Hoch et al. and also discussed by other authors. Thus, the ELDM can be a good framework of analysis in this context.

The Early-Life Decision Model (ELDM) highlights the relevant decisions that entrepreneurs can address in their startups. These decisions are grouped into four dimensions: (1) shaping the company, (2) developing the product[2], (3) establishing the market, and (4) going international. The ELDM can be applied by entrepreneurs who want to achieve success in their startups, and should take into consideration all types of decision that are distributed by the four dimensions.

To obtain these dimensions, van Cann et al. conducted structured interviews with the founders of 16 dutch software companies [6]. Through these interviews, the authors analyzed the various decisions that were made by the founders, with both positive and negative impact. The dimensions of the ELDM are represented in the form of a four-leaf clover, because some of the participants in the study considered that luck was a key factor in the success of their companies. This four-leaf clover is represented in Fig. 1.

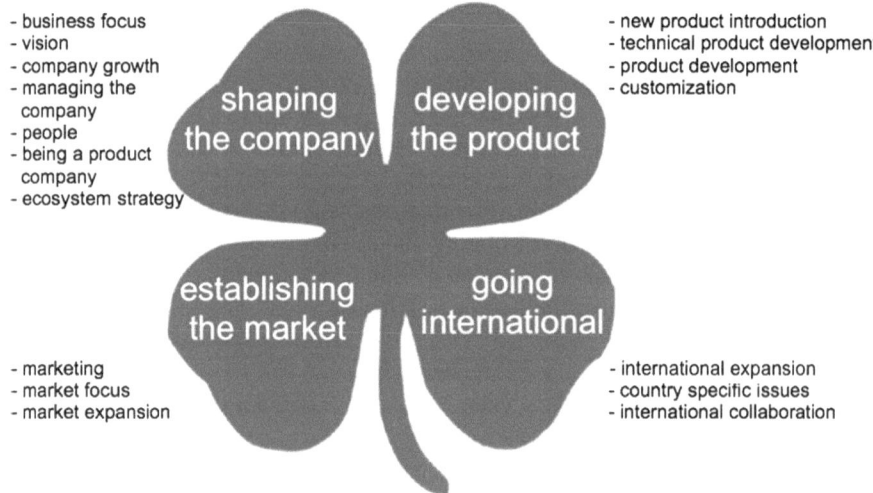

Fig. 1. Early-life Decision Model (ELDM) for software entrepreneurs [6].

In total, the clover covers 17 types of decision indicated by the participants of the study, where each one belongs to a study dimension. The "shaping the company" dimension is the most important to be analyzed, because it is considered as the starting point of startups. The "developing the product" dimension represents decisions that can be made in the course of both early and later phases of the startups life cycle, when for example the product is extended or innovation is tried. The "establishing the market" dimension is also very important for the business, and finally the "going international" dimension, which does not apply to many startups, since it requires more employees, resources and experience in

---

[2] The original designation is 'product development'.

the market. The impact of decisions related to these dimensions is significant in the progress of the companies.

Although this manuscript explores the four ELDM dimensions, more attention is given to the "shaping the company" dimension, since it is the first step of many startups to achieve success. Additionally, it is the most consistent dimension in the decisions presented by the participants in [6]. Therefore, in this first dimension, the decisions concerning the beginning of the life cycle of a start-up are considered. These decisions include (1) the definition of the business focus, (2) the establishment of a vision, (3) the design of the company's growth strategy, (4) the issues related to the management of the company, the people, and the human capital, (5) the decision about selling products, services, or both, and (6) opportunities and constraints related to the ecosystem. Additionally, this is the dimension that contains the largest number of decision types.

It is important to mention here how the principles of the Business Model Canvas suggested by Osterwalder and Pigneur and the logic of the Lean Startup approach proposed by Eric Ries can be related to the ELDM.

Osterwalder and Pigneur [4] propose a template for business modeling, composed of nine building blocks: (1) the value proposition, (2) customer relationships, (3) channels, (4) customer segments, (5) key activities, (6) key resources, (7) key partners, (8) revenue streams, and (9) cost structure.

Furthermore, Eric Ries founded the Lean Startup movement with the aim of supporting the creation and management of startups, notably in fostering a new vision on the way in which these companies develop and launch their products in the market [3]. The Lean Startup approach gives particular attention to the initial phase of a startup. It is mainly concerned with three aspects: (1) the way in which a value proposition is built, based on the market fit principle between the product and the customer/market; (2) the concept of a minimum viable product (MVP); and (3) the need for a continuous adjustment or pivoting of the business model. The goal of any startup is to build, in the shortest possible time, the products and services that customers are willing to pay, suggesting an iterative and recursive approach based on the cycle "Build-Measure-Learn".

3   Research Method

In qualitative research, the researcher seeks to understand the whole phenomenon in question and to capture the context of global research. He has few preconceived ideas and he dedicates a considerable part of the research effort to interpret the events that occurred [9]. The collection of data is done without using formal and structured instruments, and the researcher emphasizes subjectivity to understand and interpret the data, analyzing in a systematic and inductive way the information obtained, which is usually narrated in the first person through semi-structured interviews. Thus, semi-structured interviewing was the method selected for the collection of the data in the different companies involved in this study.

Planning the Interview. In the process of planning and organizing the interviews, the following aspects were taken into consideration:

- definition of the inclusion criteria to select the companies to be involved in this research study;
- preparation of the documents necessary for conducting the interviews;
- definition of a list of companies that could be included in the study;
- identification of candidate interviewees from the list of companies;
- submission of invitations to participate in the study.

Selecting the Companies. Some of the inclusion criteria previously identified were defined on the basis of the ones defined in the design of the ELDM [6] and in the study on innovation and entrepreneurship reported in [10]:

- being a Portuguese company active in the market;
- having headquarters in the region;
- being in the market for about 5 years (i.e., between 3 and 7);
- having at least three employees;
- having obtained profits during its existence;
- being a software company that offer value to customers;
- being interested in participating/collaborating in the study.

Our initial set of companies was comprised of 21 companies, from which 15 were effectively included in the study.

Interview Guide. Subsequently, the documents needed to carry out the interviews were elaborated. Two scripts of the interview were created and a confidentiality document was sent to each participant. The script that guided the interview is composed of the following parts:

1. General information: this part consists of topics needed to generate control variables, related to information about the respondent and the company;
2. Business design and market entry strategy: it is composed of issues and topics related to the definition of the market, the market entry strategy, and the internal and external constraints to the initial strategy;
3. Business growth strategy: concerning key moments in business growth and development, the evolution of the value proposition and changes in the relationship with the market and the business model;
4. Economic and financial aspects: it contains issues and topics on the cost structure and sources of revenues, investment, financing and profitability, and business management practices;
5. Final aspects: to give to the respondent the opportunity to give his/her opinion or suggestions and to give space for questions that may emerge from the interview.

Pilot Interview. A pilot interview was prepared to test the interview guide, in order to correct and improve some aspects. Other objectives in performing this interview were (1) to prepare how to conduct the interview, (2) to gain experience in the collection of data, (3) to realize if the average time previously established for each part of the interview was correctly estimated, and obviously (4) to collect the first set of informations.

Interviewees. For each selected company, a co-founder was identified who held a leadership position in the company, because he/she is usually a person who knows well the business. In this process, several persons who held positions of leadership in the selected companies were identified (preferably CEOs and CTOs), to proceed to invite them to participate in the research study.

Data Analysis. After the interviewing process, the collected data was analyzed and processed. For data identification and categorization, a software application (NVivo) for qualitative data analysis was used. An analysis of the cases was carried out individually and a cross-examination was also conducted. Additional information about the companies was collected and an individual follow-up report was sent to each one for validation purposes.

Companies. The 15 software companies that agreed to cooperate in our study were categorized in three different groups, based on their value propositions (i.e., the type of systems they develop). Software companies develop software systems which refer to the result of executing a project [11]. In this study, each category includes five companies classified as:

1. Own projects (OP): development of a portfolio of own projects, i.e., the company takes the initiative to develop its own software products, web platforms, and/or mobile applications;
2. Bespoke projects/services (BP): development of applications/systems tailored to customers;
3. Own projects and Bespoke projects/services (OP&BP): this group includes companies that simultaneously address the two previous profiles.

The most relevant determinants for each decision type that characterize each dimension of the ELDM were identified and discussed in the three groups of companies.

4 Analysis of Findings

The internal and external determinants found throughout this study were taken into account to analyze the type of decisions made by software startups. These determinants are focused on the "shaping the company" dimension suggested in the ELDM. Additionally, we present the results in a four-quadrant matrix that allows a comparison/analysis among different types of companies, internal determinants vs. external ones, and the respective impact.

4.1 Internal and External Determinants

The analysis of the information from the 15 companies allow us to conclude that the decisions were composed of several fundamental determinants, which can be divided into two groups: internal determinants and external determinants.

These determinants were identified and analyzed. Here, the ones that characterize the category "shaping the company", are presented and discussed.

Business Focus: The internal determinants are related to internal decisions of the company, that is, decisions taken by the co-founders at the beginning of the business, such as the beginning of the activity and the foundation of the company, the business models adopted and the chosen value proposition. On the other hand, external determinants are related to external business factors, such as the fact that the company was born in an academic context, the business areas, and the markets explored.

Vision: The internal determinants are based on decisions taken by business leaders, which directly influenced their internal functioning. The external determinants are related to decisions that influenced the relationship between the companies and the market approached.

Company Growth: Internal determinants are based on decisions taken by the business leaders, who have influenced the internal growth of the companies, such as the robustness of the value proposition, the first acquisitions, and the initial investment. The external determinants are related to the received (financial) support, such as obtaining external investment from several entities.

Managing the Company: The internal determinants are related to the resources of the companies, namely human resources and technological equipment. External determinants are related to the access to supplies, external inputs and general facilities.

People: The internal determinants are based on decisions taken by business leaders at the beginning of the activity, such as the number of co-founders, their expertise, and the first contractors and subcontracts. The external determinants are related to factors prior to the beginning of the business activity and therefore not controllable by the co-founders. These include the institutions of higher education where the responsible person got his/her degree, their academic areas, the professional experience of the co-founders, their age when founding the companies, as well as experience in leadership roles and/or participation in academic groups.

Ecosystem Strategy: These determinants are related to external factors of the companies. After an analysis of the strategic ecosystem of the companies, a set of three external determinants were defined: (1) the entry into the market, (2) the established partnerships, and (3) the external support of various entities.

4.2 ELDM Matrix

Once the analysis of the data collected in each type of decision of the four dimensions comprising the ELDM, a matrix divided into four quadrants was created as illustrated in Fig. 2. It considers a horizontal axis (relative to the three

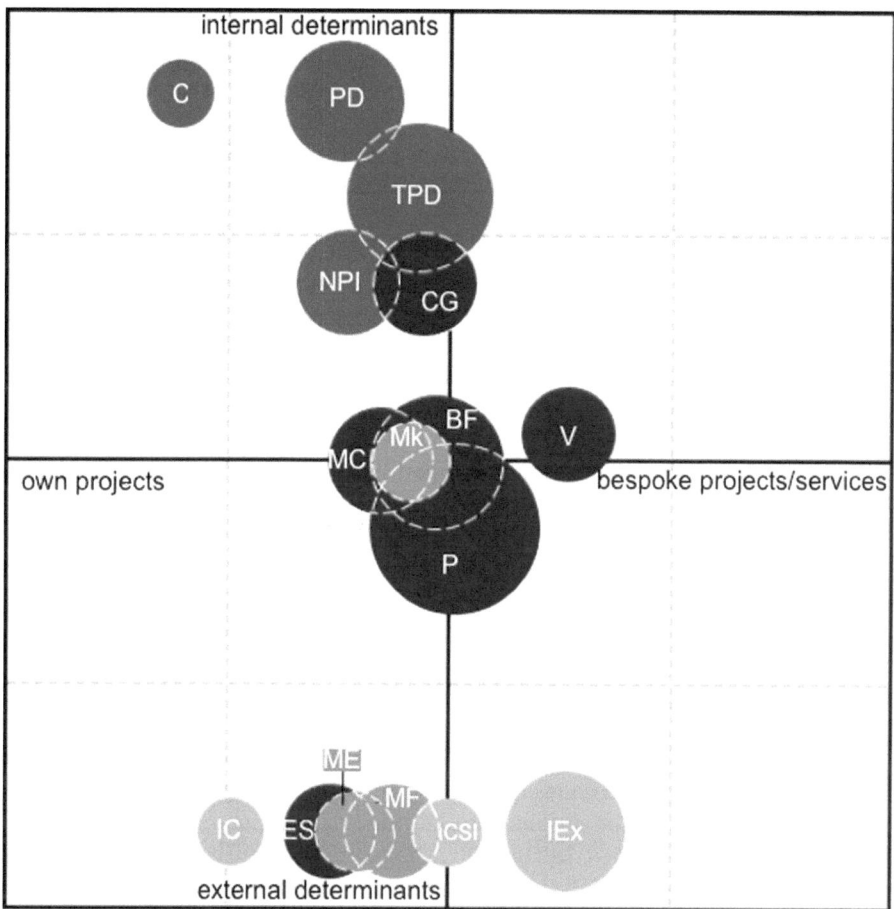

Fig. 2. ELDM matrix and determinants by company category. Dimensions "shaping the company" (BF - business focus, V - vision, CG - company growth, MC - managing the company, P - people, ES - ecosystem strategy); "developing the product" (NPI - new product introduction, TPD - technical product development, PD - product development, C - customization); "establishing the market" (Mk - marketing, MF - market focus, ME - market expansion);"going international" (IEx - international expansion, CSI - country specific issues, IC - international collaboration)

groups of companies) and a vertical one (relative to the type of determinants). As one moves from left to right along the horizontal axis, the group of companies gradually varies from the ones with own projects to those that offer services (with the origin of the axes representing both aspects). On the vertical axis, as one moves from the bottom to the top, the type of determinants begins to be exclusively external and becomes totally internal (with the origin representing an equal contribution of internal and external determinants).

Due to the large number of identified determinants (a total of 60), it was decided to refer to the 16 types of decision actions presented in the ELDM. Indeed, as stated by Cann et al., categorizing the decisions gives a basis for the analysis of the high number and variety of early-life decisions [6]. In order to position each type of decision on the matrix, its tendency in terms of the three groups of companies identified was considered. As an example, one can verify in the matrix that the type of decisions related to 'People' influences companies with both own products and services (even if slightly displaced to the services), and that the type of decisions related to 'Customization' has a greater influence on companies with own projects. The same applies to the vertical axis of the matrix. For example, one can verify that the aspects related to the 'Technical Product Development' presents more internal determinants than external ones, and that 'International Collaboration' is more related to external than internal determinants.

Once the position of each type of decision has been defined in the matrix, the radius of its representative circle was calculated. For this calculation, the number of determinants identified in the 16 types of decisions was taken into account. In this way, the radius dimension depends on the quantity of the identified determinants. As an example, one can notice that 'International Expansion' presents more (in this case, five) determinants than the specific issues of the country (in this case, just one).

Then, four different colors were assigned to the dimension which they belong to. Despite the different shades presented, the color chosen for all determinants was the green, because it is a allusive color to the luck factor, which is important to the success of companies. The tonality was gradually attributed to each dimension according to the number of identified determinants and the influence they had in the case studies. In this way, the tonality with the greatest dark hue was assigned to the dimension that presents the highest number of determinants, and which had the greatest impact on the study cases. On the other hand, the lightest hue is related to the dimension with the smallest number of identified determinants, and which had the less significant impact on the case studies.

5   Discussion

In this section, we discuss the main findings of the study presented in this manuscript, according to the four main dimensions of the ELDM and distinguishing internal from external factors. We also propose an extension of the ELDM, with a new learning dimension. Finally, some validity threats are discussed.

5.1   Shaping the Company

After a first analysis of the elaborated matrix, one verifies that "shaping the company" is the most present dimension in the two business configurations (own projects and service provision) and the most balanced in terms of the number of internal and external determinants (14 internal and 15 external), compared with the remaining three ELDM dimensions. In fact, Ries [3] gives special importance to this dimension as a key source for companies to achieve success.

Among the six types of decision that make up this dimension, the 'People' one presents the biggest number of identified determinant (four internal and five external). It is also the largest of the 16 types and it occupies a central place in the matrix. In both cases, and as in the analysis carried out in the 15 cases that were studied, special attention was given to the innovation factor (present in the 'Vision' decision), considered a central aspect to the success of the companies and achieved through creativity and differentiation.

5.2   Developing the Product

It is possible to verify that "Developing the product" is the dimension with the second largest number of determinants (14 internal and three external). We can conclude that this dimension is especially dependent on decisions taken and internal factors occurring within the company, thus becoming a more controllable dimension for entrepreneurs. Although they were presented in both axes, the identified determinants had a greater influence on the companies with own projects.

Some of the factors mentioned in the study on software development in startups [12] were proven in the analysis of the 15 study cases. Other factors to take into account and which have been found in almost all of the 15 cases of study are related to the execution of a thorough pre-market study and the existence of good software project management.

5.3   Establishing the Market

The "establishing the market" dimension is present in the two considered axes and has less determinants identified than the first two dimensions. Almost all of the identified determinants are external to the business (one internal and six external) and therefore it depends on market factors.

5.4   Going International

Internationalization is the only dimension that does not occur in all companies of this study, since some of them chose to exclusively address the national market to start the business and to expand the value proposition. This also occurs in the study carried out in [6], which mentions that we do not find this dimension in many startups. International collaboration is the determinant that further deviates from the balance of the two axes, having a greater influence on own projects. Additionally, the majority of the identified determinants have a greater impact on the bespoke projects/services.

5.5   The Learning Dimension

During the interviews, in addition to the factors that influenced, positively, the start of the business of the 15 companies involved in this study, others were also mentioned that hindered the entry into the market and influenced the course of the business. It also aroused interest in the opinion of respondents about the factors leading startups to failure.

In fact, startups are companies facing a number of challenges. As already indicated, they usually have little or no operational history, have no experience in management, are limited in the resources at their disposal, face multiple influences, and are highly affected by the dynamism of technologies and markets [5,12]. According to a study conducted on the development of software in startups [12], it was also found that self-destruction is another factor that leads many startups to failure at the beginning of the activity [13], and that the aggressiveness of the market and the strong competition leads them to operate in chaotic environments [14,15].

According to Ries [3], it is critical for the startups to acquire knowledge resulting from the experience obtained throughout the software development process, even in the first months of the companies. This confirms the idea that it is necessary to have a constant learning of the whole process when a company is started, a factor considered by Ries as essential to foster its sustainability. In fact, this factor proves essential to better orient the business, in order to make known to all stakeholders which are the most/less important aspects that lead the businesses to success.

Therefore, based on the results collected among the 15 companies that are part of this study, an adapted version of the ELDM is proposed. This extended ELDM version takes into account the learning factor, as verified in many of the companies of this study and considered to be a fundamental issue to the business of startups [3] (Fig. 3).

Although this version retains the format of the initial version of the model, i.e., a four-leaf clover, a flower was added (notably the clover flower) with the indication of the acquired learning that results from the difficulties felt, the mistakes made, the realization of pivots, and the experience acquired throughout the process of developing a company. In this way, a more dynamic dimension is given to the model proposed in [6], by also considering the Lean Startup approach [3].

5.6   Validity Threats

A series of issues may influence the results of this exploratory study, such as the bias that could be introduced by the researchers who performed the study or the observed data set. In the following, we consider the threats to validity, in a way to discuss the acceptance and accuracy of the findings presented here.

We should not claim that the results are representative of all software startups, or can be generalizable to other economic fields. Though, they provide insights from a set of 15 software startups, located in Portugal. However, even

difficulties felt
mistakes made
conducting pivots
experience acquired

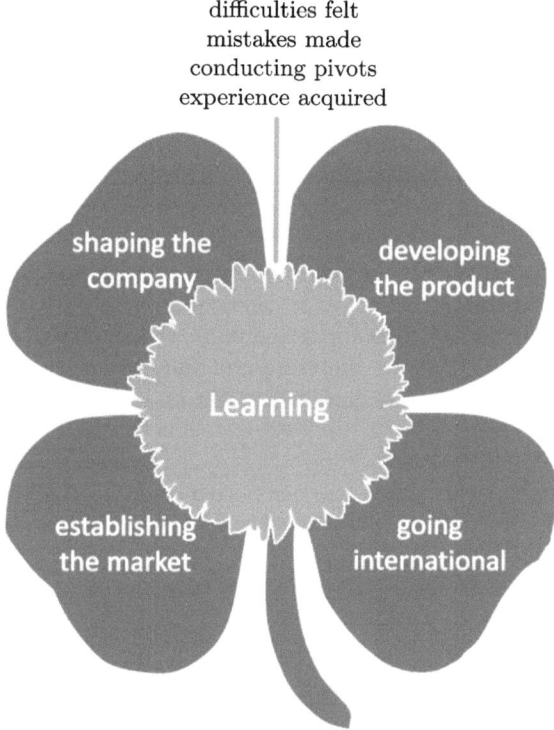

Fig. 3. Extended version of the ELDM with the learning dimension.

if the total number of companies is relatively low, they equally cover the three considered types of companies.

During the field study, two researchers were responsible for interviewing the participants, collecting and organizing the data, and processing the results. The two authors conducted the analysis of the gathered data, so there is a risk related to the interpretation of the findings. Nevertheless, we tried to mitigate this validation threat by the use of a software application for the analysis of qualitative data, with follow-up reports that were sent to the interviewees and by discussing the preliminary results at length with all the researchers, supporting the triangulation of the data.

6   Conclusions

Several conclusions were obtained, such as the impact of each determinant on the groups of companies identified, as well as the type of internal and external determinants identified in the various aspects of the business. It was also possible to verify that the existence of determinants, which make it difficult for companies to enter the market, influence the course of the business, and that the learning acquired through them and the experience lived during the activity of the company, is essential for business sustainability.

Once analyzed the 15 case studies in this research and reviewed the literature, it can be stated that the experience obtained and the learning acquired throughout the process of opening and growing a company, influences the decisions taken by all the actors in the process. These decisions are important to analyze and define which market entry strategies to adopt, taking into account internal and external determinants and the type of company.

In a broader perspective, the various determinants are important in both axes, with a slight tendency towards the companies with own projects. In this way, those who want to open a company to develop their own projects should have more attention to the (internal and external) determinants that can affect the business, such as decisions taken and other factors considered as fundamental.

Acknowledgements. This work was supported by COMPETE: POCI-01-0145-FEDER-007043 and FCT (Fundação para a Ciência e a Tecnologia) within the Project Scope: UID/CEC/00319/2013.

References

1. Busenitz, L.W.: Entrepreneurial risk and strategic decision making: it's a matter of perspective. J. Appl. Behav. Sci. **35**(3), 325–340 (1999). https://doi.org/10.1177/0021886399353005
2. Nowak, M.J., Grantham, C.E.: The virtual incubator: managing human capital in the software industry. Res. Policy **29**(2), 125–134 (2000). https://doi.org/10.1016/S0048-7333(99)00054-2
3. Ries, E.: The Lean Startup: How Today's Entrepreneurs Use Continuous Innovation to Create Radically Successful Businesses. Crown Publishing Group, New York (2011)
4. Osterwalder, A., Pigneur, Y.: Business Model Generation: A Handbook for Visionaries, Game Changers, and Challengers. Wiley, Hoboken (2010)
5. Sutton, S.M.: The role of process in a software start-up. IEEE Softw. **17**(4), 33–39 (2000). https://doi.org/10.1109/52.854066
6. van Cann, R., Jansen, S., Brinkkemper, S.: Software business start-up memories: Key decisions in success stories. Palgrave Macmillan (2013)
7. Miettinen, O., Mazhelis, O., Luoma, E.: Managerial growth challenges in small software firms: a multiple-case study of growth-oriented enterprises. In: Tyrväinen, P., Jansen, S., Cusumano, M.A. (eds.) ICSOB 2010. LNBIP, vol. 51, pp. 26–37. Springer, Heidelberg (2010). https://doi.org/10.1007/978-3-642-13633-7_3
8. Hoch, D.J., Lindner, S.K., Roeding, C.R., Purkert, G.: Secrets of Software Success: Management Insights from 100 Software Firms Around the World. Harvard Business School Press, Massachusetts (2000)
9. Saunders, M., Lewis, P., Thornhill, A.: Research Methods for Business Students. Prentice Hall, New York (2009)
10. Instituto Empresarial do Minho: Innovation and entrepreneurship: 15 national success case studies. Technical report, IEMinho (2011) (in Portuguese)

11. Fernandes, J.M., Machado, R.J.: Requirements in Engineering Projects. LNMIE. Springer, Cham (2016). https://doi.org/10.1007/978-3-319-18597-2
12. Paternoster, N., Giardino, C., Unterkalmsteiner, M., Gorschek, T., Abrahamsson, P.: Software development in startup companies: a systematic mapping study. Inf. Softw. Technol. **56**(10), 1200–1218 (2014). https://doi.org/10.1016/j.infsof.2014.04.014
13. Crowne, M., Why, : software product startups fail and what to do about it: Evolution of software product development in startup companies. In: IEEE International Engineering Management Conference (IEMC), vol. 1, pp. 338–343 (2002). https://doi.org/10.1109/IEMC.2002.1038454
14. Eisenhardt, K.M., Brown, S.L.: Time pacing: competing in markets that won't stand still. Harv. Bus. Rev. **76**(2), 59–69 (1998). https://hbr.org/1998/03/time-pacing-competing-in-markets-that-wont-stand-still
15. MacCormack, A.: Product-development practices that work: How internet companies build software. MIT Sloan Manage. Rev. **42**(2), 75–84 (2001)

Opportunity Exploitation in Software Startups.
A Human Capital View

Pertti Seppänen[✉], Kari Liukkunen, and Markku Oivo

M3S/M Group, University of Oulu, FI 90015 Oulu, Finland
{pertti.seppanen,kari.liukkunen,markku.oivo}@oulu.fi

Abstract. *Background* – Transforming a business opportunity to a valid business case is a crucial process of an early-stage software startups. Prior literature on entrepreneurship defines two types of opportunity exploitations, opportunity discovery and opportunity creation, and proposes models describing the exploitation processes. The factors affecting startups' abilities to conduct the exploitation are, however, addressed only to a limited extend in prior research. *Aim* – This research aims at increasing the knowledge on those factors by studying empirically the effects of the available human capital on the opportunity exploitation processes in software startups. *Method* – We conducted a multiple-case study on a group of software startups in Italy, Norway and Finland. We focused on the founders of the startups, examining their opportunity processes, their human capital, and the interdependencies between the opportunity processes and human capital. *Results* – Our results are in line with the findings of prior research, which point out that *uncertainty* is the key differentiator between the opportunity discovery and creation processes. The results reveal, however, that both process types *co-exist* in the early stages of software startups, independently of how the opportunity was initially recognized, and also highlight *missing human capital* as a key reason for the uncertainty. We conclude that in software startups the availability of human capital plays a bigger role in the exploitation of opportunities than their types, discovered or created, because even exploitation of a-priori existing opportunities turn to opportunity creation processes in case of human capital shortages.

Keywords: Software startup · Opportunity discovery theory
Opportunity creation theory · Product development process
Human capital theory

1 Introduction

Founding a software startup is a realization of a business opportunity. Identifying an opportunity, innovating a product or service fitting to the opportunity, and being able to turn the innovation to a business case are crucial tasks of an early-stage software startup. The phenomena of opportunity exploitation have been studied from the perspectives of business case creation by several authors. Alvarez et al. [1, 2] presented the opportunity discovery and creation theories, and Sarasvathy [3] the effectuation theory. Ries [4], Bosch [5], and Ojala [6] propose startup models describing the processes of a successful business case creation.

© Springer Nature Switzerland AG 2018
K. Wnuk and S. Brinkkemper (Eds.): ICSOB 2018, LNBIP 336, pp. 142–156, 2018.
https://doi.org/10.1007/978-3-030-04840-2_10

The opportunity discovery theory focuses on opportunities that exist independently of direct human involvement, waiting to be discovered by alert individuals or teams [1, 2]. The opportunity creation theory, in turn, suggests that new opportunities are created by individuals or teams working actively to initiate new businesses [1, 2], instead of just looking for existing opportunities. The effectuation theory focuses on phenomena caused by the unavoidable uncertainty of building up a new enterprise [3].

The opportunity discovery and creation theories [1–3] and the startup models [4–6] address the exploitation of opportunities by focusing on the innovations and the processes to create business cases, paying less attention to the new enterprise's abilities to conduct the exploitation processes. That leaves a gap in knowledge, what are the factors affecting these abilities. In this research, we studied the opportunity exploitation in software startups from the viewpoint of the human capital [7]. We opted for human capital (HC) because it was identified as a key contributor of startups' business performance in the prior literature on entrepreneurship [7–9].

For this study, we used the term opportunity exploitation to address the evolution of both discovered and created opportunities. We divided the human capital into three broad dimensions, human capital in business, human capital in software, and human capital in application technology. We defined the application technology as all other technology areas but software, used to implement the product.

The research was conducted on eleven startups in four European locations. It aimed at identifying the characteristics of the startups' opportunity exploitation processes, defining the founders' human capital, and exploring how the human capital affects the exploitation processes.

For our study, we asked the following research questions:

RQ1: What are the characteristics of the software startups' opportunity exploitation processes?
RQ2: What are the effects of the founders' human capital on the opportunity exploitation processes?

Our results indicate that, independently of the circumstances how the opportunity originally appeared, the opportunity exploitation in software startups is a process where (1) the characteristics of both opportunity creation and discovery *co-exist*, (2) the founders take actions typical for one or another theory on a *context-dependent* and *situational* basis, (3) a determining factor of the process type is the *uncertainty*, and (4) the *human capital* is both an origin of, and a means to manage, the uncertainty.

The rest of this paper is structured as follows. Section 2 focuses on the background of and the motivation for the study, reviewing prior research on the opportunity discovery and creation theories and the HC theory. Section 3 presents the research design, including the case selection and research data analysis. Section 4 deals with the results, and Sect. 5 discusses the study's findings and relevance. Section 6 concludes the paper and offers suggestions for future research.

2   Background

In this section, we review prior research on the opportunity exploitation and the human capital in order to gather the theoretical basis for our empirical study. This study is based on theories of opportunity creation and opportunity discovery, as defined by Alvarez and Barney in [1], Alvarez et al. in [2], and by Sarasvathy in [3, 10], and on the human capital theory as defined by Becker in [7].

2.1   Prior Research on Opportunity Discovery and Opportunity Creation

The opportunity discovery theory [1, 2] assumes that business opportunities exist as objective phenomena, just waiting for getting discovered. The theory proposes that such opportunities are generated autonomously by changes in competitive imperfections that in turn are based on changes in the business environment. Discovering new business opportunities created by such changes is then depending on an individual's abilities to discover them, on the individual's 'alertness' to the opportunities.

The prior existence of opportunities enables the alert individuals or teams to figure out a product or service addressing the discovered opportunity [1, 2]. The predictability of the exploitation outcome is the key attribute of the discovery theory, out of which its other characteristics derive.

The opportunity creation theory, in turn, proposes that opportunities can be created by actions of individuals or teams [1, 2]. The creation theory proposes that the opportunity creation process itself is the driving force that changes the business environment. It creates totally new customer demands or markets, and creates a slot in the business environment for the new product or service [1, 2]. The non-existence of a prior competitive imperfection means that the outcome of the opportunity creation process cannot be defined in advance. Like the predictability of the exploitation outcome is the key of the discovery theory, the uncertainty of the outcome is the key of the opportunity creation theory.

The key differences of the theories are presented in Table 1.

Sarasvathy studied creation of new firms in [3], and defined an approach of human reasoning to address the uncertainty of the creation process, effectuation, as an opposite of a more traditional causation. She defines effectuation as on actor-dependent process, where the goal is to tackle contingences instead of reaching a pre-defined or known target [3, 10], typical for opportunity creation. Causation, in turn, is a reasoning process driven by a pre-defined target, typical for discovered opportunities. The means to reach the target and their selection criteria are defined to fit the target [3, 10]. The key differences of causation and effectuation are presented in Table 2.

An existing opportunity provides an entrepreneur with a possibility to run the process with causation-type reasoning. Creating an opportunity, in turn, is a process where an entrepreneur's effectuation-type actions bring the exploitation from her early aspirations towards more tangible goals.

Table 1. General assumptions of opportunity discovery and creation theories [1]

	Opportunity discovery	Opportunity creation
Nature of opportunities	Opportunities exist independently of entrepreneurs	Opportunities don't exist independently of entrepreneurs
Nature of entrepreneurs	Differs from non-entrepreneurs in advance by being more 'alert' for the opportunities	Do not necessarily differ from non-entrepreneurs in advance
Nature of decision making context	Risky	Uncertain
Decision making	Decisions based on risk evaluations	Iterative, inductive, and incremental decision making
Human resource practices	Recruitment of task-specific human capital	Recruitment of general and flexible human capital

Table 2. Selected differences of causation and effectuation [3]

	Causation	Effectuation
Target	Target is known	Aspirations of possible targets, means for striving for the target
Decision making criteria	Criteria helping to choose between means to achieve the target	Criteria helping to choose between alternatives provided by the available means
Competencies employed	Focusing on utilizing knowledge	Focusing on exploiting possibilities
Nature of unknowns	Predictable aspects of an uncertain future	Controllable aspects of an unpredictable future
Outcomes	Competitive products for existing markets	New products for new markets

Ojala reports in [6, 11] a longitudinal study on the business model creation of a Finnish ICT company. The study verifies empirically the opportunity exploitation theories [1–3, 10], stating that an opportunity creation is an iterative process, where the entrepreneur verifies the values of her actions by responses from the markets and adjusts the next steps accordingly. One of the key findings of Ojala [6, 11] is that an opportunity created once isn't necessarily stable, but needs further modifications driven by changes in technology, customer preferences, and markets. Based on the findings, Ojala presents an iterative model for business model creation and development [6].

The lean startup model [12] and the early-stage software startup development model [5] propose iterative processes to validate the business feasibility of an product idea. The validation is implemented in a build-measure-learn (BML) loop, the purpose of which is to identify a product with a problem-solution fit and a product-market fit.

2.2   Prior Research on Human Capital Theory

The HC theory [7] describes the effects of human capabilities and talents on the performance and success of human activities at many levels, ranging from individuals to nations, and finally to the mankind. Applied on entrepreneurship, the research on the HC theory studies individuals' and teams' contribution to a firm's business performance from the viewpoint of capabilities, knowledge, and talents [13].

Bosma et al. studied Dutch startups and found that investing on the entrepreneur's human and social capital had a significant effect on the startups' business performance [8]. Unger et al. [14], in turn, discovered that a priori existing capabilities and skills contributed more to the success of new enterprises than education or learning. Contrary findings were made by Martin et al. [15] indicating that entrepreneurship-specific education was a valid source of entrepreneurship-specific HC.

Shrader and Siegel found that an enterprise's long-term performance was strongly affected by the fit between the enterprise's strategy and the team's experience, especially the team's technical experience [16]. Hatch et al. [17] found that gaining a team's experience from external sources reduced learning.

The relationship between an entrepreneur's HC and the radicalness of the innovation was studied by Marvel and Lumpkin [18]. The study divided the experience in two dimensions, the experience depth and the experience breadth, and concluded that the experience depth affected positively to the innovation radicalness while the experience breadth did not. Partly opposite result was concluded by Lazear indicating that entrepreneurs were generalists with several skills, but not necessarily experts in any specific area [19].

The results of the prior research manifest the importance of the entrepreneur's proper human capital for the success of a new enterprise. However, at a more detailed level they are mixed, giving reasoning for the objective of our study.

3   Research Methods and Design

To answer the research questions, we studied a group of software startups following the guidelines set up by Runeson and Höst for case study research in software engineering [20]. Runeson and Höst propose a five-step process: (1) designing the study, (2) preparing the data collection, (3) collecting the data, (4) analyzing the collected data, and (5) reporting. We opted to use interviews of key persons as the data collection method [20, 21] and a combination of thematic and narrative synthesis as the data analysis method [22], as presented in detail in the following sub-sections.

3.1   Designing the Study

The target group of our study were founders and other key persons of software startups. We interviewed eleven persons from twelve software startups, including one startup in Italy, two startups in Norway, and nine in Finland. Eleven case startups created own software-intensive products, while one offered software services. We contacted software startups in a snowballing process using local startup incubators as the starting point (Table 3).

Table 3. Descriptions of the case founders.

	Location	Product type	Founder(s)	Experience of founder(s)
A	Finland	Embedded product	Team	Professionals
B	Italy	SW product	Team	Professionals and students
C	Norway	SW product	Team	Just graduated
D	Norway	SW product	Individual	Just graduated
E	Finland	Embedded product	Team	Professionals, internal startup
F(a, b)	Finland	Embedded products	(a) Individual (b) Team	(a) and (b) Professionals
G	Finland	SW product	Individual	Professionals
H	Finland	SW product	Individual	Just graduated
I	Finland	SW product	Team	Professionals
J	Finland	Embedded product	Team	Professionals
K	Finland	SW service	Team	Professionals

The founder F founded first a startup alone and then another as a team member. Both startups targeted to products for the health and fitness business segment, and we handel them in a single case. Out of eleven product-developing startups five had established businesses, two were discontinued, and four had functional prototypes under testing. The service provider had a ready service concept to offer.

3.2 Collecting and Analyzing the Research Data

The research data were gathered by utilizing semi-structured interviews and applying the key informant technique as defined in [21]. Most interviewees were founders or co-founders. One interviewee was a chief executive officer (CEO), who was hired to run the administration, but had a founder-level understanding of his company. The interviews were conducted face-to-face, recorded, and transcribed, following the thematic interview guides [23]. All interviews were held in English, they lasted 60–90 min, and altogether 106 pages of transcribed data were gathered.

For the research data analysis we opted to use a combination of thematic synthesis and narrative synthesis, as presented in [22]. We started the analysis with a thematic synthesis utilizing the deductive approach, as presented in [24]. The initial codes of the deductive synthesis were derived from the research questions and from the utilized theories. The thematic synthesis was conducted by using NVivo11 tool. The list of the identified themes is shown in Table 4a.

Coding revealed that the theme human capital consisted of several different areas, as proposed by [19]. Based on the initial findings we divided the human capital further to three more detailed themes, as shown in Table 4b.

The next step was a narrative synthesis of the research data, as presented in [22]. In the narrative synthesis, we broadened the view defined by the thematic synthesis by two additional viewpoints, (1) the idea background, and (2) the refinements to the idea and the opportunity. In order to outline the strength of the human capital we defined a three level scale, as shown in Table 5.

Table 4a. Themes identified in the thematic synthesis.

Theme	Description
Founders	Individual founder or a team
Product	Product or service innovation
Opportunity	Business opportunity
Opportunity discovery	Discovery approach utilized
Opportunity creation	Creation approach utilized
Uncertainty	Type of experienced uncertainty and possible ways to manage it
Opportunity realization	Actions taken in the exploitation process of the opportunity, their results, covering both the initial idea and its potential modifications
Human capital	Founders' human capital
Iteration count	Complexity of the iterative opportunity exploitation process, including pivoting [12]
Learnings	Customer feedback and other lessons learned in exploitation

Table 4b. Themes of human capital.

Human capital	Knowledge and understanding on…
HC on business	The potential business, the customers, and the opportunity's value to the customers
HC on software development	Software development needed when realizing the opportunity
HC on application technology	Application-specific technology other than software

Table 5. Human capital scale for narrative synthesis.

HC	Description
Good	The founder has earlier experience, good skills and knowledge on the specific human capital area, is an expert
Medium	The founder has some experience, reasonable skills and knowledge on the specific human capital area, but isn't an expert
Limited	The founder has no or little experience, missing skills and knowledge on the specific human capital area

4   Results

In this section, we discuss the results of our study. The findings of the narrative syntheses are shown Tables 6a and 6b, and summarized in the following.

Table 6a. Summary of the findings of startups A, B, C, D, E, F

Case	A	B	C	D	E
Founders	Team of three professionals, careers in software industry	Professor, team of students	Two just graduated	Just graduated	Team of internal startup of a mid-sized company
Product	Underwater ultrasound device	Service for photo sharing and selling	Service for selling tickets to events	Intelligent emergency call service	IOT device platform
Idea background	Discovered similar product	Ideas were sought in an academic course on startups	Founders were looking for something to start with	Own accident, entrepreneurship training	Host company set up an internal startup incubator
Opportunity	Simpler, cheaper, and technically better product	Service for s specific customer segment	Simpler and cheaper product, new customer segment	Local variant of a known service with new functionality	Entering growing markets with an IOT platform for multitude of vertical use cases
Discovery	The competitor product	Yet another sales channel for photos	Product discovered through own experiences	Entrepreneurship training, family member's proposal	Idea from a national idea bank by the internal incubator
Creation	How to reach a simpler, cheaper, and better product				
Uncertainty	Targeted customers, technology	Finding customers	Opportunities, personnel, funding	Personnel, funding	None
Realization	Product with different technologies from competitor	Internet service for photo selling, initial base of 32.332 photos from 54 photographers	Internet service for ticket selling	An emergency call with positioning support and personal health information	IOT device platform with versatile functionality
HC business	Medium: founder was a serial entrepreneur	Limited	Limited: just graduated	Limited: just graduated	No data available
HC SW	Good: strong SW experience	Good: strong SW experience	Limited: just graduated	Limited: just graduated	Good: strong SW experience
HC app	Medium experience on ultrasound devices	Not applicable	Not applicable	Not applicable	Good: strong application experience
Learnings	Feedback from early customers	Difficulties in starting business	Difficulties in developing software	Difficulties in developing software	Normal product development
Iterations	Two customer segment and several technical solution iterations	Iterations in customer case creation	One iteration in business ideas, several iterations in team setup and SW development	Several iterations in team setup and SW development	Normal product development
Refinements	Refinements in technical solutions to realize the opportunity	More efforts on service marketing, technical improvements	Changes in team personnel and responsibilities, acquiring more HC	Changes in team personnel and responsibilities, acquiring more HC	Increasing number of vertical use cases

Table 6b. Summary of the findings of startups G, H, I, J and K

Case	Fa, Fb	G	H	I	J	K
Founders	Founder in a startup (a) and a co-founder in another (b)	Founder with long professional career in software industry	Just graduated	Two founders with long managerial careers in software industry	Team with long professional careers in software industry	Team with long professional careers in software industry
Product	Two products for physical exercise	Graphical user interface platform for smart devices	Service for improving aircraft maintenance processes	Internet service for nurseries and families	Wireless anti-noise earplugs	On-site IT support services for industrial customers
Idea background	Several years' maturing periods for both ideas, slow activation	Several years' maturing period	Founder's work in the maintenance of a big airline	Need for new job after lay-offs	Own experiences, lay-offs	Need for new job after lay-offs
Opportunity	New innovations for on-line measurement of human body	Superior UI platform through deployment of latest technology	Ideas how to improve the data management of aircraft maintenance processes	New way for communications replacing manual message sending	Wireless anti-noise earplugs	Highly qualified, professional IT support
Discovery	Slow forethought of both ideas	Own experiences with similar functionality	Own experiences with the aircraft maintenance work	Family member's proposal	Own experiences	Own experiences
Creation	How to create functional solutions	How to create functional solutions			How to create wireless solutions	
Uncertainty	Technology	Technology	None	SW competencies	Technology	None
Realization	Two instruments for human body measurements, a and b, (case a abandoned)	Scalable graphical user interface platform, optimization to small smart devices	Services for improving aircraft maintenance processes	Internet service for communications and photo sharing	Wireless anti-noise earplugs developed	On-site IT support services based on a commercial platform, specific full-time support concept
HC business	Limited	Good: experience in the business of graphical user interfaces	Good: personal experience	Medium: some experience in internet services	Medium: experience on audio functionality of smart devices	Good: strong experience in IT services
HC SW	Good: strong SW experience	Good: strong SW experience	Good: strong SW experience	Limited	No data available	Good: strong experience in SW
HC app	Limited	Not applicable	Not applicable	Not applicable	Medium: strong and weak areas	Not applicable
Learnings	Difficulties in application-specific technology	Several implementation approaches trialed, but not offering good enough functionality or quality	Normal product development	Need for hiring persons with software development competencies	How to handle size and functionality requirements	Learnings from customers
Iterations	Two product ideas to the same customer segment, two startups	Two implementation approaches failed, own development finally selected	Minimum-viable product, otherwise normal product development	Normal product development	Normal product development	Normal product development
Refinements	Abandonment of first idea due to technical problems, new idea with known technology	Different implementation approaches, focus on software quality	Normal product development	Normal product development	Normal product development	Creation of customer segments and support concepts

Most of the founders were experienced professionals. In three cases the founder was a just-graduated person, though founder H had strong software knowledge and work experience in the customer organization. Even experienced founders had areas of limited or missing human capital. HC on software was the strongest area in our study group. Only three founding teams were good in all relevant HC dimensions.

Out of eleven cases we identified three partial opportunity creation and one full creation cases. All partial opportunity creation cases had also characteristics of opportunity discovery. The idea of case F was a totally new innovation. Failing in developing new technology was the main cause of the abandonment of the idea. Both iterative and linear opportunity exploitation processes were identified. The linear ones were tied to founders with good human capital, or to a fairly straightforward product.

All but two cases faced uncertainty during the opportunity exploitation process. We were able to identify three types of uncertainty sources, all typical for startups: (1) problems with technology, (2) problems with customer and markets, and (3) problems with funding. In four cases the application-specific technology was the biggest source of the uncertainty. Not being able to identify and hire competent personnel for software development was the main cause of uncertainty in three cases. Creating the customer base was uncertain in two cases. The main means to cope with the technology-related uncertainty were iteration and networking. Funding uncertainty was tackled by deploying a variety of funding sources.

5 Discussion

In this section, we first present the answers to the research questions and discuss our findings in the context of the opportunity exploitation theories [1–3, 6, 10] and human capital theory [8, 14, 16–19], [8, 14, 16–19]. Then follows the discussion on the validity of our findings, and their relevance to the academia and to practitioners.

5.1 Answering the Research Questions

RQ1: What are the characteristics of the software startups' opportunity exploitation processes?

In several cases of our study we could identify characteristics of both opportunity creation and discovery processes [1, 2], as well as characteristics of effectuation and causation [3, 10]. Out of eleven cases we categorized four as creation processes. In all four cases the opportunity was to create business by new, ambitious technical solutions that were not existing without the founders' actions. From the business perspective cases A, G and J were, however, fairly clear opportunity discovery cases, because the products were targeted to existing markets with existing products. The innovation of case F(a) was such a new one that even the business case was uncertain.

Out of the seven opportunity discovery cases, five showed clear characteristics of discovery. In those cases the opportunity was existing independently of the founders: similar products were existing and the opportunity was tied to development of a new product for different customer segments or simply to development of competitor to well-known but growing markets. Cases B and H were different. In case B the product was not a new one, neither its development turned out to be technically challenging. However, the exploitation process turned to a creation-type one on the business side. In case H the product was a unique one targeted for a unique customer. There were no similar products nor competitive imperfections, but the exploitation process created a new slot in the business environment [1]. However, it was a most typical opportunity discovery process with an alert individual, a predictable outcome, and the uncertainty tackled already before founding the enterprise by a successful minimum-viable-product [12].

RQ2: What are the effects of the founders' human capital on the opportunity exploitation processes?

The human capital of the founders of our case startups varied from very strong to weak. HC on software was the most common good HC dimension. HC on business and on application-specific technology could be limited also in cases of founders with a good HC in software.

In our cases existing or missing HC was not identified as a direct determining factor between the initial opportunity creation and discovery. Out of the four opportunity creation cases, only one founder had a strong expertise in all relevant HC dimensions. Similarly, in cases with opportunity discovery, the founders' HC compositions varied from limited to good in all three HC dimensions.

The founders' HC profiles had a strong correlation with the uncertainty and the iterative nature of the opportunity exploitation process. Missing HC in a certain HC dimension tended to predict iterative processes, and good HC linear processes, though there were variations to both directions.

Compensation for the missing HC was common in our research group. The research data reveal that the typical compensation means varied between the HC dimensions: (1) in case of business HC a common compensation was based on networking, (2) in case of software HC on hiring qualified work force, and (3) in case of application HC on networking and learning by iterating.

5.2 Opportunity Exploitation in Software Startups

Our categorization of cases to creation and discovery, presented in Sect. 5.1, is a simplifying overview based on the direction a particular case tends to incline. More significantly, our results indicate that in a practical situation the opportunity creation and discovery characteristics *co-exist* in the very same opportunity exploitation process – not only offer two explanation models of it. The founders' actions according to a specific theory and utilizing a specific reasoning model seems to be a *context-dependent* and *situational* choice varying over the topics of the opportunity exploitation process.

The uncertainty, mentioned as a differentiator between opportunity creation and discovery in [1], was identified in both creation and discovery cases. What are then the factors causing the uncertainty, and leading to a parallel deployment of creation and discovery processes?

We seek the answer by taking a look on the iteration, learnings and refinements rows of Tables 6a and 6b. The cases with a linear development process and learnings and refinements along to a normal product development carried characteristics of opportunity discovery processes. Excluding case I, the cases were characterized by founders being relatively good in relevant HC dimensions, business, software, and application. In case I the founders could compensate for their HC shortages through networking and recruitment, leading to a linear opportunity exploitation process.

Excluding case G, the iterative cases were characterized by shortages in one or several human capital areas. In case G the founder had strong experience in all relevant HC dimensions. He needed, however, three iteration rounds to figure out the technology solutions that fulfilled the functionality and quality targets he defined for the product.

The research data coded as learnings reveal that in the cases with a linear development process the learnings were such experiences from own actions and customers that are typical in a managed product development. In the iterative cases, in turn, the learnings were related to the founders' shortages in one or several HC dimensions.

Our findings gave a mixed picture of the nature of the entrepreneurs compared to the non-entrepreneurs. The opportunity discovery theory assumes that the entrepreneurs are more alert to the existing opportunities than non-entrepreneurs, while the creation theory points out the entrepreneurs' focus on contingencies [1]. The research data reveal that all founders but two were actively looking for new opportunities, but the level of alertness, sources of the ideas, and focus on contingencies varied.

By combining two crucial elements of a software startup's early stages, the business opportunity and the founders' capabilities to exploit it, our study deepen the knowledge on how software startups are created. It gives new perspectives to Ries' lean startup model [12], which has in the recent years gained popularity among the startup researchers. It indicates that iterative learning, as proposed by the lean startup model's build-measurement-learn cycle, happens not only in the customer interface but also internally in a startup, covering both the business-related and the technical aspects.

5.3 Effects of Human Capital on Opportunity Exploitation in Software Startups

The results of our study are in line with the results of studies on the human capital [8, 14, 16], pointing out the value of the entrepreneur's HC to the startup's business performance. The entrepreneur's good HC in relevant areas seems to make the opportunity exploitation process smoother and faster, which in turn lays a better basis for the enterprise's overall success and performance. The results do not, however, support the findings of [17], claiming that HC from external sources would be less valuable for startups. Instead, in our cases HC from external sources seemed to be a common and successful compensation for the founders' HC shortages.

We could identify the two dimensions of HC pointed out in [18], HC depth and breadth. From the perspective of HC, our results indicate that shortages in any HC dimension of our study increase uncertainty and iteration. The findings of [19], indicating that entrepreneurs are generalists without being experts in any specific area, were not fully supported in our study.

We could identify the unbalance between the human capital and the challenges as the key reason for the uncertainty. Especially clear the relationship was in cases where challenging application-specific technology was needed. In two cases, the founders' HC shortages prevented them from hiring competent software development resources, which was then the key source of the uncertainty.

The above reveals two items in our research determining between opportunity creation and discovery as well as between effectuation and causation: (1) the founders' own human capital, and (2) their possibilities to compensate for the shortages. As long as there are HC shortages the exploitation process tends to be iterative and follow the characteristics of the opportunity creation [1–3, 10] – independently of whether the opportunity originally was an existing discovered one, or a created one.

Correspondingly good, available HC tends to direct the exploitation process towards the opportunity discovery type [1–3, 10].

5.4 Validity Discussion

We discuss the validity of our findings from four viewpoints, construct validity, internal validity, external validity, and reliability [20].

The construct validity concerns whether the operational measures that are studied really represent what the researcher has in mind and what is investigated according to the research questions [20]. We conducted our study by using well-established research methods for qualitative research. We used semi-structured interviews of the founders of software startups for gathering the research data [21]. The interviews and data analysis were conducted by the first author. The analysis of the data was carried out by following established guidelines of qualitative analysis [24], and the results were reviewed by the co-authors.

The internal validity concerns examination of causal relations [20]. When studying whether a factor effects the investigated factor, other uncontrolled, possibly unknown factors may affect the investigated factor and threaten the internal validity of the research [20]. From our research data, we were able to identify a relationship between an iterative exploitation process and the shortages in the founders' human capital. There may be, however, other factors leading to an iterative exploitation process, not covered in this research. Therefore, we can only conclude that missing human capital seems to be one source of uncertainty.

The external validity concerns the generalizability of the findings [20]. The limited amount of study cases restricts the external validity of our findings, though the research covered a fairly broad palette of different startups in Italy, Norway and Finland.

Reliability concerns the dependency of the data and analysis on the specific researcher [20]. To address the reliability issues we utilized peer work in our study. The interview schema was created together with two experienced researchers. All interview data was recorded, and the data was transcribed by an external transcription service. Analyzing the data and concluding the findings was done by the first author and reviewed by the co-authors.

5.5 Relevance to Academia and Practitioners

We studied the early stages of software startups, identifying and exploitation the business opportunities, from the perspective the founders' human capital, their capabilities, knowledge, and experience. Our research had an empirical focus, studying the real-life embodiments of the utilized theories. Our results give the academia new interesting research perspectives by indicating that the two theoretical approaches for opportunity exploitation, creation and discovery processes [1], co-exists in the early stages of the same software startup. In our study, we focused on the founders' human capital as a factor affecting the deployment of these two processes. Our study gives a model for future studies of other factors affecting opportunity exploitation in software startups.

By having a practical focus our study provides new entrepreneurs with in-depth knowledge on how to bring a discovered opportunity or an opportunity aspiration towards more tangible ideas and products. Our study indicates that a successful exploitation of an opportunity requires a broad palette of technical and business-related human capital. It points out that an entrepreneur needs access to that human capital, and proposes that networking, hiring capable work force, and learning by iterating are the basic means to gather it.

6 Conclusions and Future Research

In this study we empirically explored how a group of software startup founders exploited the opportunities, on which the founders were building their startups. We utilized the multiple-case study method, collecting the research data from semi-structured interviews of the founders or founding team members. We identified embodiments of both the opportunity creation and discovery theories in the same opportunity exploitation processes.

We found that missing human capital was a reason for the uncertainty typical for opportunity creation and effectuation cases. The effect of the founders' human capital shortages to the opportunity exploitation processes was independent of whether the opportunities were originally discovered or created ones. Our results indicate also that the deployment of the opportunity discovery and creation processes was context-dependent and situational, varying not only between the case founders, but also between different problem areas of the same process. We further identified that the uncertainty caused by missing human capital was tackled by networking, hiring capable work force, and learning by iterating.

Our study focused on a factor affecting the opportunity exploitation processes in software startups and, thus, contributed both the theories of entrepreneurship and empirical research on software startups with new knowledge. Studies seeking for other factors and studies with bigger sample sizes and a broader geographical coverage would contribute in deepening the knowledge and generalizing our results.

Acknowledgments. This study was partly funded by TEKES as part of the HILLA program. We thank the members of the Software Startups Global Research Network that supported this study, especially Anh Nguyen Duc and Pekka Abrahamsson for their help in gathering the empirical data.

References

1. Alvarez, S.A., Barney, J.B.: Discovery and creation: alternative theories of entrepreneurial action. Strateg. Entrep. **26**, 11–26 (2007)
2. Alvarez, S.A., Barney, J.B., Anderson, P.: Perspective-forming and exploiting opportunities: the implications of discovery and creation processes for entrepreneurial and organizational research. Organ. Sci. **24**, 8–13 (2012)
3. Sarasvathy, S.D.: Causation and effectuation: toward a theoretical shift from economic inevitability to entrepreneurial contingency. Acad. Manag. Rev. **26**, 243–263 (2001)

4. Ries, E.: The Lean Startup, pp. 1–28. Crown Business, New York (2011)
5. Bosch, J., Holmström Olsson, H., Björk, J., Ljungblad, J.: The early stage software startup development model: a framework for operationalizing lean principles in software startups. In: Fitzgerald, B., Conboy, K., Power, K., Valerdi, R., Morgan, L., Stol, K.-J. (eds.) LESS 2013. LNBIP, vol. 167, pp. 1–15. Springer, Heidelberg (2013). https://doi.org/10.1007/978-3-642-44930-7_1
6. Ojala, A.: Business models and opportunity creation: how IT entrepreneurs create and develop business models under uncertainty. Inf. Syst. J. **26**, 451–476 (2016)
7. Becker, G.S.: Human Capital: A Theoretical And Empirical Analysis With Special Reference To Education. National Bureau of Economic Research, New York (1993)
8. Bosma, N., Van Praag, M., Thurik, R., De Wit, G.: The value of human and social capital investments for the business performance of startups. Small Bus. Econ. **23**, 227–236 (2004)
9. Becker, G.: Human capital revisted. J. Chem. Inf. Model. **53**, 1689–1699 (1994)
10. Sarasvathy, S.D.: Effectuation: Elements of Entrepreneurial Expertise. Edward Elgar Publishing, Northampton (2009)
11. Ojala, A.: Discovering and creating business opportunities for cloud services. J. Syst. Softw. **113**, 408–417 (2016)
12. Ries, E.: The Lean Startup: How Today's Entrepreneurs Use Continuous Innovation to Create Radically Successful Businesses. Random House LLC, New York (2011)
13. Hitt, M.A., Bierman, L., Shimizu, K., Kochhar, R.: Direct and moderating effects of human capital on strategy and performance in professional service firms: a resource-based perspective. Acad. Manag. J. **44**, 13–28 (2001)
14. Unger, J.M., Rauch, A., Frese, M., Rosenbusch, N.: Human capital and entrepreneurial success: a meta-analytical review. J. Bus. Ventur. **26**, 341–358 (2011)
15. Martin, B.C., McNally, J.J., Kay, M.J.: Examining the formation of human capital in entrepreneurship: a meta-analysis of entrepreneurship education outcomes. J. Bus. Ventur. **28**, 211–224 (2013)
16. Shrader, R., Siegel, D.S.: Assessing the relationship between human capital and firm performance: evidence from technology-based new ventures. Entrep. Theory Pract. **31**, 893–908 (2007)
17. Hatch, N.W., Dyer, J.H.: Human capital and learning as a source of sustainable competitive advantage. Strateg. Manag. J. **25**, 1155–1178 (2004)
18. Marvel, M.R., Lumpkin, G.T.: Technology entrepreneurs' human capital and its effects on innovation radicalness. Entrep. Theory Pract. **31**, 807–828 (2007)
19. Lazear, E.P.: Balanced skills and entrepreneurship. Am. Econ. Rev. **94**, 208–211 (2004)
20. Runeson, P., Höst, M.: Guidelines for conducting and reporting case study research in software engineering. Empirical Softw. Eng. **14**, 131–164 (2009)
21. Marshall, M.N.: The key informant technique. Family Pract. **13**, 92–97 (1996)
22. Cruzes, D.S., Dybå, T., Runeson, P., Höst, M.: Case studies synthesis: a thematic, cross-case, and narrative synthesis worked example. Empirical Softw. Eng. **20**, 1–32 (2014)
23. Lethbridge, T.C., Sim, S.E., Singer, J.: Studying software engineers: Data collection techniques for software field studies. Empirical Softw. Eng. **10**, 311–341 (2005)
24. Cruzes, D.S., Dybå, T.: Recommended steps for thematic synthesis in software engineering. In: International Symposium on Empirical Software Engineering and Measurement, pp. 275–284. IEEE (2011)

Changing and Pivoting the Business Model in Software Startups

João M. Fernandes$^{(\boxtimes)}$ⓘ and Paulo Afonsoⓘ

Dept. Informática and Dept. Produção e Sistemas/Centro ALGORITMI,
Universidade do Minho, Braga, Portugal
`jmf@di.uminho.pt`, `psafonso@dps.uminho.pt`

Abstract. In a company, its business strategy and business model undergo changes throughout its life. These changes can be induced or forced externally or they can result from a deliberate strategy to improve the business performance and to achieve success. Certain changes can lead to a major change in the business model of the company (i.e., a pivot). Such change or innovation in the business model can occur in various of its dimensions. According to Osterwalder and Pigneur, there are four epicenters of change and innovation to be taken into consideration. In this manuscript, fifteen Portuguese software startups were studied using essentially semi-structured interviews to gather the information. The data was processed with a software application for qualitative data analysis. The main results are related to a dynamic process of evolution and change of the business model in software startups. In particular, we have identified that the changes in the business elements that support the production of the value proposition (left-hand side of the Business Model Canvas) affect the elements that explain the strategy of delivering the value proposition to customers (right-hand side of the Business Model Canvas).

Keywords: Software companies · Startups
Business model · Strategic innovation

1 Introduction

The business strategy and business model undergo changes throughout the company's life, in order to improve its performance and success. For example, the difficulty in gaining customers can lead to a major change in the business model of a company (i.e., a pivot). A pivot is a special change designed to test a fundamental new hypothesis about a product or business model and assumes itself as an important engine for growth and consolidation of the business [1]. Pivots can be interpreted in a broader way considering, not only radical or high-impact changes, but also more specific or incremental changes that are gradually changing the company's course and the configuration of the business. Since pivots have a significant impact on the business model of the company and on its success, it

© Springer Nature Switzerland AG 2018
K. Wnuk and S. Brinkkemper (Eds.): ICSOB 2018, LNBIP 336, pp. 157–171, 2018.
https://doi.org/10.1007/978-3-030-04840-2_11

is important to understand this phenomenon. Unfortunately, the literature still offers few contributions about this topic.

Terho *et al.* [2] studied how pivots can change business hypotheses. Their work includes three case companies (all small software startups from Tampere, Finland) and map the pivot effects on the business hypotheses. They found out that the pivots can be identified by changes in the Lean Model Canvas and that pivots usually occur in groups.

The study conducted by Bajwa *et al.* [3] focused on understanding the pivoting processes of software startups and on identifying the triggering factors and pivot types. Their initial results show that the pivots are triggered by various factors, namely negative customer feedback.

Osterwalder and Pigneur highlight four epicenters of change and innovation in the business model [4]. Voelpel et al. suggest a systematic structure for the reinvention of the business model, thus enabling entrepreneurs to evaluate the business models of their companies [5]. The change in the business model is also presented in the literature in the context of strategic innovation. Entrepreneurs have to decide, at the strategic level, three basic questions [6]:

- **Who** will be the customers?
- **What** type of products/services should be offered?
- **How** products/services should be offered in an efficient way?

Osterwalder and Pigneur also add the question "how much", which expresses how much a company can get profits from its products/services [4]. Thus, according to these authors, the business model can be divided into four pillars (who, what, how [7], and how much), and each of them can be translated into a main element of the business model. These four pillars can be translated into four main business model elements that can then be further decomposed [8]:

- **Product elements**: a company's value proposition;
- **Customer relationship elements**: how a company comes into contact with customers and what kind of relationships it wants to establish with them;
- **Infrastructure management elements**: type of activities, resources, and partners needed to provide the product elements and customer relationship elements;
- **Financial aspects elements**: revenue streams and pricing mechanisms for a company, i.e., how the company makes money through the other three elements.

In this manuscript, fifteen Portuguese software startups, all located at Braga, were studied using essentially semi-structured interviews to gather the information. The data was processed with NVivo, a popular software application for qualitative data analysis.

The remainder of this paper is structured as follows. A description of the Business Model Canvas (BMC) is given in Sect. 2. Some issues related to business change and innovation is discussed in Sect. 3. Section 4 presents the research methodology. In Sect. 5, the major results of this study are analyzed and discussed. Finally, Sect. 6 concludes the paper and presents some opportunities for further work.

2   Business Model Canvas

A business model describes the logic of creating, delivering and capturing value by an organization [4]. It must be simple, clear and easy to understand, but not too oversimplifying the complexity of the functioning of a particular company. By addressing, in a conceptual way, the business model, it can be harnessed, modeled, understood, shared, observed, measured, and simulated.

Stähler considers business models as a new analytical unit for innovation [9]. Indeed, the business model can be seen as a way to tell a good story, aiming to align employees on the type of value to be created in a particular company.

Many authors have proposed different models for addressing the business of a company. For example, Alt and Zimmermann [10] consider the six following business elements. **Mission**: A critical part of the business model is developing a high-level understanding of the overall vision, strategic goals and the value proposition including the basic product or service features. The **Structure** determines the roles of the different agents involved and the focus on industry, customers and products. **Processes** provide a more detailed view on the mission and the structure of the business model. **Revenues** are the "bottom line" of a business model. **Legal issues** influence all aspects of the business model and the general vision. **Technology** is an enabler and a constraint for IT-based business models. Also, technological change has an impact on the business model design.

This manuscript considers the popular Business Model Canvas (BMC), proposed by Osterwalder and Pigneur [4] that consists of nine components as shown in Fig. 1:

- **Value Proposition (VP)**: It should focus on the problem that will be solved, in the needs that customers want to see satisfied and, in the products, and/or services to offer to each segment of customers.
- **Customer Segments (CuS)**: Customers are grouped in different segments according to their needs, behaviors, and other specific attributes.
- **Channels (CH)**: Through channels of communication, distribution and sales, companies reach their customer segments and deliver the value propositions.
- **Customer Relationships (CR)**: Relationships (personal and automated) between a company and its customers.
- **Revenue Streams (RS)**: Set of forms of business monetization.
- **Key Activities (KA)**: activities that support the value creation process inherent to the business model.
- **Key Resources (KR)**: Main resources (e.g., human, physical, technical) that support the main activities.
- **Key Partnerships (KP)**: Suppliers and company partners that contribute to the optimization of the business model and to the reduction of business risks.
- **Cost Structure (CoS)**: Implies recognizing and understanding all the costs involved in the business operation.

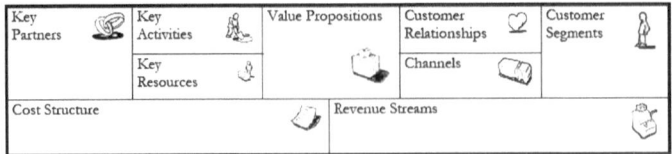

Fig. 1. Business model canvas [4].

This model, used and tested whole over the world, was used during this study and the components that comprise it cover the four most relevant areas of a given business: customers, supply, infrastructure and financial viability.

Some studies refer to BMC and connect it with other models. Cann et al. suggest the use of a model for software entrepreneurs to help startups to succeed and survive in the initial phases [11]. This model, called Early-Life Decision Model (ELDM), identifies 17 different types of decisions that can be taken in a daily basis at companies in order to achieve market success. These types of decisions are grouped into four major dimensions (shaping the company, developing the product, establishing the market, and going international), and 12 of the identified decision types may be contained in the BMC. Some types of decision can be placed on more than one BMC component, and some components may contain more decision types in a particular category than others.

3   Business Model Change and Innovation

In order to remain viable on the market, a company may need to change its business model over time.

Osterwalder and Pigneur claim that each of the nine components that are part of the BMC can be a starting point to innovate the business model of a company [4]. They also consider four epicenters that can be starting points for the innovation of business models:

- **Resource-driven epicenter:** This type of epicenter allows to expand or transform the business model of the company, through the innovations originated in the company's infrastructure or through a partner.
- **Offer-driven epicenter:** Innovations from this kind of epicenter create new value proposals to be delivered to the customer. The emergence of these new value proposals therefore alter the other components of the business model.
- **Customer-driven epicenter:** These innovations are based on the needs of each client, in the facilitated access or in the increase of the convenience.
- **Finance-driven epicenter:** The innovations of this type of epicenter arise from finance, pricing mechanisms or from reduced cost structures.

These four types of innovation epicenters of the business model are important mechanisms for a better understanding of the components where changes can occur and the components that will be affected by them. In any case, all the innovations that depart from resources, value proposition, customers, and the financial dimensions affect the other components of the business model.

Linder and Cantrell interviewed 70 business executives and analysts, and their study aimed to identify a roadmap for operations managers to lead the change in their business models [12]. This study presents a list of 39 different ways to change the business model, ranging from narrowing or expanding the target market to changing the production of products for services.

Voelpel et al. suggest a systematic structure for the reinvention of the business model, thus enabling entrepreneurs to evaluate the business models of their companies [5]. After conducting a literature review on the subject, these authors found that there has been little guidance on how to remodel business models. The reconfiguration of the business strategy and the dynamic capabilities of the company are some of the factors contributing to the development of a new business model.

As a result of this study, a wheel-based model was developed to illustrate the reinvention of the business model (Fig. 2). This wheel allows entrepreneurs to know how to operationalize and measure the development of new business models. It presents the interactive (systemic) flow of the four dimensions in the reinvention of the business model: (1) customers; (2) technology; (3) business system infrastructure; and (4) economics/profitability. The wheel allows companies to continuously try to reinvent themselves, iterating the process throughout the four dimensions.

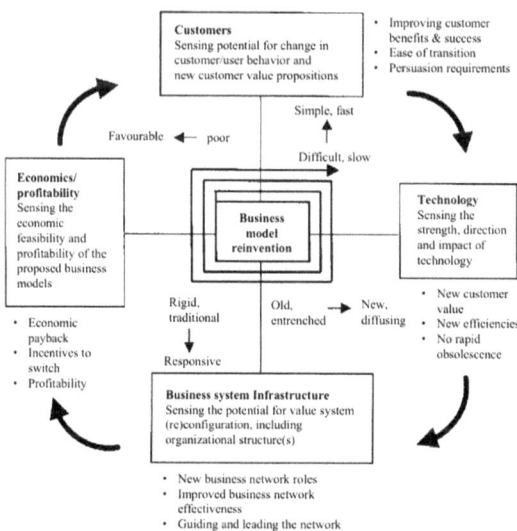

Fig. 2. Reinventing the business model [5].

In many cases, for companies to survive and succeed in the market, they must be able to change the business strategy during their lifecycle.

Among the different types of strategies, one can highlight the growth strategy. The following approaches can be followed by a given company [13]:

- It can acquire companies in a distribution channel, thus approaching the final consumers of its products (vertical integration);
- It can acquire competitors, thus increasing not only its size, but also its sales volume and its market share (horizontal integration);
- It can diversify its business;
- It can merge with another company, causing them to become just one.

Growth strategies can be divided in four types [14]:

- **Innovation:** Some companies are concerned with constantly innovating their products/services, to allow them to keep ahead of their competition;
- **Internationalization:** By entering into the markets of other countries, some companies can grow and increase their sales volume;
- **Joint venture:** Two companies can join for the development of a product to be placed on the market;
- **Expansion:** Some companies are looking to expand their business in the market segment where they currently operate.

Several authors refer various types of strategies that can be adopted, contributing to the growth of the business. According to Markides [7], "strategic innovation occurs when a company identifies gaps in the industry positioning map, decides to fill them, and the gaps grow to become the new mass market". These gaps can be interpreted as customer segments, needs that they seek to see supplied or new forms of production, delivery or distribution of products/services. A company can develop, proactively and in an organized way, a new business model: redefining the WHO, redefining the WHAT, redefining the HOW. Additionally, answers to the three key questions should be obtained: (1) who should be selected as a client? (2) what products/services and value propositions we offer to the selected clients? (3) how to offer these products/services in a cost-efficient form? [7].

Ries considers that the strategy that a startup applies must include a business model, a product road map, a perspective about partners and competitors, and ideas about the characteristics of the customer [1]. This strategy has as a final result the product to be developed by the startup in its first years of existence.

4   Research Methodology: Semi-structured Interviews

This section describes the research approach followed during the study reported in this manuscript. The semi-structured interview was the method selected for the collection of the data in the different companies involved in this study, because it presents adequate characteristics for the purpose of this research.

The interviews must be well organized and structured in order to obtain quality data, and they can take place in four key steps: (1) identification of the interviewees; (2) preparation of the interview; (3) conducting of the interview;

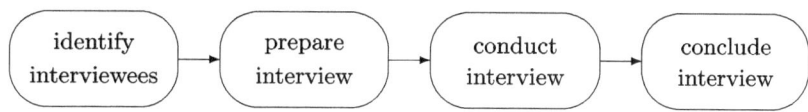

Fig. 3. Main steps of an interview.

and (4) conclusion [15]. These four steps were carried out in the interviews conducted in this study (Fig. 3).

The semi-structured interview was used as a way to gather the data for this study. A characteristics of this type of interview is the use of a previously-elaborated guide [16]. A guide offers to researchers support at the time of gathering verbal data in the interviews they perform. The semi-structured interview combines the features of structured and unstructured interviews. In this type of interviews, it is necessary for the interviewer to create a certain dynamics and to control the way how the interview takes place.

Interview Script. The interviewer needs to prepare some key questions to be asked during the interview. The interview script was elaborated based on the BMC and the ELDM. During its elaboration, the script was changed several times, so that the questions were placed in the most appropriate order, were not ambiguous, and permitted the interview to not exceed 60 min. The guide used for the interviews in this study was structured as follows:

1   General information
1.1   Information about the interviewee (education, role, experience)
1.2   Information about the company (location, size, business)
2   Business modeling and market entry
2.1   How the company was initially modeled (mission, vision, staff)
2.2   Product and market (initial product, initial market)
2.3   Market entry strategy
2.4   Internal and external restrictions
3   Business growth strategy
3.1   Key moments in the business growth
3.2   Evolution in the value proposition
3.3   Changes in the relationship with the market
3.4 Changes in the business model
4   Economic-financial issues
4.1   Cost structure and revenue streams
4.2   Investment, funding, and profitability
4.3   Business management

Planning the Interview. At this stage, (1) the inclusion criteria were established, (2) the interview script and the confidentiality document were edited, (3) a pilot interview was conducted to identify the aspects to be corrected/improved in the script and to better prepare the conducting of the interviews, (4) the companies that could be considered in the study were identified, and (5) the contacts with the companies were established.

Interviewees. This study was conducted in Portuguese software startups, all with their headquarters in the city of Braga. The 15 companies that agreed to cooperate in our study were categorized in three different groups, based on their value propositions (i.e., the type of software systems they develop). In this study, each category includes five companies classified as:

1. Own projects (OP): development of the portfolio's own projects, i.e., the company takes the initiative to develop its own software (mass-market) products, platforms and/or mobile applications;
2. Bespoke projects/services (BP): development of applications/systems tailored to customers;
3. Own projects and bespoke projects/services (OP&BP): this group includes companies that simultaneously address the two previous profiles.

A summary of the companies, anonymously designated from A to O, is provided in Table 1. Among the 15 collaborators (i.e., one per company) that were available to be interviewed, 13 held the position of CEO and the remaining two were CTOs. Only two of these 15 persons were not co-founders of the companies. Although it was not possible to meet with a co-founder in these two companies, the CEOs had a good knowledge about the company history and its evolution from the beginning of their activities. In some cases, additional questions were asked during the interviews, according to the answers that were provided.

Interview Analysis. This phase was characterized by the transcription of the interviews, production and validation of the reports. For each interview, the respective transcript was made (except in one case, since the CEO did not allowed the interview to be audio recorded). During the transcription, when new questions arose or when some issues required further clarifications, the interviewee was contacted again. When the transcript of each interview was considered as complete, it was sent to the interviewee for validation.

The data standardization was carried out iteratively. The process was stopped when we got adequate conditions for coding the interviews and analysing in the NVivo program (software for qualitative data analysis). The use of the NVivo program proved essential for this work, as it allowed us to group the data into topics and to identify similar aspects among the participating companies.

5   Analysis and Discussion

The main results and findings of this study are discussed in this section, namely the most relevant aspects related to the building blocks of the BMC and how they changed and evolved in the considered startups. The key moments and the decisions in terms of business model change are also highlighted.

Table 1. Characterisation of the companies. Turnover refers to 2015 and is presented in thousands of Euros.

Cpy.	Found. year	Category	Workers	Turnover	Interviewee	Date
A	2012	OP & BP	11	500	CEO	May & Aug 2016
B	2011	BP	11	250	CEO	May & Jul 2016
C	2012	BP	10	200	CEO/co-founder	May 2016
D	2011	OP & BP	17	n/a	CEO/co-founder	May 2016
E	2010	OP	12	1.000	CTO/co-founder	May 2016
F	2008	BP	15	n/a	CEO	May 2016
G	2013	OP	8	n/a	CEO	Jun 2016
H	2008	BP	7	180	CEO/co-founder	Jun 2016
I	2013	OP	7	50	CEO/co-founder	Jun 2016
J	2011	OP & BP	8	170	CEO/co-founder	Jun 2016
K	2013	OP & BP	3	50	CEO/co-founder	Jun 2016
L	2013	BP	11	560	CEO/co-founder	Jun 2016
M	2013	OP	6	50	CEO/co-founder	Jul 2016
N	2011	OP & BP	14	1.200	CEO/co-founder	Jul 2016
O	2014	OP	9	0	CTO/co-founder	Aug 2016

5.1 Results

By analyzing how each of the nine BMC components have changed between the key moments that characterize the life of each company, one was able to identify which one had the highest number of changes. A score, ranging from zero (minimum score) to three (maximum score), was established to measure the change level of the BMC components (see Table 2).

Table 2. Score assigned to the change in the BMC components.

	Meaning
	The BMC component had ...
Zero	... not undergone any major changes
One	... few and small changes
Two	... significant changes
Three	... completely changed (pivot)

Figures 4 and 5 summarize the main results of business model change in the 15 companies that were studied. In Fig. 4 we can see how each component of the business model of each company has evolved or changed ranging from white (no relevant changes were identified) to dark blue (when pivoting or radical change was found). Figure 5 presents the number of changes by component in the three types of companies and in aggregate. The dimension or the level of change is indicated by the accumulated points in each building block of the business model canvas.

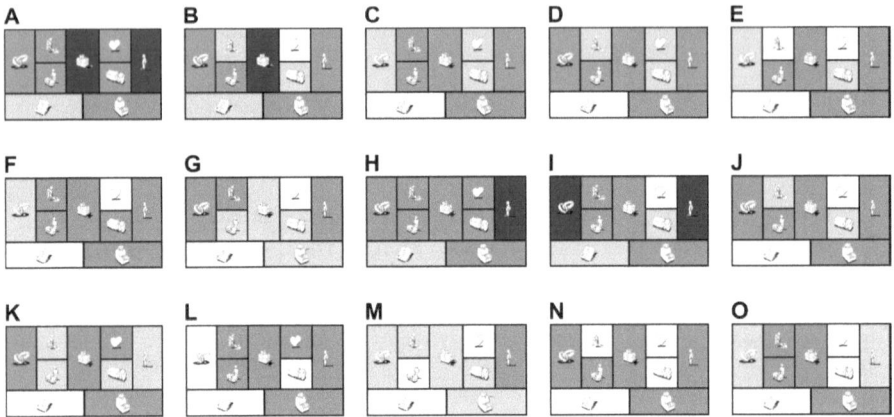

Fig. 4. Scores assigned to measure the change in all BMC building blocks for each company. Dark blue = 3; blue = 2; light blue = 1; white = 0. (Color figure online)

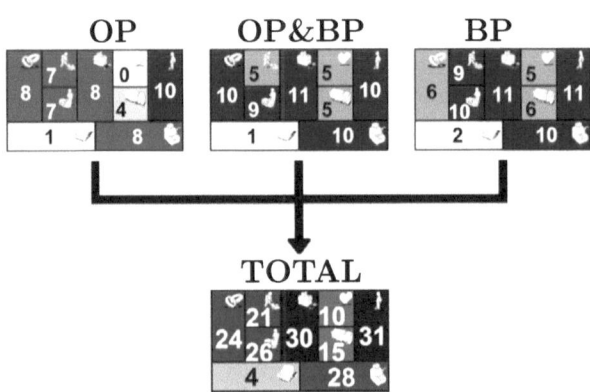

Fig. 5. Scores assigned to measure the change in all BMC building blocks for the three types of companies (OP, OP&BP, BP) and in aggregate (TOTAL).

5.2   Discussion

These results corroborate some assumptions found in the literature (e.g., Oster-walder and Pigneur's epicenters of change [4] and the three dimensions of strategic innovation suggested by Markides [7]), but also give new insights on this process. Taken into consideration the exploratory nature of this research, these findings ask for further validation through in-depth case studies or a survey approach but they offer already interesting and additional issues for discussion. Some of these findings are discussed below.

The Most Stable Components in the BMC

In the companies considered in this study, most of the components of the business model changed but some did not show relevant changes. It is the case of the CoS building block in the left-hand of the BMC. Apparently, software startups may evolve and change during the first years of life but such changes do not impact significantly on the overall cost dimension of the company. Curiously, activities and resources tend to change more significantly than the overall cost structure. This may suggest that these companies face changes with impact on operations, but without overall financial impact.

Furthermore, in the right-hand of the BMC, the components CR and CH changed much less than most of the other components on the "emotional" side of the BMC, particularly the former. We may ask why these business building blocks do not change so frequently or significantly. Indeed, some of the companies increased the number of communication channels used (e.g., social media, participation in events) but, on the other hand, we also realized that others have been disinvesting in their channels. One may assume that these components were already well established at the beginning of the business and no particular evolution was needed or demanded. But, such inertia may also result from opposite reasons. These two components represent more detailed aspects of the business model that may be develop later or remain underdeveloped in the first years when business effectiveness is predominant. They also ask for additional and specialized skills and knowledge related to marketing and business management that are not priorities in the initial rounds of hiring new collaborators. This kind of successive waves of development in the business model is a very common business strategy where technical skills come first and soft or business skills development happen later. Indeed, the reduced changes in these two important components that we can find in more complete and sophisticated business models may indicate some underdevelopment and limitations that should be mitigated.

As in the case of the CR component, CH has evolved slightly more in BP companies. In general terms, when the three types of companies are compared, OP companies tend to show less significant changes in their business model when compared to BP ones.

The Most Dynamic Components of the BMC

Firstly, only a few components experienced very significant changes (pivoting) and those were the VP and CuS dimensions of the business model. The CuS was the right-hand side BMC building block where the most significant changes were observed and, particularly, in the cases of BP and OP&BP companies. OP companies are not so agile as BP ones in changing products and services offered what may result in a higher risk of the business. Indeed, some OP companies are still focus on the same products since the company was launched. Even if OP companies are constantly improving the product, adjusting it to the market needs and expectations, those changes are more incremental than radical e.g., new versions of the initial product.

On the other hand, BP companies are more dynamic, for example, two of these companies made a pivot in their value proposition what represents a radical change of the business model. Furthermore, it was observed in the companies interviewed that, as the value proposition evolved (e.g., with new products or services), new sources of revenue were added to the company's business model - which forced changes in this component. There is, therefore, a causal relationship between the value proposition and the sources of revenue. Thus, beyond identifying the causes of changes in business models, also the impact of these changes on the other elements of the business model should be analyzed. This aspect is discussed next.

The Most and the Less Interrelated Components of the BMC

The left-hand components of the BMC related to the rational of the business or the way how the value proposition is produced are apparently more interconnected than the components related to the emotional side of the business model (presented in the right-side of the model) because the components of the latter apparently can change/evolve more independently. The components of the left-hand of the business model (i.e., KA, KR and KP) change in a more interrelated way and more significantly. On one hand, changes in the key resources are essentially related to hiring more collaborators and that occur more often in BP companies. On the other hand, key partnerships, if not established at the beginning tend to only occur much later when the companies have more experience in the market and are able to align them with company's business strategy.

Sources of Change and Impacts

A change in a particular BMC component may have an impact on other components. The type of impact that the change in certain BMC components caused in the remaining components was analyzed. It was concluded that:

- A change in a BMC component may not affect the remaining eight components but adjacent components tend also to change;
- All the components on the left-hand side of the BMC (excepting CoS) and the CuS component on the right-hand were the ones with the greatest impact on the business model of the 15 companies;
- The VP component and all components belonging to the right side of the BMC (excepting CH) were the most affected by the changes that have occurred;
- The propagation of an "earthquake" (which are starting points for change and innovation in business models) does not necessarily follow what is suggested by the four epicenters proposed by Osterwalder and Pigneur [4].

Key Moments and Decisions

Finally, we highlight the most significant key moments/decisions that were identified as drivers of change in the business model of the studied software startups. They pushed or justified changes in different BMC components. The collected key moments and decisions driving changes in the business model are:

- *Value proposition*: innovation, product development;
- *Customer segments*: the first clients, addressing new (or more) clients, internationalization;
- *Customer relationship*: acquiring new clients, changing customer relationship;
- *Channels*: better communication through social networks;
- *Revenue streams*: venture capital investment, increasing sales;
- *Key resources*: increasing the number of employees, retaining/attracting experienced employees, hiring skilled employees for specific positions;
- *Key activities*: changing the software development process, addressing the maintenance of the products, addressing branding and marketing;
- *Key partners*: changing unsuccessful partnerships, establishing technical partnerships;
- *Cost structure*: N/A.

Changes in the value proposition and customer segments are related and are those with more impact in the business model representing a major change or pivot. This was the case of companies A and N.

Initially, the product of Company A had some acceptance and quickly attracted close to 20 customers. However, the product does not solve a real problem from the perspective of the market and sales were not enough to support the expenses of the company. Thus, after a year of its launch, the product was discontinued. Company A had to abandon the first product and decided to redefine its strategy and its business model. With the departure of two shareholders, the company chose to provide web services and web design in order to generate cash flow to finance the investment in its own products and changed the focus to the international market namely, the USA.

Company N developed an electronic government system and established a contract with four municipalities. However, this happens in the crisis period and under the economic supervision of the Troika in Portugal. As a consequence, all the funding that would have allowed the four municipalities to buy the product was cancelled. Thus, Company N decided to focus on new business areas in the company namely, an e-commerce solution, a CRM tool, and also web development services. The company decided to develop tailored made software for its customers and a significant restructuring of the business was made.

5.3 Validity Threats

A series of issues may influence the results of this exploratory study, such as the researchers who performed the study or the observed data set. In the following, we consider the threats to validity, in a way to discuss the acceptance and accuracy of our findings.

The use of the BMC may be criticized. There are multiple models to address the business models of a company, like [17]. However, the BMC is nowadays the most used one and it is particularly popular to support the creation of startups.

We do not claim that our results are representative of all software startups, or to be generalizable to other economic fields. Though, they provide relevant insights from a set of software startups. The number of companies is relatively low, even if they the three considered types of companies are equally covered.

During the field study, two researchers were responsible for interviewing the participants, collecting and organizing the data, and processing the results. More than one author drew the conclusions from the gathered data, so there is a risk related to interpretation of the findings. Furthermore, we tried to mitigate this validation threat by the use of a software application for the analysis of qualitative data, with follow-up reports that were sent to the interviewees and by discussing the preliminary results at length with all the researchers.

6   Conclusions

For the data collection from the participating software companies, it was necessary to prepare a set of tools that can be used in similar studies. The interview script, based on the list of questions made in the BMC and ELDM, can be used when conducting the interviews in such studies. The data collected through the interviews and web search allowed to form a very thorough and detailed database. The analysis of some of these data may be the starting point for the realization of new studies within the software companies.

For a better understanding of the components that have evolved in different ways in the business model of each company, it was necessary to develop a score system, in the range 0–3 as shown in Table 2. This system has allowed the identification of the components that have more and less evolved for each of the three identified groups of companies and can be used in other similar studies.

The four types of epicenters that Osterwalder and Pigneur (2011) present as possible starting points for the innovation of business models were verified when analyzing the data and results. In this study, it was also found that the "quake" propagation does not necessarily follow and that change in a particular component may not affect all adjacent BMC components.

Finally, some opportunities for further work can be highlighted. In-depth case studies can be performed in some of the companies that took part in this study. Another possible opportunity is related to compare the business strategies of mature software companies vs. startups, which in this case implies extending the analysis to more companies (namely, mature ones). Coleman and O'Connor show that the previous experience of the person that manages the development work is the main influencer on the process a company initially uses [18]. This may provide a good trigger to study if the same happens with respect to the business approach followed by startups.

Acknowledgements. This work was supported by COMPETE: POCI-01-0145-FEDER-007043 and FCT Fundação para a Ciência e a Tecnologia within the Project Scope: UID/CEC/00319/2013.

References

1. Ries, E.: The Lean Startup: How Today's Entrepreneurs Use Continuous innovation to Create Radically Successful Businesses. Crown Publishing Group (2011)
2. Terho, H., Suonsyrjä, S., Karisalo, A., Mikkonen, T.: Ways to cross the rubicon: pivoting in software startups. In: Abrahamsson, P., Corral, L., Oivo, M., Russo, B. (eds.) PROFES 2015. LNCS, vol. 9459, pp. 555–568. Springer, Cham (2015). https://doi.org/10.1007/978-3-319-26844-6_41
3. Bajwa, S.S., Wang, X., Duc, A.N., Abrahamsson, P.: How do software startups pivot? Empirical results from a multiple case study. In: Maglyas, A., Lamprecht, A.-L. (eds.) ICSOB 2016. LNBIP, vol. 240, pp. 169–176. Springer, Cham (2016). https://doi.org/10.1007/978-3-319-40515-5_14
4. Osterwalder, A., Pigneur, Y.: Business Model Generation: A Handbook for Visionaries, Game Changers, and Challengers. Wiley, Hoboken (2010)
5. Voelpel, S.C., Leibold, M., Tekie, E.B.: The wheel of business model reinvention: how to reshape your business model to leapfrog competitors. J. Chang. Manag. **4**(3), 259–276 (2004). https://doi.org/10.1080/1469701042000212669
6. Abell, D.F.: Defining the Business: The Starting Point of Strategic Planning. Prentice-Hall, Englewood Cliffs (1980)
7. Markides, C.: Strategic innovation. MIT Sloan Manag. Rev., 9–23 (1997). (Spring). https://sloanreview.mit.edu/article/strategic-innovation/
8. Osterwalder, A., Pigneur, Y.: Modeling value propositions in e-business. In: 5th International Conference on Electronic Commerce (ICEC 2003), pp. 429–436. ACM (2003). https://doi.org/10.1145/948005.948061
9. Stähler, P.: Business models as an unit of analysis for strategizing. In: International Workshop on Business Models, Lausanne, Switzerland, pp. 4–5 (2002)
10. Alt, R., Zimmermann, H.-D.: Preface: introduction to special section – business models. Electron. Mark. **11**(1), 3–9 (2001). https://doi.org/10.1080/713765630
11. van Cann, R., Jansen, S., Brinkkemper, S.: Software Business Start-up Memories: Key Decisions in Success Stories. Palgrave Macmillan, Basingstoke (2013)
12. Linder, J., Cantrell, S.: Changing business models: Surveying the landscape. Technical report, Accenture - Institute for Strategic Change, May 2000
13. Wright, P., Kroll, M.J., Parnell, J.A.: Strategic Management: Concepts and Cases, 4th edn. Prentice Hall, Upper Saddle River (1998)
14. Oliveira. D.: Planejamento estratégico: Conceitos, metodologia e práticas, 26th edn. Atlas, São Paulo, Brazil (2009). In Portuguese
15. Fernandes, J.M., Machado, R.J.: Requirements in Engineering Projects. LNMIE. Springer, Cham (2016). https://doi.org/10.1007/978-3-319-18597-2
16. Edwards, R., Holland, J.: What is qualitative interviewing? The 'What is?' Research Methods Series. Bloomsbury Publishing (2013)
17. Maurya, A.: Running Lean: Iterate from Plan A to a Plan That Works. O'Reilly Media, Sebastopol (2012)
18. Coleman, G., O'Connor, R.: An investigation into software development process formation in software start-ups. J. Enterp. Inf. Manag. **21**(6), 633–648 (2008). https://doi.org/10.1108/17410390810911221

From MVPs to Pivots:
A Hypothesis-Driven Journey
of Two Software Startups

Dron Khanna[1]([⊠]), Anh Nguyen-Duc[2], and Xiaofeng Wang[1]

[1] Free University of Bozen-Bolzano, 39100 Bolzano, Italy
{dron.khanna,xiaofeng.wang}@unibz.it
[2] University of Southeast Norway, 3800 Bø i Telemark, Norway
anh.nguyen.duc@usn.no

Abstract. Software startups have emerged as an interesting multiperspective research area. Inspired by Lean Startup, a startup journey can be viewed as a series of experiments that validate a set of business hypotheses an entrepreneurial team make explicitly or inexplicitly about their startup. It is little known about how startups evolve through business hypothesis testing. This study proposes a novel approach to look at the startup evolution as a Minimum Viable Product (MVP) creating process. We identified relationships among business hypotheses and MVPs via ethnography and post-mortem analysis in two software startups. We observe that the relationship between hypotheses and MVPs is incomplete and non-linear in these two startups. We also find that entrepreneurs do learn from testing their hypotheses. However, there are hypotheses not tested by MVPs and vice versa, MVPs not related to any business hypothesis. The approach we proposed visualizes the flow of entrepreneurial knowledge across pivots via MVPs.

Keywords: Software startup · Lean startup
Entrepreneurial journey · Minimum viable product · Pivot

1 Introduction

The software industry has witnessed a growing trend of the development of software products by small teams of people with limited resource and little operating history. Despite this global movement of high-tech entrepreneurship, the majority of software startups fail within two years of their creation, primarily due to self-destruction rather than competition [1]. The number will be much higher when counting startup teams which have not reached the launching milestone. It is known that there is no common recipe for entrepreneurs to be successful. It is difficult to frame successes and failure from startups [2], as each startup will have a unique evolution path depending on an abundant amount of context factors. Lean startup, a common methodology among entrepreneur, emphasizes the role of validating business ideas via building MVPs. It is also common that a pivot

K. Wnuk and S. Brinkkemper (Eds.): ICSOB 2018, LNBIP 336, pp. 172–186, 2018.
https://doi.org/10.1007/978-3-030-04840-2_12

occurs after a series of MVPs are created [3,4]. Such a startup journey is also an artefact-creating process, given that major milestones for startups (namely: pitching events, first paid customer and fund-raising) tight to certain artefacts. Entrepreneurship research provides a grounded foundation that startup is an emergent sequence of events, in which an event is both, path dependent on prior processes and contingent on contemporaneous processes [1,5–7].

While it is useful for an entrepreneur to view entrepreneurial development from an MVP-creating process perspective, it is more important for them to know what they can learn from their MVPs. Ries mentions the Build-Measure-Learn circle in his method [8]. The concept of the loop explains that build stage is based on the hypothesis formulated by an entrepreneur. In order to test the hypothesis, an experiment has to be configured. Learning is intended during the testing of hypothesis [9]. Therefore, this loop could also be regarded inter-preted as a traditional scientific hypothesis-metric-experiment loop. The cycle that starts with the hypothesis and ends with a prototype to test the hypoth-esis. While exercising the loop, the earlier a startup realizes a hypothesis is wrong, the quicker it should be updated and retested [9]. However, the cycle does not directly imply what software entrepreneur actually learn from their previous experience embedded in MVPs. Software startup teams are excessively focused on the developing a better software solution and delivering a prototype to its customer. Individuals exercising so many experiments to win the software development timeline, often neglect the learning involved in software startups [10]. The objective of this study is to understand the entrepreneurial learning from an MVP-creation process. We assume that entrepreneur has predetermined business ideas, which are formed as a hypothesis, that is validated by building MVPs. Therefore, adopting MVP as the unit of analysis, our research questions are RQ1: *Do entrepreneur learn from formulated hypotheses for their business and product?* RQ2: *Are their corresponding MVPs for a formulated hypothe-sis?* The study is organized as follows: Sect. 2 presents a background about startup development and entrepreneurial artefacts. Section 3 describes our study design, case description, data collection and data analysis. Section 4 presents the entrepreneurial journey of two software startups: Startuppuccino and MUML AS. Finally, Sect. 5 presents the discussion and concludes the paper.

2   Background and Related Work

To explore our research questions, we articulate two theoretical fields: startup development and entrepreneurial artefacts as illustrated in Fig. 1. On the grounds of software engineering, a startup doing experiments contributes with knowledge on software development process, techniques and their outcomes. The procedure to carry out experimentation helps the startup team to better predict, under-stand and develop the software development process [11].

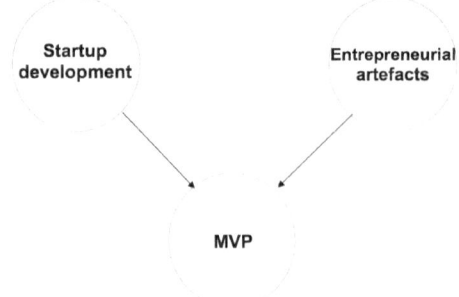

Fig. 1. Theoretical aspects of MVP's

2.1 Startup Development

Lean Startup [8] as a methodology for entrepreneurship has become increasingly popular in the past several years, evidenced by dedicated conferences and global Lean Startup meet-ups. As a result, it starts to enter entrepreneurship education programs as the main topic too. The Lean Startup approach was inspired by the lean concepts of focusing on the efforts that create value for customers and eliminating waste during entrepreneurial processes [8]. However, since the customers are often unknown, what customers could perceive as value is also unknown. Therefore, entrepreneurs should get out of the building to involve the customers since day one [12]. Lean Startup advocates to build the product iteratively and deliver to the market as quickly as possible for earlier feedback [8]. Lean Startup is essentially a hypothesis-driven approach [13] which bases entrepreneurial decisions on evidence and validated learning. To capture customer value, an entrepreneur should start a feedback loop that turns an idea into a product, learning whether to pivot or persevere. This can be done by developing an MVP using agile methods to collect customer feedback about the product [8]. The feedback becomes the input to improve the product and validate the hypothesis. As a result, the startup might pursue new directions of the business or continue and scale it [14]. Figure 2 is a high-level representation of the Lean Startup methodology. Pivots in software startups are common to occur and discussed by various scholars. According to Ries [8], it is a kind of change done to validate the startup hypothesis about a product, business model and the engine of growth. Bajwa et al. in their study refer to various different types of pivots that can happen in startups: Zoom-in, Zoom-out, Customer Segment, Customer need, Platform, Business Architecture, Value Capture, Engine of Growth, Channel, Technology, Complete and Side project [4]. A startup journey can be seen as a process of creating entrepreneurial artefacts [15]. According to the science of artificial, one of the schools of theory adopted in entrepreneurship research [16], an artefact is defined as an interface between the internal team and its surrounding environment. MVP is one type of artefact created as a result of the entrepreneurial process. As a core concept of Lean startup [8], MVP is a

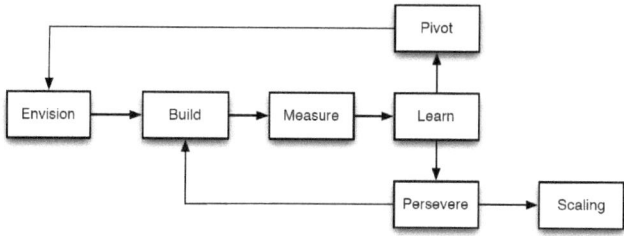

Fig. 2. Lean startup process model [14]

version of a new product which allows a team to collect the maximum amount of
know-how about customers with the least effort [8]. Eric Ries listed several types
of MVPs, for example, an explainer video, a landing page, a wire-frame, and a
single feature prototype [8]. In Software Engineering context, Nguyen Duc et al.
discussed the throw-away prototype and the evolutionary prototype as an MVP
[17]. MVP is also considered as a type of boundary object in startup context [3].

2.2   Theoretical Model of Startup Evolution

Based on the Build-Measure-Learn approach, hypothesis about both product
and customer should be formed and validated using MVPs [8]. The loop repeats
and moves forward, from problem-solution space to product-market space and
eventually to scaling. Lindgren and Münch present a study about experiment-
driven product development in the startup context. The authors describe
the product development as a series of linear increment of experiments [18].
Fagerholm et al. propose a framework for the continuous experiment which
includes the elements of the lean startup [19]. This type of experiment points
out the importance of continuous testing in order to support the development
process to achieve the high-end product. Continuous in this context refers to
running many iterations of Build-Measure-Learn feedback loop. In addition to
whisking the experiment Fagerholm et al. provides the description of required
artefacts, tasks and roles [18,19]. This experiment-driven process facilitates the
development of MVP or minimum viable features (MVF) and supports the plan,
implementation and analysis of experiments. Holmström et al. study describes
the Hypothesis Experiment Data-Driven Development (HYPEX) model which
helps to blend the experiments with the customer in the software development
process. The HYPEX model aims at reducing the customer feedback loop. Hence
this leads to less development pressure in the software development process. Similar to the approaches mentioned earlier Nguyen et al. represents the evolution of
startups via double loop model of sense-making [20]. We formed a process-based
framework to realize the entrepreneurial process as in Fig. 3.

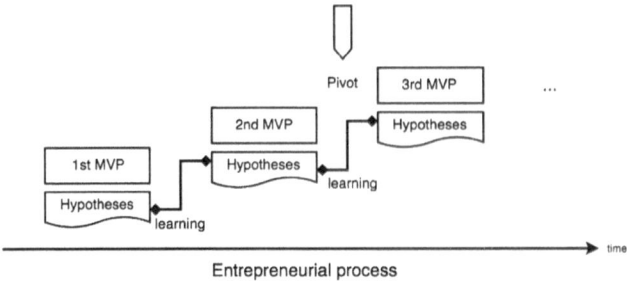

Fig. 3. Hypothetical process of artefact-driven startup evolution

3   Research Approach

This section describes the research methodology adopted to study our cases. Given startups are a dynamic and multi-influenced environment, our initial plan was to conduct an exploratory case study. Further, in the research process, our data was dominated by participant observations due to the fact that all of the paper authors were heavily involved in the startup cases. This motivated us to conduct a tailor ethnography study [21]. Ethnography derives from traditional anthropology aiming at telling a credible, rigorous, and authentic story, giving voice to people in their local context [22]. The central focus of ethnography is to provide rich, holistic insights into people's views and actions, as well as the scenario where they behave, through the collection of detailed observations and interviews [23]. There have been some attempts to adopt ethnography in software engineering context [24]. In this type of study, ethnographic methods are helpful in generating rich and detailed accounts of software project teams, their interactions with project stakeholders, and their approaches for delivering products, as well as in-depth accounts of their experiences [24]. Hence, we would like to adopt the approach to leverage all contacts and insights we have from the cases.

3.1   Case Description

A case was selected from our convenient sample. We defined four criteria for our case selection: (1) a startup that operates for at least six months, such that their experience can be relevant, (2) a startup that has at least a first running prototype, (3) a startup that has at least an initial customer set, first customer payments or a group of users, (4) a startup that has software as core value of their business. We eventually decided to study the hypothesis-driven journey of two startup cases: case 1: Startuppuccino and case 2: MUML AS.

Case 1. The startup is named after the name of the developed application, Startuppuccino [25], which is based at the Free University of Bozen-Bolzano in the northern part of Italy. Startuppuccino started with the experience and observation of two team members who are also university teachers. The initial idea of the teachers was to recommend good software tools to initiate and support startups that miss key skills in their teams (e.g., design, web development) [26]. Commonly, early-stage startups lack resources and look for some startup tools in order to launch their idea and test the product solution fit. Later, the idea pivoted into an educational platform that aims at helping entrepreneurship educators in providing students with better learning experience during their courses. Tools were also recommended to users at this level. So far the journey of Startuppuccino did three pivots: (1) startuptools.club, (2) MineToolz and (3) current version running as Startuppuccino [25].

Case 2. MUML AS is a spin-off from a Norwegian social media company. The CEO of the company quit the job and sought for a technical team to develop a hyper-local news platform. She started with the business idea and hiring several consultants, freelancers and contractors to realize and refine the idea. After that, a CTO joined the team and started a prototyping contract with a Vietnamese outsourcing team. The team was selected after a bidding process to ensure the lowest price quote. The contract was made based on six-milestone delivery and payments were made after each milestone. The outsourcing team worked in a Sprint-based approach adopting Sprint planning and retrospective meetings, burn-down chart and communication via social media. After nine months of collaboration, the CEO stated that it was a positive experience regarding the value perceived. The outsourced team was offered to be a part of the startup.

3.2 Data Collection

Semi-structured individual interviews [27] and participant observation were used to collect data since they enable enough focus on the topic of interest, but also flexible structures to discover unforeseen information. Table 1 shows outlook of the data collection instrument. An interview guide was slightly different between two cases, between different people in the same case and even between the same interviewee subject. However, we asked three types of questions: (1) warm-up question about the current context of the interviewees related to business and product development, (2) past experience question to investigate how the interviewees did in certain project scenarios in the past and (3) lessons learnt questions to capture the beliefs that emerged or evolved from the project experiences. Most of our performed observations are active participation, in which researchers are members of the startups, actively involving in business development, decision making, product development and customer interaction. When counting observations with predefined research goals, there were six planned observation sessions conducted in MUML AS and ten planned observation sessions were conducted in Startuppuccino. The researchers came to observed sessions with a clear research goal in mind, sometimes with a check-list. Field note was done after the observation. In case of Startuppuccino, the observation of actions and thoughts

Table 1. Data collection instrument

Cases	Data collection	Amount
Startuppuccino		
	Planned participant observation-strategic meetings	10
	Interview with entrepreneur	4
	Artefacts: Trello, pitching videos, dairy project plan, project charts, kanban board	Various
MUML AS		
	Planned participant observation-strategic meetings	6
	Interviews with entrepreneur	3
	Artefacts: pitching documents,trello, bitbucket, user research, project plan, Development contract	Various

were captured in a startup diary. Data triangulation was done by looking at project's artefacts, such as project plan, meeting notes, technical document and project management board. By triangulating our data sources and our instruments, we addressed issues of validity and obtained comprehensive insights into the application of ethnographic methods.

3.3   Data Analysis

Interview transcripts and observation diary were available for analysis. We adopt-ed a narrative analysis by going through the scripts, identifying the relevant piece of text and labelled them by codes representing: business, product ideas and descriptions of MVP. Combining with extra materials, we came up with a list of hypotheses and MVPs. Hypotheses were either directly stated or indirectly explained by an interviewee. We also noted the timestamps when a hypothesis or an MVP occurs. The connections among hypotheses are interpretative and conducted by all co-authors of the work. For instance, the connection between hypotheses is interpreted by their semantic meanings. Most of the connections between hypotheses and MVPs are evident from our data. After that, a cross-case analysis was done to identify commonality and difference between two cases. This was done on top of the previous analysis of hypotheses and MVPs in each case.

4   Results

This section describes our finding with regards to each case. First, we explain the Startuppuccino and then the MUML AS journey with the list of hypotheses formulated, then the MVPs that were created, the pivots that occurred and finally the relationship diagram between hypotheses and MVPs.

4.1   Entrepreneurial Journey of Startuppuccino

With regards to RQ1, we found that in Startuppuccino entrepreneurs had some initial ideas and assumptions about customer problems. Table 2 shows that most of the hypotheses relate to the customer problems, which is based on their business model canvas. Some hypothesis, for example, H04, was derived after obtaining the new knowledge from testing a previous hypothesis, i.e H02 and H03. Hence, we formulated a parent-child relationship between these hypotheses. The hypotheses are also temporally ordered; H01 is the first hypothesis and H07 is the last hypothesis in the investigated time-frame. During the postmortem analysis, we were also able to identify the MVPs that are associated with these hypotheses, as described in Table 3. We identify 7 MVPs (in which the pivots occurred at M02, M05, M07 as marked *) and 7 hypotheses as described in Tables 3 and 2. MVPs were described with their types and how they were built in the startups. The MVP is numbered chronologically: M01 is the first MVP and M07 is the last one within our investigated time-frame. Pivots are evidence of visible knowledge and experience transfer in Startuppuccino. M02 is a zoom-in pivot, where a major change occurred in the team, targeted market, UX design of the product. M05 is a customer segment pivot, coming with new team members and vision change. M07 is the least knowledge transfer as it was a complete pivot, where the whole business model got changed.

Table 2. Hypotheses formulated in Startuppuccino journey

	Parent	Hypothesis	Tested-In
H01		Entrepreneurs have less time and resources to build startup so they need assistance from startup tools	
H02		Entrepreneurs need right startup tool at right time for very early stage startups	M02
H03	H02	People would like to see video on platform, Users like to grasp the idea quickly	M02, M03
H04	H02, H03	People prefer a video with real users stating the idea	M02, M04
H05		Entrepreneurs/students need a better platform with guidance from mentors to intiate/run the startup	M05
H06	H05	Users like to grasp the idea quickly	M05
H07		Students could know better about the startup course, Educators could get support to run the startup course	M07

Table 3. MVPs build in Startuppuccino journey

	MVP	Description
M01	Mockup	made to visualize, understand the very first idea clearly
M02*	Landing page	made just enough for the market/users
M03	Explainer Video	made so that users understand the idea quickly, made to retain users on the landing page
M04	Explainer video	made with real users at the startup weekend
M05*	Concierge	made with vision to provide support, entrepreneurs/students with startup tools and guidance provided by mentors
M06	Explainer Video	made so that users understand the idea quickly made to retain users longer on platform
M07*	Concierge	made with vision changed to provide platform to support entrepreneurship education made with vision to support educators teaching course

4.2   Entrepreneurial Journey of MUML AS

With regards to RQ1, Table 4 shows that most of the hypotheses relate to the business objectives driven by their business model canvas. The hypotheses are also chronologically ordered; H01 is the first hypothesis and H14 is the last hypothesis in the investigated time-frame. During the postmortem analysis, we were also able to identify the MVPs that are associated with these hypotheses, as described in Table 5. We identify 13 MVPs (in which the pivots occurred at M03 and M13) and 14 hypotheses as described in Tables 5 and 4. MVPs were described with their types and how they were built in the startups. The MVP is numbered chronologically: M01 is the first MVP and M13 is the last one within our investigated time-frame. In MUML AS, two pivots happen, which occurred by building a new MVP (M3 and M13) based on previous learning from customer needs and product design. M03 is a customer need pivot, which is quite disconnected from its previous MVP. However, the learning experience regards to UX design and customer involvement remained the same with those in previous MVPs. M13 is a technology pivot, where new market research results in a new technical platform. Only the platform was changed here, all the knowledge about the customer, product design and business model remained the same.

4.3   Findings from Cross-Case Analysis

We observe some commonalities in terms of hypothesis and MVP development in the two startup cases: With regards to RQ1, we found that startups do actually learn during entrepreneurial evolution and the learning can be marked with

Table 4. Hypotheses formulated in MUML AS

ID	Parent	Hypothesis	Tested-In
H01		People are interested in hyper-local news around them	M01 M02, M12
H02	H01	People are interested in a sub-set of news depending on geographical context	
H03	H01	People are interested in trusted,validated news	M09
H04	H01, H02	People are interested in news in other locations as well	M07
H05		People are willing to share hyper-local news around them	M01, M12
H06	H05	People are interested in sharing news via interesting sharing mechanism	M09, M10
H07		People are interested in news displayed in a map	M04
H08	H07	People like to see news headline in the map	M04, M06
H09	H07	People like to be able to configure the radius of news they can receive	M08
H10	H01, H07	People would like to see picture and less text	M04, M06, M07
H11	H10	People would like to see picture, live stream video as well	M10
H12	H05	There is a way to trigger people to post news	M09
H13	H12	A camera-ready button triggers the willingness to capture a photo and share	M09
H14	H12	Gamification can help users to engaged into the system	M12

either hypothesis testing or MVP creation. However, the overall learning does not occur systematically and linearly. The relationship between hypotheses and MVPs is non-linear. The theoretical model of startup evolution includes a series of incremental experiments that involves hypothesis testing. In both cases, we find that the actual model of hypothesis testing in startups is more complicated. It is not straightforward that a hypothesis is associated with an MVP. In some cases, a business hypothesis is tested by multiple MVPs, at different times in the startup life-cycle. Validating one hypothesis can lead to another hypothesis (parent-child relationship). In some cases, one hypothesis can be derived from multiple parent hypothesis. Some hypotheses are so complex that they are fully tested by the very late MVPs. We also observe some MVPs that answer multiple hypotheses. These are often important MVPs that turn into commercial products. With regards to RQ2, We capture the relationship between hypotheses and MVPs as in the Fig. 4. In the figure, the dashed link represents the temporal

Table 5. MVPs build in MUML AS journey

ID	MVP	Description
M01	Explainer Video	Firstly made to express the business idea
M02	Mockup	Created by a consultant company to communicate ideas
M03*	Mockup	Created in just in mind, use to communicate the idea with CEO, with designers and development team
M04	Single feature	The first implemented features include Mapview, Listview of a news
M05	Single feature	No new feature added but changing a lot relating to the interfaces
M06	Evolutionary	Adding detail view, location, features to the app
M07	Evolutionary	Channel feature
M08	Evolutionary	Map configuration feature
M09	Evolutionary	Camera button
M10	Evolutionary	Live story feature, preparing for two pitching events and a makerfaire
M11	Landing page	Formal page of the startup
M12	Evolutionary	User management and gamification feature
M13*	Evolutionary	Making the new version of MUML AS for Android devices It was previously applied for iphone only.

relationship or the evolution flow over time of the startup. The white-head arrow links represent the parent-child relationship of the hypotheses. The black-head arrow links represent the evolution of MVPs. It is also used for the association link between a hypothesis and an MVP. In the case M1 there is no link with the hypothesis as the MVP was never validated. In the case of M2, which was built on top of M1, the pivot occurred hence it is highlighted green. In reference to the case of M5 and M6, the pivot occurred during M5, but M6 was tested at the same time of M5. Both MVPs were developed in parallel around the same time. In relation to RQ2, we found that there are NO correspondences between hypotheses and MVPs. According to Lean Startup, learning occurs while validating pre-defined hypotheses. However, we find in both cases that some MVP is built without an association to a hypothesis. The MVP is built either as an extension of a previous one or with the push from customer and market demands. There are also hypotheses not tested. Startup founders recognize that derived hypotheses were not fully covered by MVPs. Some are skipped due to intuitive reasons; some are skipped mistakenly. Moreover, we found that pivot can be captured from the MVP-creation approach. A pivot marked by a new MVP often inherits learning from the previous MVPs. Typically, the pivoted MVP will start from scratch. This means an MVP before the pivoted one, is typically considered as a throw-away prototype. There are also situations in which a pivoted MVP

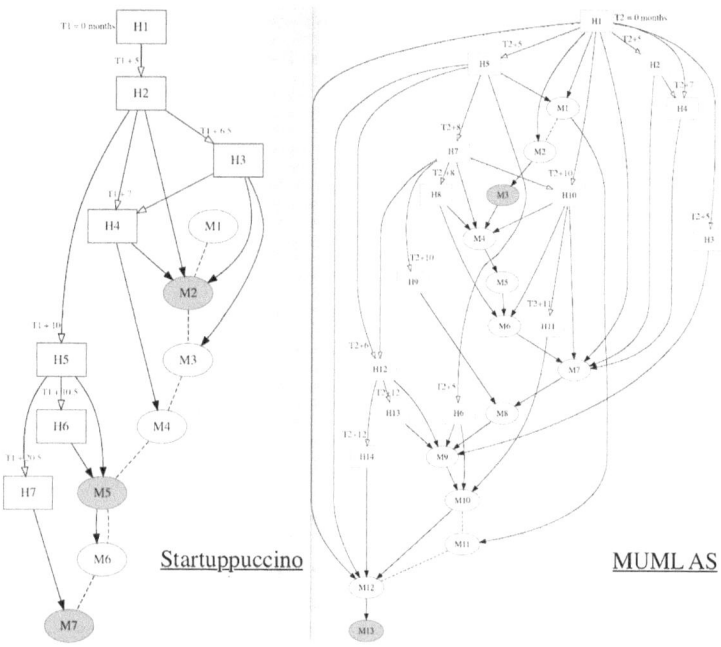

Fig. 4. Relationship between hypotheses and MVPs in startuppuccino and MUML AS

reuses source code from the previous MVPs. In our cases, the reuse also involves a significant refactoring and change of code bases. A pivoted MVP is also found to be associated with a new (sub) hypothesis disconnected with the previous hypothesis.

5   Discussion and Conclusions

This study describes the hypothesis-driven journey of two software startups expedition which started with forming the hypothesis, building MVPs and pivots that occurred. Lean Startup and previous studies on software startups have neglected the relationship between hypothesis and MVPs or considered them in an ideal context. We found that entrepreneur does learn from testing their hypotheses, however, they do not always focus on hypothesis formulation and hence, the relationship between business objective to test and MVPs to build is not always straightforward. Through two case studies, we observed that a relationship between hypothesis and MVPs is non-linear and incomplete. We also proposed an approach to visualize the startup journey from capturing the Hypothesis-MVP relationships. From our cases, it seems that the amount of learning entrepreneur have depends on user involvement and their existing knowledge about market, industry and technology. Little user involvement might lead to little experience gained from testing hypotheses. For an entrepreneur, it is crucial to solving the urgent problem of a user, although a startup has to face a complete pivot. This could be time-consuming and a big move for a startup to deal with, but beneficial too. Moreover, an entrepreneur should grab every opportunity to experiment with MVPs. Furthermore, the need and effectiveness of having a strong business driver for a startup are important. Last but not least, with the usefulness of visualizing startup journeys demonstrated in this paper, an entrepreneur can find the journey maps an useful tool for reflecting and reviewing possible gaps in the business and product development. We are not aware of a specific toolset for this purpose in the market. However, an entrepreneur can use generic graph tools, such as Graphviz, GraphTea and Plotly and follow the approach described in this paper. There are several threats to validity worth to discuss [28]. One internal threat of validity is the bias in data collection, as data might not represent a comprehensive story. In order to mitigate this threat, we selected CEOs during the postmortem analysis, who have the best understanding about their startups. We used all opportunities for interviewing relevant people of our cases in this context of the study. We also used artefacts (Trello, project charts, kanban board, dairy) during postmortem to increase our understanding of the cases. With both startups, we also acted as startup team members, which enables a lot of insights beyond interviews. Another internal threat to validity regards how reliable the reported cases are. This ensured that all of the authors have not only theoretical background about software startups but also hands-on experience. A construct threat to validity is a possible inadequate description of constructs. An external threat to validity is the representativeness of our selected cases. Both of the cases are small startups. Besides, the startup decisions on MVP might be influenced by individual personalities. Future research can validate results from this work by systematic adoption of the approach in a larger set of cases. We also call for a development of a specific toolset to visualize startups hypotheses, MVPs, and the connections among them. The toolset will definitely highlight the learning and experience flow during the entrepreneurial development.

References

1. Fletcher, D.E.: Entrepreneurial processes and the social construction of opportunity. Entrepreneurship Reg. Dev. **18**(5), 21–440 (2006)
2. Song, M., Podoynitsyna, K., Van Der Bij, H., Halman, J.I.: Success factors in new ventures: a meta analysis. J. Prod. Innov. Manag. **25**(1), 7–27 (2008)
3. Duc, A.N., Abrahamsson, P.: Minimum viable product or multiple facet product? the role of mvp in software startups. In: Sharp, H., Hall, T. (eds.) XP 2016. LNBIP, vol. 251, pp. 118–130. Springer, Cham (2016). https://doi.org/10.1007/978-3-319-33515-5_10
4. Bajwa, S.S., Wang, X., Duc, A.N., Abrahamsson, P.: Failures to be celebrated: an analysis of major pivots of software startups. Empirical Softw. Eng. **22**(5), 2373–2408 (2017)
5. Sarasvathy, S.D.: Effectuation: Elements of Entrepreneurial Expertise. Edward Elgar Publishing, Cheltenham (2009)

6. Venkataraman, S., Sarasvathy, S.D., Dew, N., Forster, W.R.: Reflections on the 2010 AMR decade award: whither the promise? moving forward with entrepreneurship as a science of the artificial. Acad. Manag. Rev. **37**(1), 21–33 (2012)
7. Lichtenstein, B.B.: Generative Emergence: A New Discipline of Organizational, Entrepreneurial, and Social Innovation. Oxford University Press, New York (2014)
8. Ries, E.: The Lean Startup: How Today's Entrepreneurs Use Continuous Innovation to Create Radically Successful Businesses. Crown Books, New York (2011)
9. Müller, R.M., Thoring, K.: Design thinking vs. lean startup: a comparison of two user-driven innovation strategies. In: Leading through Design, vol. 151 (2012)
10. Khanna, D.: Experiential team learning in software startups. In: International Conference on Agile Software Development. Springer, Cham (2018)
11. Basili, V.R., Selby, R.W., Hutchens, D.H.: Experimentation in software engineering. IEEE Trans. Softw. Eng. **7**, 733–743 (1986)
12. Blank, S.: The Four Steps to the Epiphany: Successful Strategies for Products that Win. BookBaby, Cork (2013)
13. Eisenmann, T., Ries, E., Dillard, S.: Hypothesis-driven entrepreneurship: the lean startup. Harvard Business School Entrepreneurial Management Case No. 812–095 (2012)
14. Wang, X., Khanna, D., Abrahamsson, P.: Teaching lean startup at university: an experience report. In: International Workshop on Software Startups (IWSS) Co-located with 22nd ICE/IEEE International Technology Management Conference (2016)
15. Selden, P.D., Fletcher, D.E.: The entrepreneurial journey as an emergent hierarchical system of artifact-creating processes. J. Bus. Ventur. **30**(4), 603–615 (2015)
16. Simon, H.A.: The Sciences of the Artificial. MIT Press, Cambridge (1996)
17. Nguyen Duc, A., Wang, X., Abrahamsson, P.: What Influences the Speed of Prototyping? An Empirical Investigation of Twenty Software Startups. Norwegian, Cologne (2017)
18. Lindgren, E., Münch, J.: Raising the odds of success: the current state of experimentation in product development. Inf. Softw. Technol. **77**, 80–91 (2016)
19. Fagerholm, F., Guinea, A.S., Mäenpää, H., Münch, J.: Building blocks for continuous experimentation. In: Proceedings of the 1st International Workshop on Rapid Continuous Software Engineering, pp. 26–35. ACM (2014)
20. Nguyen Duc, A., Seppänen, P., Abrahamsson, P.: Hunter-gatherer cycle: a conceptual model of the evolution of startup innovation and engineering. In: 1st Workshop on Open Innovation on Software Engineering, ICSSP (2015)
21. Sharp, H., Dittrich, Y., De Souza, C.R.: The role of ethnographic studies in empirical software engineering. IEEE Trans. Softw. Eng. **42**(8), 786–804 (2016)
22. Fetterman, D.M.: Ethnography: Step-by-Step, vol. 17. Sage, Thousand Oaks (2010)
23. Reeves, S., Kuper, A., Hodges, B.D.: Qualitative research methodologies: ethnography. BMJ Br. Med. J. **337** (2008)
24. Passos, C., Cruzes, D.S., Dybå, T., Mendonça, M.: Challenges of applying ethnography to study software practices. In: 2012 ACM-IEEE International Symposium on IEEE Empirical Software Engineering and Measurement (ESEM), pp. 9–18 (2012)
25. Khanna, D., Mondini, M., Pantiuchina, J., Stillittano, G., Wang, X.: Experiment with MVPs: the First Startuppuccino Steps to a Lean Edtech Startup. In: Agilealliance (2017). https://www.agilealliance.org/resources/experience-reports/experiment-with-mvps/

26. Edison, H., Khanna, D., Bajwa, S.S., Brancaleoni, V., Bellettati, L.: Towards a software tool portal to support startup process. In: Abrahamsson, P., Corral, L., Oivo, M., Russo, B. (eds.) PROFES 2015. LNCS, vol. 9459, pp. 577–583. Springer, Cham (2015). https://doi.org/10.1007/978-3-319-26844-6_43
27. Myers, M.D., Newman, M.: The qualitative interview in IS research: examining the craft. Inf. Organ. **17**(1), 2–26 (2007)
28. Runeson, P., Höst, M.: Guidelines for conducting and reporting case study research in software engineering. Empirical Softw. Eng. **14**(2), 131 (2009)

Author Index